W9-CNA-254

Free Public Library
Township of Hamilton
1 Municipal Drive
Hamilton, NJ 08619

About Island Press

Island Press is the only nonprofit organization in the United States whose principal purpose is the publication of books on environmental issues and natural resource management. We provide solutions-oriented information to professionals, public officials, business and community leaders, and concerned citizens who are shaping responses to environmental problems.

In 2002, Island Press celebrates its eighteenth anniversary as the leading provider of timely and practical books that take a multidisciplinary approach to critical environmental concerns. Our growing list of titles reflects our commitment to bringing the best of an expanding body of literature to the environmental community throughout North America and the world.

Support for Island Press is provided by The Nathan Cummings Foundation, Geraldine R. Dodge Foundation, Doris Duke Charitable Foundation, Educational Foundation of America, The Charles Engelhard Foundation, The Ford Foundation, The George Gund Foundation, The Vira I. Heinz Endowment, The William and Flora Hewlett Foundation, Henry Luce Foundation, The John D. and Catherine T. MacArthur Foundation, The Andrew W. Mellon Foundation, The Moriah Fund, The Curtis and Edith Munson Foundation, National Fish and Wildlife Foundation, The New-Land Foundation, Oak Foundation, The Overbrook Foundation, The David and Lucile Packard Foundation, The Pew Charitable Trusts, The Rockefeller Foundation, The Winslow Foundation, and other generous donors.

The opinions expressed in this book are those of the author(s) and do not necessarily reflect the views of these foundations.

Water Follies

All streams flow into the sea;
yet the sea is not full.
To the place the streams come from,
there they return again.

—Ecclesiastes 1:7

WATER FOLLIES

Groundwater Pumping and the Fate of America's Fresh Waters

Robert Glennon

ISLAND PRESS

Washington • Covelo • London

333.91
GLE
c1

3 1923 00427601 6

Copyright © 2002 Robert Glennon

All rights reserved under International and Pan-American Copyright Conventions. No part of this book may be reproduced in any form or by any means without permission in writing from the publisher: Island Press, 1718 Connecticut Avenue, N.W., Suite 300, Washington, DC 20009.

ISLAND PRESS is a trademark of The Center for Resource Economics.

Library of Congress Cataloging-in-Publication Data
Glennon, Robert, 1944–
  Water follies : groundwater pumping and the fate of America's fresh waters / Robert Glennon.
      p. cm.
Includes bibliographical references and index.
  ISBN 1-55963-223-2 (hardback : alk. paper)
  1. Water-supply—United States. 2. Groundwater—United States. 3. Water use—United States. 4. Water consumption—United States. I. Title.
  TD223 .G58 2002
  333.91'0413'0973—dc21   2002007977

British Cataloguing-in-Publication Data available

Book design by Brighid Willson

Printed on recycled, acid-free paper ✸

Manufactured in the United States of America
09 08 07 06 05 04 03   8 7 6 5 4 3 2

To Karen

Contents

Water Follies

Introduction

The idea of selling spring water came to Eric Carlson in 1997, when he observed trucks filled with water as they traveled up and down Maine highways. To Carlson, it was an epiphany: "I was like, 'Wow! Water is valuable enough to truck around?' From that moment on, I just got wicked psyched that I was going to do this." Carlson teamed up with Hugh Hastings, who owned land with a bubbling brook in Fryeburg, Maine, to supply spring water to Poland Spring water company, which bottles the water under the Ice Mountain label.

Out of a small clapboard house, Carlson and Hastings operate their fully automated system of pipes, pumps, and software. A trucker pulls up at their facility, uses a computer keypad to punch in the code numbers, and fills up the tanker. A computer records the amount of water taken. It is a very slick operation. It cost them $150,000 in capital outlay, but, as Carlson describes it, "Now, at the end of the month, I push a button and the printer spits out a bill. I pop the bill into the mail, I get a check, and once a month I go to the bank and deposit it. It's the best thing ever." I should think so. In 1999, their first year of operation, Carlson and Hastings sold more than 15 million gallons to Poland Spring. A conservative estimate suggests that the pair grossed approximately $300,000. With room for considerable expansion, that's not a bad return on a $150,000 investment.

Bottled water as a food commodity has recently taken America by storm. Although drinking bottled water is a custom well established in Europe and South America, due partly to fears about the quality of public water supplies, bottled water consumption in the United States totaled only 415 million gallons in 1978. By 2001, consumption had risen 1,300 percent to 5.4 *billion* gallons, or about 43 billion sixteen-ounce bottles.

Now the fastest-growing product among the top fifty supermarket categories, bottled water has become the American public's second-largest non-alcoholic beverage expenditure. Sixty percent of Americans drink the stuff.

The explosion in sales prompted PepsiCo to begin marketing its own bottled water, Aquafina, and Coca-Cola to launch its Dasani brand. Coke also saw an opportunity to expand the market, if only it could persuade restaurant customers to switch from tap water to bottled water. In 1998, in partnership with the Olive Garden restaurant chain, Coke began an aggressive campaign to reduce "tap water incidence." The campaign, named "Just Say No to H_2O," taught the Olive Garden's servers selling techniques to steer customers from tap water to "a profitable beverage."

Even McDonald's began offering its own spring water in July 2000 in a twenty-ounce plastic bottle, complete with a red top and a yellow mouthpiece. A *New Yorker* cartoon recently captured this bottled-water phenomenon with a befuddled supermarket shopper staring at an aisle sign that read simply: "Water." In most supermarkets, the aisle dedicated to soft drinks and mixers has between one-third and one-half of the shelf space filled with bottled water.

The profits from bottled water are huge, thanks to an extraordinary retail markup. Better-known brands of spring water may fetch between $4.50 and $7.50 per gallon. Bottled water provides much higher profit margins than carbonated beverages and other drinks. It has a higher retail value than milk, oil, gasoline, or, paradoxically, many commodities made with water, such as Coca-Cola.

But even profit margins come with a price tag attached, and in the case of water, we all pay the costs, though few of us are aware of them. The water that more than half of Americans drink comes from underground aquifers—large repositories of water once thought to be as ubiquitous and plentiful as the air we breathe. This groundwater, we now know from the science of hydrology, is part of a hydrologic cycle that provides freshwater to lakes, rivers, and streams. Groundwater pumping disrupts this cycle. It steals water from our rivers and lakes, but because it does so very slowly, we don't notice the effects until they are disastrous. And they are.

Groundwater pumping in the United States has increased dramatically in just the past few decades. For domestic purposes alone, groundwater use jumped from 8 billion gallons per day (bgd) in 1965 to approximately 18.5 bgd in 1995, or sixty-five gallons for every man, woman, and child in the country. But domestic consumption, including for bottled water, is only a small fraction of the country's total groundwater use—almost 28 *trillion* gallons in 1995. Farmers used two-thirds of that to irrigate crops; the mining industry, especially for copper, coal, and gold production, pumped approximately 770 billion gallons. Groundwater constitutes more than 25 percent of the nation's water supply. Groundwater pumping has become a global problem because 1.5 billion people (one-quarter of the world's population) depend on groundwater for drinking water and because the earth's population is expected to jump from 6 billion to 8 billion by 2025.

This excessive pumping of our aquifers has created an environmental catastrophe known to only a few scientists, a handful of water management experts, and those unfortunate enough to have suffered the direct consequences. Quite remarkably, *no* books or magazine articles have focused on the impact of groundwater pumping on the environment. Yet groundwater pumping has caused rivers, springs, lakes, and wetlands to dry up, the ground beneath us to collapse, and fish, birds, wildlife, trees, and shrubs to die. In the Southwest, we have seen verdant rivers, such as the Santa Cruz in Tucson, become desiccated sandboxes as cities pumped underground water until the surface water disappeared. Around Tampa Bay, Florida, groundwater pumping has turned lakes into mudflats and has cracked the foundations of homes. These illustrations offer a glimpse of the future, as operations such as the Carlson-Hastings facility cater to the voracious demand of a burgeoning population. But they also make a point that is easy to overlook: freshwater is becoming scarce, not just in the arid West, with its tradition of battling over water rights, but even in places we think of as relatively wet.

To illustrate the contention surrounding America's thirst for groundwater and its impact on the environment, we need only consider recent events in Waushara County, in the heart of Wisconsin.

A major beneficiary of the bottled-water craze is The Perrier Group of America, a subsidiary of Perrier Vittel S.A. (a French company), which itself is owned by Swiss-based Nestle Corporation—the world's largest food and beverage company. Most consumers know Perrier as the importer of green bottles of spring water from France. But Perrier also sells bottled water under fourteen other brand names, including Arrowhead, Calistoga, Deer Park, Zephyrhills, Poland Spring, Ozarka, and Ice Mountain. Indeed, Perrier has become the largest U.S. bottler of water (ahead of

Pepsi and Coke), with a 32 percent market share. In 2001, Perrier's U.S. revenues grew 23 percent to $2.1 billion. Worldwide, Nestle markets bottled water under seventy-two brands in 160 countries. In 2001, its global revenues from bottled water totaled $4.5 billion.* To supply its needs in the United States, Perrier relies on approximately fifty locations around the country, yet it must relentlessly search for new sources to satisfy the growing demand.

Among other places, Perrier looked to the Mecan River in Wisconsin. A gin-clear, hard-water, spring-fed stream, the Mecan River originates in a set of small ponds fed by water from Mecan Springs. One of the state's most popular trout streams, the Mecan River sustains large populations of wild brown, brook, and rainbow trout. Its clear water and insect hatches make the river particularly attractive to fly anglers. Most flies used by anglers are tiny imitations of extremely small mayflies, caddis flies, or other aquatic insects. But in June each year, the Mecan witnesses a hatch of the most famous of all mayflies—the *Hexagenia limbota*, known simply as "the Hex."

Imagine yourself as a trout trying to eke out your subsistence by consuming insects the size of a child's fingernail, when suddenly at dusk thousands upon thousands of mayflies with a wingspan exceeding two inches fall to the surface and twitch or float. A feeding frenzy ensues. Reclusive, mature brown trout, sage veterans of the war with fly anglers and alert to an angler's tiniest miscue, find themselves unable to resist gorging on the Hex. When trout respond in this fashion, you can only imagine the reaction of fly anglers, who happily shun jobs, spouses, children, friends, food, and drink to fish the Hex hatch.

The Mecan River is a wonderful place, thanks to decades of work by the Wisconsin Department of Natural Resources (DNR). The state has had the good sense to protect its abundance of exceptional natural resources, including blue-ribbon trout streams, crystal-clear lakes, wild rivers and waterfalls, native prairies, and deciduous and evergreen forests. Beginning in 1957, the state gradually acquired over 6,000 acres on the Mecan River and surrounding tributaries, now known as the Mecan River Fishery Area. It has also undertaken extensive efforts to improve the stream and fish habitat by reinforcing the riverbanks with rocks, planting bank cover, and

---

*This tremendous growth led Nestle, in April 2002, to change Perrier's corporate name to Nestle Waters North America, Inc.

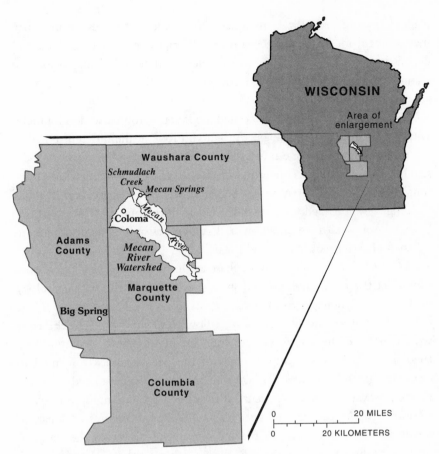

Location of the Mecan River watershed of Wisconsin.

placing boulders at strategic locations to deflect flows and encourage fish runs. The program has been spectacularly successful, and the state now controls over 50 percent of the land on the most important twenty-nine-mile section of the Mecan River.

But Wisconsin also has an interest in economic development. In 1999, the state used offers of tax breaks, free airline tickets, and the support of key state officials to woo Perrier to locate a bottling plant in Wisconsin. An article in the *Milwaukee Journal Sentinel* documented the letters, e-mail messages, and other contacts between state officials and Perrier. Wisconsin Commerce Secretary Brenda Blanchard wrote Perrier officials that "our goal is to help you locate at one of our Wisconsin sites."

In December 1999, Perrier proposed a 250,000-square-foot bottling plant that would employ as many as 250 people and represent an initial investment from Perrier of $35 million. Perrier approached the state for permission to drill a well on state-owned land near Mecan Springs. It wanted to pump the spring water through a pipeline to its bottling plant about a mile away.

Local real estate brokers welcomed the Perrier proposal as development without environmental damage. "When you look at the different types of industry, you can't get one much cleaner. There is no pollution, no noise," said one broker. Others, concerned about the local economy, favored a bottling plant that would pay wages between $12 and $18 an hour. Debbie Dehling, a waitress, endorsed the economic development: "We need jobs here. As soon as kids are old enough, they move away. There's nothing here for them. Perrier would be good for us."

Environmental groups were aghast at the prospect. They knew how important the cool, underground spring water was to the fragile ecology of the river, particularly to the health of its trout. Even a reduction of one cubic foot per second (7.5 gallons) in flow from the springs to the river would increase the river's temperature and damage fish spawning and larval rearing. A new group, Friends of the Mecan, quickly formed to organize against Perrier, in part with bumper stickers that blared "No Way Perrier." Elward Engle, who spent his career as a DNR employee working to restore the Mecan, reacted with alarm: "We spent millions of dollars to repair that stream. It's one of the most beautiful places on the Earth. A place of healing, like a sanctuary. But it is a delicate balance. A trout stream is warm in the winter and cold in the summer. If that changes, the stream can die."

From Perrier's perspective, the company has an economic incentive to maximize its profit by selling water from a common resource—the aquifer. Perrier need not pay the costs of whatever environmental degradation occurs. Instead, it transfers these costs—what economists call externalities—to neighboring landowners, fly anglers, other recreationalists, and society at large. These costs do not appear on Perrier's balance sheet. They never show up on a tax bill, on a monthly statement, or as an appropriation item. They are costs to the environment: degraded rivers, endangered species, depleted springs, dying trees, lost wetlands, ruined fisheries, altered flora, and threatened fauna.

Some Perrier sites nationwide have received the endorsement of local elected officials and business and community leaders. In Poland Spring,

Maine, a relatively new pumping plant appears to have the general endorsement of the community. As part of the deal, Perrier pledged $1 million to fund land acquisition on the pristine St. John River and to reestablish rare, native plants. The executive director of The Nature Conservancy in Maine, Kent Wommack, complimented Perrier: "We've always found them to be innovative and wanting to do the right thing as opposed to the minimum for the environment. They're doing good work here." Perrier has long portrayed itself as an ethically and environmentally conscientious corporation. Rob Fisher of Perrier commented about the situation in Poland Spring: "If we cause anybody's wells to go dry because of our operation, we've already made the commitment to replace [the wells]." Jane Lazgin, a public relations spokeswoman at Perrier headquarters in Greenwich, Connecticut, asserted that there is no evidence of the company's sites in the United States affecting any water supply. Concerning the Mecan River, she added: "Environmental stewardship is not only the right thing to do for nature and our neighbors, it is also in our best long-term interests to do business in a conscientious manner." She has noted that the company could hardly stay in business if it went around the country destroying aquifers.

Perrier's arguments have considerable merit, although two caveats are in order. First, we must recognize the conflict between short-term profits and long-term ecological balance. A multinational corporation has an enormous profit-maximizing incentive to pump an aquifer dry if it will make a profit doing so and if the company can avoid paying damages or other penalties for environmental harm. If the aquifer goes dry, the company simply moves its pumps to another aquifer. Second, Perrier may be a good steward of aquifers around the country, but protecting aquifers does not necessarily protect the environment. An aquifer may contain plenty of water, but pumping from it may harm a nearby river, stream, or wetland.

In the Mecan River case, local political and elected officials soon weighed in, expressing grave doubts about the propriety of allowing a private corporation to exploit resources beneath state-owned land in an area that the state has tried to protect for decades. In February 2000, Perrier abandoned its efforts to secure state approval for its pumping from state-owned land. The opposition appeared to prevail.

But there's more to the story. Since 1998, Perrier had also been negotiating with private landowners to drill test wells adjacent to the Mecan River. Perrier drilled two test wells on land owned by James Kengott near

Schmudlach Creek. A terrific little brook trout stream, Schmudlach Creek has extremely cold water and plays a critical role in the health of the Mecan River. Mecan Springs water is quite cold when it emerges from the earth but quickly warms in the ponds because of the sun. In contrast, the water in Schmudlach Creek is highly oxygenated and quite cold; when it flows into the Mecan, it lowers the temperature in the river, thus producing absolutely ideal spawning conditions. Any reduction of flow in Schmudlach Creek would affect not only the volume but also the temperature of the Mecan. Tests of the Mecan River have disclosed an enormous number of trout in the Mecan just below where Schmudlach Creek enters, suggesting that this reach is critical to wild trout reproduction. The danger is apparent. Perrier's test well is located sixty feet from Schmudlach Creek, a small stream with a flow between 1,350 and 2,250 gallons per minute (gpm). Perrier proposed to pump 500 gpm, which would devastate the creek and have catastrophic consequences for the Mecan River.

But the state can't halt Perrier's commercial operation if the well is drilled on private property. Under Wisconsin law, Perrier must get a permit from DNR for any high-capacity well that pumps over 100,000 gallons per day (gpd), and Perrier's well would pump 720,000 gpd, but the only ground for denying a permit is if the well would interfere with a municipal water supply. The Perrier well would not. In addition, Wisconsin groundwater law follows the "reasonable use" doctrine: landowners may pump as much water as they want, so long as the pumping does not unreasonably harm adjoining landowners. Under this system, the burden is on the neighbors to prove that they have been harmed, a task made exceedingly difficult because the law on groundwater pumping does not consider a reduction in surface flows in creeks and rivers as harm. Put another way, the law is virtually ignorant of hydrologic reality.

Political pressure is another matter, however. In February 2000, hundreds of local residents attended a meeting in Coloma, Wisconsin, to express their displeasure at Perrier's proposal to pump from private property near the Mecan River. The negative reaction prompted Perrier to "regroup and reevaluate." Perrier then announced that it was abandoning efforts to locate its facility in the Mecan River watershed. "We've listened [to the public reaction] and we are moving on," noted Perrier spokeswoman Jane Lazgin.

Ironically, Perrier could have spared itself the trouble and been happily pumping away, but for a curious regulatory fiction. It could have obtained water with the same chemical content as the water from Schmudlach Creek if it located the wells one or two miles away. Locating the wells at this distance would lessen the impact on the river and virtually ensure the end of local opposition. However, as a marketing strategy, Perrier has no interest in this water even though it is virtually identical.

To understand Perrier's reluctance, one must understand a set of byzantine regulations promulgated by the U.S. Food and Drug Administration (FDA). These 1996 regulations define in great detail "spring," "artesian," "natural," "seltzer," "flavored," and "mineral" water. Water pumped from wells a couple of miles away from the Mecan would be deemed "artesian" water under the FDA regulations. However, Perrier wants to market "spring" water because it has greater cachet among the American public and commands a much higher price. The FDA regulations define spring water as "water . . . from an underground formation [that] flows naturally to the surface of the earth. . . . Spring water shall be collected only at the spring or through a bore hole . . . feeding the spring." In other words, for Perrier to market "spring" water, the well must be close enough to the spring to satisfy the FDA definition.

The FDA rules create a perverse, though unintended, incentive to harm the environment by pumping groundwater from a well so close to a spring that it reduces the spring's flow. Wisconsin water law and the FDA regulations share a common flaw: both ignore hydrologic reality.

⸺ ⸺

The laws regulating groundwater pumping often flout the scientific principles of hydrology. Our legal system has created rules that foster the economic interests of those who benefit from using water. Once a public good, water has become a commodity and, depending on the location, a highly valuable one. As water becomes more scarce, it will fetch higher prices, and people will go to greater lengths to secure rights to it. As private corporations vie for the extraordinary profits to be earned from bottled water, cities are frantically searching for new supplies of water to accommodate population growth and, most often, are turning to groundwater as the solution. In Florida, one of the wettest states in the Union, groundwater pumping in the Tampa Bay region increased 400 percent to 255 million gallons per day between 1960 and 1996. As a result, fewer than ten of the area's 153 lakes are "healthy." Yet pumping is expected to rise another 170 percent by 2020. Meanwhile, the state of Florida is embroiled in a struggle with Georgia and Alabama over control of the Apalachicola-Chattahoochee-Flint River basin. Water withdrawals and groundwater pumping in Georgia have increased exponentially to slake the thirst of Atlanta's burgeoning suburbs and the state's farmers. It is sobering to consider that this interstate water war is situated in the East, not the West.

As groundwater pumping increases, we, as humans, suffer the costs. If you place a frog into a pot of cold water on the stove, then turn on the heat and increase it gradually, the frog won't know enough to jump from the pot. The heated water will eventually kill the frog. With groundwater pumping, we may not notice the changes as they slowly occur over years. Stark consequences—such as rivers that dry up—are apparent. In contrast, pumping that causes a gradual decline in the number of birds, butterflies, fish, or trees diminishes our enjoyment of the resource in imperceptible steps.

There is the additional problem of determining the causal relationship between groundwater pumping and environmental degradation. Sometimes the facts aren't clear. Scientific uncertainty attends many disputes over whether pumping will have a specific impact on a particular river or spring. Some of this debate is in good faith, an honest disagreement about what the evidence suggests and the computer models predict. Other positions seem animated by gross self-interest. With so much money at stake, Perrier and other companies pay consultants handsome fees to help obtain lucrative permits to pump. After a Perrier hydrologist in Wisconsin concluded that the company's pumping would not damage the environment, the *Sheboygan Press* editorialized: "Pardon us for being skeptical, but what else could he say given that he's on the company payroll." In Florida, Perrier proposed to pump 657 *million* gallons per year from a well near a spring, yet the company's hydrologist testified at a 1999 hearing that "[y]ou will not be able to detect" a change in the nearby river's flow. My hydrologist colleague Tom Maddock contemptuously dismisses hydrologists who make such extravagant claims as "hydrostitutes."

— —

In Wisconsin, Perrier gave up on the site near the Mecan River but, in September 2000, received a permit from the state for a plant in Adams County. As of June 2002, it is unclear whether that plant will be built. Meanwhile, Perrier has continued its search for new sources.

- In June 2001, Perrier announced that it was buying Bennett Hill Spring, one of several springs that give Boiling Springs, Tennessee, its name. Perrier has promised the town of 1,023 residents good-paying jobs at the bottling facility. The local newspaper described the announcement as "one of the best-kept secrets" in Macon County. It has the blessing of Governor Don Sundquish, who met with Macon County officials, Perrier executives, and the owners of Bennett Hill Spring to finalize the sale.
- In August 2001, with the assistance of $12 million in incentives and the support of Michigan governor John Engler's administration, Perrier began construction of a plant in Mecosta County, about fifty miles north of Grand Rapids. The plant became operational in May 2002 and will pump up to 575,000 gallons per day for Perrier's Ice Mountain brand.
- In January 2002, after an elaborate ribbon-cutting ceremony attended by a veritable "who's who" of southern California power brokers, Perrier began construction of a 383,000-square-foot bottling facility on the Morongo Indian Reservation near Riverside, California. The plant will supply spring water to Perrier's subsidiary, Arrowhead Mountain Spring Water, and will employ 260 workers.

In Perrier's relentless quest, we see only the tip of the iceberg of excessive groundwater pumping. The remainder of this book aims to shed light on the impact of groundwater pumping on the environment in the United States. In communities and watersheds around the country, we find groundwater being used to accommodate population growth; to supply private homeowner wells; to irrigate blueberries, and grow potatoes, alfalfa, wheat, and oats; to mine gold and coal; and to support tourism in national parks and forests. The localities range from Tampa Bay to Down East Maine; from Minnesota to California's Central Valley; from the suburbs north of Boston to the Hopi Reservation in Arizona; and from Grand Canyon National Park to coastal regions of Florida. This book tells the story of groundwater in each of these places.

I tell these stories for their poignancy and occasional perversity and because each story poses a conflict of values that explains how and why we use water. We will consider the conflicting water claims of wild blueberries versus wild Atlantic salmon; of a coal slurry pipeline versus springs sacred to the Hopi people; of San Antonio's premier tourist attraction, River Walk, versus endangered species in springs from the Edwards

Aquifer; of trophy homes, lawns, and swimming pools in affluent Boston suburbs versus a river used for public recreation; of fast-food french fries versus a blue-ribbon trout stream; of endangered Pacific chinook salmon versus Sacramento's suburban sprawl; and of growth in Atlanta versus a tiny community based on oyster fishing.

The stories range from the tragic to the comic to the tragicomic. Writing about water use, policy, management, and law demands both a sense of irony and a sense of humor. In the years between World War I and his death in 1970, Rube Goldberg drew cartoons of absurdly complex and convoluted machines and contraptions that would perform basic tasks, such as scratching a mosquito bite. His drawings so tickled the funny bone of the country that Webster's dictionary has a listing for "Rube Goldberg . . . accomplishing by complex means what seemingly could be done simply." This book's stories involve proposed "solutions" that would make even Rube Goldberg smile. These water follies unmask human foibles, including greed, stubbornness and, especially, the unlimited human capacity to ignore reality.

Chapter 1

The Worth of Water in the United States

"True conservation of water is not the prevention of its use. Every drop of water that runs to the sea without yielding its full commercial returns to the nation is an economic waste."
—Herbert Hoover (1926)

On July 4, 1997, NASA's Pathfinder landed on Mars, and its little rover, Sojourner, captured the hearts and the imaginations of people around the world. In succeeding days and weeks, NASA's Mars Web site was overwhelmed with hits from curious citizens who were captivated by the crisp images that Pathfinder returned to Earth. Among its most significant scientific discoveries, Pathfinder offered clear evidence of the past existence of water on Mars. The images suggested that Mars may once have been a warm, wet place. The rolling terrain and variety of rocks offered testimony to an ancient past when Mars was beset by massive floods. These discoveries tantalizingly raise the possibility that there was once life on Mars. Billions of years ago, a thick blanket of carbon dioxide clouds may have kept the surface of Mars warm enough for a long enough time that life could develop. The prerequisite of life is liquid water.

Water is the essence of life, the core of chemistry, the prime component of the human body; it covers two-thirds of the surface of the earth. Without it, life ceases. With it, life can flourish. In the American Southwest, Pueblo societies cherished water. Its scarcity led them to pray to water deities in hope of rain. Peoples such as the Anasazi and the Hohokam (between 1000 A.D. and 1300 A.D.) developed irrigation systems to harness this precious resource. They sought to cultivate sufficient food to subsist; they sought to adapt to the environment rather than to dominate it. Many native myths and traditions celebrated water as sacred, the lifeblood of Mother Earth.

In contrast, most Americans, even those of us living in the Southwest, take water for granted. Turn on the tap, and water flows for cooking and drinking. Jump in the shower, wash off the dirt, and feel refreshed. Turn on the hose to wash the car or water the lawn and garden. Most Americans' involvement with their water supply occurs once a month when they write a small check to the local water utility. Some cities do not even have a separate charge for water. In these cities, people are literally free to use as much water as they desire.

Why? We've been spoiled by excess. The European colonists of North America came to a continent with abundant, untapped natural resources, including water. Many settlers aspired to reap the economic value of those resources. To a considerable extent, the story of settlement involves the exploration, extraction, harvesting, and exploitation of these resources. It began with fur trappers and hunters, continued with gold and silver miners, then turned to mining copper, oil, and gas, to logging, and to commercial harvesting of salmon stocks. It has continued with water.

In the eighteenth century, the American colonists borrowed the English law of riparian water rights, the legal theory that owners of land abutting lakes, rivers, or streams were guaranteed the "natural flow without diminution or alteration" of the watercourse. The idea was that property was an estate to be enjoyed for its own sake and left undisturbed. In colonial America, surface water served mostly domestic needs that were relatively modest and did not involve large-scale diversion projects. By prohibiting consumptive uses or diversions of water, the natural flow doctrine served as a brake on economic development. Colonial entrepreneurs saw opportunities to harness the power of rivers for mills that would grind grain into flour or meal, but few in the American colonies wished to risk their capital without secure water rights. Recognizing this, legislatures and courts rejected the natural flow theory in favor of a rule of priority that protected the first entrepreneur against the claim of neighboring landowners to the natural flow. A river's water had become valuable as an instrument of economic development.

Although the rule of priority initially created an incentive to invest, it eventually threatened to retard economic development. In the nineteenth century, as the country began to industrialize, New England developed textile factories that relied on the powerful force of moving water to turn the gears that determined the rotational speed of spindles. This use involved impounding large amounts of water behind dams to produce sufficient force to operate the textile machines as the water was released. However, the priority doctrine protected the small gristmill against the subsequent textile mill.

Once again, the law changed course. Courts now embraced the "reasonable use" doctrine which allowed consideration of "the usages and wants of the community." In other words, the economic benefit of a textile factory to the town suddenly outweighed the prior interests of the gristmill owner. At each step in this history, the legal rules changed to favor economic development. Property rights evolved from a static concept to an instrumental component of the industrial revolution. Note, however, that the textile factories didn't permanently remove the water. After impoundment, the factories released it back to the river to flow downstream.

That was not true of mid-nineteenth-century California, where the discovery of gold bred new uses of surface water. Miners diverted water from rivers and creeks, built canals to transport the water to reach their mining claims, and constructed sluices to wash the gold ore. As the water washed over the gangue, the heavier ore settled out. Mining involves a consumptive use of water; only a small percentage of water diverted into these canals ever returned to the rivers and creeks.

Most gold mining involved unauthorized incursions onto federal property, and it is not an overstatement to suggest that the miners stole gold from federal lands. In 1848, the military governor of California, Colonel Richard B. Mason, told a group of miners: "This is public land and the gold is the property of the United States; all of you here are trespassers, but as the Government is benefited by your getting out the gold, I do not intend to interfere." In reality, the colonel had little choice, given his meager military force.

The miners lawlessly diverted water from the rivers and creeks. In the absence of legal rules or procedures, the mining camps relied on their own sense of frontier justice. Which miner had a right to divert water from which river or creek and in what quantity? The miners developed their own system of water rights, a set of rules that profoundly impacted the entire American West, not just in the nineteenth century but also to this very day.

They created the prior appropriation doctrine, a more sophisticated version of the New England priority doctrine. The essence of prior appropriation is "first-in-time, first-in-right." The first miner secured the right to divert from a stream however much water he needed. The earliest efforts to mine obtained superior rights, fixed as of the date of diversion; later miners took what was left. The diverters were "senior" or "junior" to each other based on the date each miner first turned the stream to his purposes. Unlike riparian law, this doctrine did not require the appropriators to own property on the river or stream. The prior appropriation doctrine was especially critical during years of low precipitation, when only the more senior users would receive water.

Although the prior appropriation doctrine arose in the gold mining camps, it soon spread to agricultural areas. In the East, farmers cultivated small farms, and natural rainfall provided ample water for their crops. However, as settlers moved west, the land became more arid and, as a result, growing crops was impossible without additional water. Moving water from rivers and creeks to a farmer's fields often required a major effort, particularly when the fields were several miles from the water source. Like the eastern mill operators, western farmers were understandably reluctant to undertake that effort without assurance that they would be rewarded by a consistent and reliable supply of water. The prior appropriation doctrine became a bedrock principle in agricultural communities throughout the West: it guaranteed water rights to those who invested the energy and capital to use the water productively. It fostered economic growth by encouraging farmers to construct massive canals to bring water to their lands. In some communities it stimulated joint enterprises, known as mutual water companies or irrigation districts, to share in the infrastructure costs and attendant benefits. This doctrine has been the unalterable rule of water allocation, and it still governs most uses of surface water in every western state.

One characteristic of the prior appropriation system deserves special mention. Unlike the riparian system, which treated water rights as "correlative," that is, contingent on the amount used by others on the river, prior appropriation granted the right to divert a specific quantity of water. How much water? As much as the appropriator wanted, limited only by the requirement that the water be used for a "beneficial purpose," which meant basically any use at all. In an arid region, rewarding appropriators with rights to as much water as they could divert created enormous incentives to maximize the diversions. Once the appropriator made the diversion, he now possessed a permanent legal right to that water.

Such an allocation system creates tremendous inefficiencies. It ignores the economic value of the activity, treating higher- and lower-value uses alike. It encourages economic speculation. It creates an incentive to hoard the resource because the appropriator need not pay for the resource. The government essentially gave away the water to anyone who could use it. Most importantly, allocating a specific quantity of water transformed water into a commodity, like gold or timber. The prior appropriation doctrine transformed water from a shared common resource into private property.

Over time, as western farmers irrigated additional lands with surface water, they diverted more and more water from rivers through their headgates, into their canals, and onto their fields. In many places, the farmers eventually exhausted the supply: the rivers dried up and remained dry until the next rainstorm. Additionally, many rivers became overappropriated, which means that the total quantity of water rights claimed by diverters exceeded the actual annual flow in the river. By 1898, diverters from the Boise River claimed rights to 150 times more water than the actual flow of the river. This anomaly led to the creation of the curious distinction between "paper rights" and "wet water." Perhaps only in the surreal world of western water is it possible to refer, with a straight face, to "wet water."

The prior appropriation doctrine had horrific effects. It allowed, for example, the complete dewatering of a river or creek. To early miners and farmers, the most important objective was the extraction of ore and the cultivation of land. If fish in a dewatered river died as a consequence, it seemed a small price to pay for progress. If dewatering caused the death of riverbank trees and shrubs or a decline in the number of animals and birds, those effects were accepted as inevitable by-products of the conquest of nature by human effort. Nineteenth-century settlers were not concerned with environmental protection, ecosystem management, or riparian habitat, nor did they have an aesthetic appreciation for the value of water in a free-flowing river or creek. To them, nature was to be explored, conquered, and tamed. Indeed, water law developed a curious doctrine of waste. A diverter could lose his prior appropriation right by failing to divert the water. Leaving water in the river did not conserve the water. It wasted it.

Remarkably, this system endures, though our interests and values have changed. We allocate enormous quantities of water to senior appropriators so that they can grow low-value crops. They receive this water even though others could make better use of it. The prior appropriation system is so entrenched that courts and legislatures have not yet developed the final stage of the history of riparianism: a reasonable use system that balances the utility of new water uses against those of senior appropriation rights.

The rise of the prior appropriation doctrine is often attributed to the natural aridity of the American West. The hundredth meridian runs through the middle of North and South Dakota, Nebraska, and Kansas, divides the Oklahoma panhandle from the rest of the state, and continues down through the middle of Texas. The annual precipitation west of that line ranges between five and twenty inches per year (except for the Pacific Northwest), compared with thirty to sixty inches per year east of the hundredth meridian. Aridity alone, however, cannot account for the rise of the prior appropriation system because other, equally tenable, competing systems emerged in these arid lands.

Quite tellingly, several different ethnic groups in the West recognized water rights that differed profoundly from the prior appropriation system. In some Native American communities, including the Anasazi and the Hohokam during the first millennium A.D., and the Tohono O'odham, the Hopi, and the Western Shoshone more recently, water was a sacred element of their religions. Pilgrimages, songs, and ceremonies celebrate the regenerative power of water. These tribes conceived of water in communal, not individualistic, terms. In New Mexico and California, a unique form of water rights, called "pueblo water rights," developed during the period of Spanish and Mexican domination. Under pueblo water rights, the town, or pueblo, holds water rights in trust for the benefit of the entire community. To this day, in many Hispanic communities in northern New Mexico, the allocation of water through irrigation canals, called acequias, is administered by an elected official, called the majordomo, who assures that all members of the acequia association receive an adequate supply of water. The allocation is according to need, not according to priority. In Utah, the Church of the Latter-day Saints, whose members are better known as Mormons, developed a system of water rights that served religious interests. A centralized system of decision making led to the cooperative construction of thousands of canals that produced a flourishing agricultural community in the late nineteenth century. According to the church, the water belonged to the group, not to specific individuals.

So why did prior appropriation come to dominate water rights? Rather than being an inevitable function of aridity, the prior appropriation doctrine reflects the values that European settlers embraced concerning the role of government, the legal system, and the environment. In this nine-teenth-century democratic society, government encouraged free enter-prise, the legal system fostered private property rights, and the environment was used as an instrument of economic development. In the context of this set of values, the prior appropriation system served beautifully. It stimulated economic activity by rewarding entrepreneurs with secure property rights; it also encouraged the maximum utilization of water resources.

Aridity was nonetheless important. In the United States, political boundaries seldom conform to the boundaries of watersheds, which are ridges of high land that divide an area drained by one river from areas drained by adjoining river systems. In the West, many states are simply rec-tangular swatches of prairie, lines drawn on a blank map in utter disregard of topographical features. The first person to protest such an odd system was John Wesley Powell. Though best known as the first white explorer of the Colorado River through the Grand Canyon, Powell is equally impor-tant to history as an early director of the U.S. Geological Survey (USGS). In 1878, Powell prepared a report for Congress that explained the folly of attempting to dole out federal lands to settlers based on the Homestead Act's assumption that 160 acres was sufficient land for a family farm. In the West, everything turns on water. If one had access to water, 160 acres was an enormous amount of land, but without water, 160 acres would prove sufficient only to graze a few head of cattle. Despite the soundness of his reasoning and report, Congress disregarded his advice, and the country has ignored him ever since. Instead of honoring or respecting the boundaries of watersheds, we have engineered various projects that flout or challenge hydrologic reality.

Nowhere is the effort to conquer nature to suit human needs more evident than in the role of the federal government in harnessing and exploiting the waters of the United States, particularly in the West. The West has substantial surface flows produced by the winter snowpack that melts over the course of the spring season, filling rivers and streams. The problem for farms and cities is that these flows are not always available when they are needed. By summertime, these surface flows may be reduced to a trickle. In the state of nature, there is an abundance of surface water in the springtime, when little or none is needed, and a paucity of surface flow in mid- to late summer, when the need is acute. The seasonality of this timing has been the prime impetus for creating dams. Dams create reservoirs, which serve as storage facilities, smoothing out the boom-or-bust cycle of surface water supplies by providing controlled flows that are available to downstream farmers when and as needed for their crops and to growing cities for municipal and industrial use.

Although humans have dammed rivers for centuries, the heyday of the dam-building era occurred in the twentieth century, when engineers, with considerable bravado and technological wizardry, dammed the most formidable and wildest rivers in North America. This era began with the classic effort to tame the mighty Colorado River with the construction of Hoover Dam during the 1930s. Set against the backdrop of the Great Depression, this engineering challenge dazzled the country. Although Hoover Dam is a remarkably beautiful example of art deco architecture, this technological success was achieved at no small cost: 112 men died during the effort. The creation of Hoover Dam led to a frenzy of dam building between the 1930s and the 1960s that resulted in the transformation of many of the great rivers in the West into storage reservoirs and hydroelectric generating plants. Such was the fate of the Columbia, Snake, Green, Sacramento, San Joaquin, American, Kings, Kern, Stanislaus, Salt, Gila, Verde, Missouri, San Juan, Gunnison, and, of course, the Colorado, all at the hands of engineers from the U.S. Bureau of Reclamation (Bureau) and the U.S. Army Corps of Engineers (Corps). The mighty Colorado, the once wild river that drew John Wesley Powell to raft its entire length in 1869, has become a set of storage reservoirs, a gigantic plumbing system under the control of the Bureau.

An obvious but important fact about dams is that it takes money, a lot of money, to build a dam on a major river. The private sector showed no interest in such undertakings because the risks were huge and the costs far outweighed the return on private capital. The Bureau and the Corps, whose allies included agribusiness and important members of Congress from the West, undertook such projects on behalf of farmers and cities. The immediate losers in these water projects were Native American tribes. Seldom did tribes obtain water rights from federal projects. Indeed, these projects frequently and profoundly damaged the agricultural economies on many reservations. By holding back melting snow waters until the summer, when they would be needed by Anglo farmers and cities, dams eliminated the historic springtime floods that created wide and fertile floodplains on which many tribes depended to plant beans and corn. The subsistence agricultural economies of some tribes suffered because of dams.

Today, as a result of the dam building era, we move huge quantities of water out of watersheds, often to cities hundreds of miles away. To accomplish this feat, we have engineered pumping stations with pipes that go over mountains, drilled tunnels that go through mountains, used unlined canals through the sand dunes of the Imperial Irrigation District in southern California, and built a concrete-lined canal called the Central Arizona Project that moves water from the Colorado River east to Phoenix and eventually south to Tucson, a distance of 330 miles and almost 3,000 feet up in elevation. From the Colorado River basin alone, we supply water to areas outside the basin that include Denver, Albuquerque, Salt Lake City, San Diego, and Los Angeles. We literally move water uphill to wealth and power.

As the history of riparianism and prior appropriation suggests, legal rules promoted economic development and created private property rights in water. Alas, the rules encouraged waste and placed no importance on protecting the environment. Thanks to the federal government, enormous growth has occurred in areas that lack adequate water resources, such as Los Angeles. To achieve this growth, we have engineered an elaborate infrastructure that ignores Mother Nature's hydrologic boundaries at an enormous cost to the environment.

Chapter 2

Human Reliance on Groundwater

"When you drink the water, remember the spring."
—Chinese proverb

Ubar, the fabled city of ancient Arabia known as "the Atlantis of the Sands," was an oasis for camel caravans transporting frankincense across the desert. A fortress with eight towers surrounded the only water for hundreds of miles. According to various religious myths, the city suddenly vanished into the desert sands without leaving a trace. The myths suggest that God destroyed Ubar, for it had become an evil place. Many adventurers, including Lawrence of Arabia, have searched for Ubar without success. In the 1980s, Nicholas Clapp, an amateur archaeologist, led an expedition that successfully located and unearthed Ubar.

It turns out that Ubar was not burned or sacked or destroyed by an earthquake. Somewhere between 300 and 500 A.D., it collapsed into a huge underground limestone cavern. Over time, Ubar's inhabitants had relied increasingly on a spring-fed well. According to Clapp, "Over Millennia, Ubar's great well had watered countless caravans and had been drawn upon to irrigate a sizable oasis. Handspan by handspan, its waters had receded, and the limestone shelf on which the fortress rested became less and less stable, for it was the water underneath Ubar that quite literally held the place up." The ultimate collapse probably was caused by a minor tremor from a distant earthquake, but the seismic shock cracked the limestone and caused the entire city to fall into the cavern, where it was quickly covered by desert sand. The inhabitants of Ubar, 2,300–2,500 years ago, sowed the seeds of their town's destruction by excess reliance on groundwater.

— —

The deep, rich soil of the High Plains of southwest Kansas and the Oklahoma–Texas panhandle attracted generations of homesteaders. Prospects for farming this flat, treeless area seemed bright if farmers could find water for their crops. But the region had few rivers or streams from which to divert surface water. Dryland farming was not an option for a region in which rainfall averages only twelve inches a year (compared to thirty inches received by the Midwest farm area). Perhaps there was water beneath the ground. There was. An aquifer called the Ogallala contained vast amounts of water. The problem was how to get it out of the ground.

The extraction of groundwater eloquently testifies to human ingenuity. No one knows when human beings dug the first groundwater well, but the Egyptians, the Chinese, and the Persians constructed wells as early as 2000 B.C. Using drill bits constructed from bamboo, the Chinese were able to drill as deep as 3,000 feet. In the United States, in 1807, two brothers in West Virginia drilled a well to extract brine that they distilled into salt to preserve meat, fish, and other foods. Although these early wells were drilled using humans or horsepower, by the 1830s, specially adapted steam engines powered the well-drilling equipment. In the late nineteenth century, the discovery of oil fueled rapid advances in the well-drilling industry. Yet the source of power for the pumps needed to lift oil or water from the new wells remained problematic. In the 1890s, the city of Tucson used wood to fuel steam engines to pump groundwater. In two years, the city burned 1,782 cords of wood—a scarce commodity in the desert.

In the late nineteenth century, the most popular form of energy for groundwater pumping on the High Plains was wind. Crude, homemade windmills dotted the landscape. The historian Walter Prescott Webb noted the symbolic significance of windmills: "The windmill was like a flag marking the spot where a small victory had been won in the fight for water in an arid land." Easily erected anywhere, windmills offered an ideal solution to the problem of providing water for cattle and crops. In short order, windmills appeared by the thousands all over the West. Although wind was plentiful and free, windmills were limited in their ability to lift large quantities of water from significant depths. Even a gigantic windmill—and some had twenty-five-foot diameters—could lift only about thirty-seven gallons per minute from a maximum depth of seventy or eighty feet.

For household water, High Plains farmers used reciprocal (or farmhouse) pumps—still seen at campgrounds around the country and in countless movies. As the pump handle moves up and down, it creates a partial vacuum that forces water up the pipe and out the spigot. Because the driving force is air at atmospheric pressure, the reciprocal pump can lift water only about forty feet.

In the 1890s, the development of rotary or centrifugal pumps gave High Plains farmers access to deeper groundwater aquifers. The basic principle of the centrifugal pump can be illustrated by swinging a pail of water around in a circle at the end of a rope. If we made a small hole in the bottom of the pail, water would discharge through the hole at high speed. An airtight cover placed over the top of the pail creates a partial vacuum inside the pail as water is discharged through the hole. If we replace the rope with an intake pipe, the vacuum causes additional water to flow into the pail, replacing the water that flowed out the hole in the bottom. Centrifugal pumps greatly increased the capacity for pumping large quantities of water, but ranchers and farmers needed to find a source of power to drive the pumps. They experimented with steam power but found that it required constant oversight and maintenance. However, in the twentieth century, as Henry Ford prepared to market his Model T, modifications to the internal combustion engine allowed for its use as a power source to pump groundwater. This development profoundly changed the face of western agriculture because it allowed farmers and ranchers to locate groundwater wells wherever they expected to find water.

Using windmills, steam, and gasoline engines as power, High Plains farmers tapped into the Ogallala Aquifer, which underlies portions of seven states, from Texas and New Mexico in the south, to Wyoming and South Dakota in the north. Because the region receives so little rain, the Ogallala Aquifer receives almost no natural recharge. The aquifer filled up with water from glaciers 10,000–25,000 years ago. From the 1880s to the 1930s, European farmers plowed under the High Plains and relied on the scant rainfall, surface water diversions, and shallow wells to irrigate fields to grow wheat, sugar beets, oats, corn, and alfalfa. During the Great Depression of the 1930s, depressed wheat prices caused farmers to cease planting. A series of lengthy droughts and high winds produced severe dust storms (lasting 134 days in 1937), gave the area its dust bowl nickname, and caused farmers to abandon vast amounts of land. Then, advances in technology permitted users to pump from deeper in the Ogallala at lower costs. What saved farmers on the High Plains was a massive increase in groundwater pumping from the Ogallala. Advances in technology enabled farmers to overcome the limitations imposed by Mother Nature.

During the New Deal, the principal energy source for groundwater pumps shifted from wood and gasoline engines to natural gas and electricity. Before the New Deal, only 10 percent of American farms had power-line electric service. The Rural Electrification Administration, together with hydroelectric power generated by a series of dams constructed on major western rivers, brought cheap electric power to vast areas of the rural West. In the 1930s, the technology for drilling wells and extracting groundwater was quite primitive; it was impossible to extract water from lower than seventy or eighty feet below the surface of the earth. Technological change in the ensuing years witnessed a remarkable revolution that made Ogallala groundwater a most attractive source for High Plains farmers.

The groundwater spigot was opened wide in the 1940s and 1950s, as high-lift turbine pumps, industrial and automobile engines, center-pivot irrigation systems, gear-driven pump heads, smaller diameter wells and casings, and the availability of natural gas and powerline electricity as energy sources dramatically lowered the costs for installing and operating irrigation systems. These technological developments profoundly increased the capacity of wells to extract groundwater. Large-capacity wells could retrieve water from 3,000 feet below the surface and produce 1,200–1,300 gallons per minute. These developments caused a spectacular expansion of irrigation on lands overlying the Ogallala Aquifer. Pumping increased more than 1,000 percent, from 651 billion to 7.5 trillion gallons per year. On the Texas High Plains alone, the number of wells jumped from 8,400 in 1948 to 42,200 in 1957. These wells irrigated over 3.5 million acres of land. By 1990, sixteen million acres of the High Plains were irrigated with water from the Ogallala Aquifer, as farmers grew fields of corn, milo, wheat, and alfalfa. The High Plains has become "the breadbasket of the world," part of a huge, vertically integrated agricultural industry. Cattle feedlots and beef-processing plants supply almost 40 percent of the country's dinner-table beef. In this process, the vast resources of the Ogallala seemed inexhaustible. But as early as 1940, the groundwater table had begun to plummet. In some sections of Kansas and Texas, the water table dropped more than 150 feet by 1980.

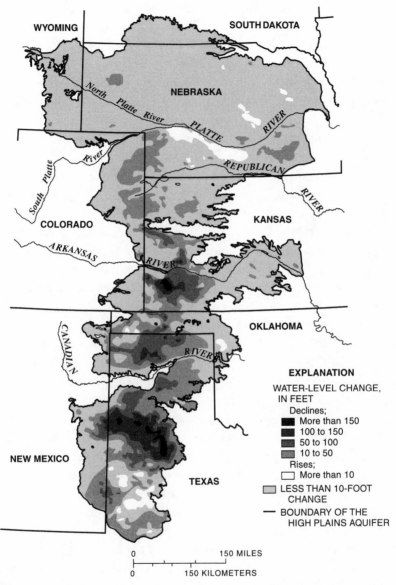

FIGURE 2.1. Groundwater level declines beneath the High Plains portion of the Ogallala Aquifer, as of 1997. Figure courtesy of the U.S. Geological Survey.

Groundwater is an extraordinarily attractive source of water for farms, mines, cities, and homeowners. First, it is available throughout the year and it exists almost everywhere in the country, including the southwestern deserts which, during the last ice age, were covered with huge freshwater lakes. Water from these lakes percolated into the ground and collected in aquifers. Unlike rivers and streams, which are few and far between in the West, aquifers exist below almost the entire region. Tapping into this supply has vastly expanded the acreage that can be commercially irrigated. Cities and farms that rely on surface water sources must construct dams to store the water for use when needed and must have canals, ditches, or other conveyance systems to bring the water to the treatment plants or fields, which might be several miles distant. A substantial amount of water is lost from the surface of reservoirs due to evaporation, and more is lost by infiltration during transmission through ditches. If the ditch is an earthen one, as many are in the West, transmission losses by infiltration may exceed 50 percent of the water diverted from the river or stream. Even if the ditch is lined, evaporation losses may be substantial. Relying on groundwater eliminates both the construction expenses and the water loss. Cities or farms that need water simply turn on the pump.

Another attraction of groundwater is its quality. Much surface water, especially in the West, is highly saline as a result of the salts that dissolve into rainwater or snowmelt as it runs off the land or percolates through the ground and into a river or stream. The Colorado River, for instance, picks up extensive salts because of the geology of the Colorado Plateau. High-elevation areas of southwestern Wyoming, western Colorado, eastern Utah, and northern Arizona were once parts of a vast inland sea. The sediments deposited during the period known to geologists as the Cretaceous period, about 65–140 million years ago, contain high concentrations of calcium, magnesium, and sodium. As the Colorado River downcuts through these thick geologic layers, the minerals dissolve in the water. Similarly, rainfall and snowmelt that move across the surface of the Colorado Plateau, draining into myriad arroyos that eventually reach the Colorado River, also pick up these soluble minerals.

Surface water quality varies enormously, even within a single river. Spring snowmelt or heavy rainfall will alter overnight the chemical composition of water in a river. As farmers divert surface flows with high turbidity—a scientific term for muddiness—into their canals and ditches, the slow flow through the conveyance system allows sediment to settle out.

The buildup of silt in the farmers' canals or ditches impedes their operational efficiency and may require the farmers to dredge the ditch. The high salinity of surface water causes other problems for farmers. When farmers irrigate their fields with highly saline water, the salts accumulate in the soil. Although some crops, such as jojoba beans, grow well under saline conditions, most high-value crops, such as citrus and other fruits, beans, grains, and legumes, are particularly sensitive to salinity. Farmers will first suffer a reduction in crop yields and, eventually, may find that they need to grow different, lower-value crops.

Salinity creates other problems for domestic users. Calcium and magnesium in water cause the water to be "hard," the reason many homeowners invest in water-softening devices that replace the calcium ions with sodium ions. Otherwise, the hard water requires using extra soap and detergent to clean dishes and clothes. Hard water may corrode a home's plumbing system and require more frequent replacement of water heaters and other appliances. It also affects the infrastructure of the municipal water supply system, usually by causing the buildup of scale on the inside of the pipes and valves, thus reducing the capacity of the system and increasing maintenance costs. Groundwater, in contrast, tends to have uniform quality and low salinity.

Last, but not least, among reasons for the use of groundwater is the nature of our legal system. In the nineteenth century, when American courts developed groundwater law, hydrology was an infant science. In 1850, the Supreme Court of Connecticut explained that water, "whether moving or motionless in the earth, is not, in the eye of the law, distinct from the earth. The laws of its existence and progress, although there, are not uniform, and cannot be known or regulated. It rises to great heights and moves collaterally, by influences beyond our apprehension. These influences are so secret, changeable, and uncontrollable, we cannot subject them to the regulations of law, nor build upon them a system of rules, as has been done with streams upon the surface." This reasoning made sense in 1850; since then, however, the law in most states has not kept pace with advances in the science of hydrology. As a consequence, the legal rules fail to conform with physical reality.

The chasm between science and law can be traced back to the work of Clesson S. Kinney, a Utah lawyer who published *A Treatise on the Law of Irrigation* in 1894. Kinney believed that an inexhaustible supply of water lay underground and flowed in "subterranean or underground watercourses."

Kinney divided these underground watercourses into "known" channels, which contained "subflow" or "underflow," and "unknown" channels. Kinney believed, and the courts agreed, that surface water law (prior appropriation) should determine rights to water in the "known" channels, and the reasonable use doctrine should determine rights to water in the "unknown" channels. Kinney's basic, albeit flawed, concept was that some groundwater was connected to a river or stream and flowed in a geologic formation beneath the surface water in "known" channels, while other groundwater percolated, like water through your Mr. Coffee machine, through the ground in "unknown" channels. Given this understanding, it made sense to apply the legal rules of prior appropriation to water that supposedly flowed underground in the known channels, as though these channels were simply underground rivers or streams. All other underground water, by hypothesis inexhaustible in supply, was therefore available for pumping under the legal rules of reasonable use.

In fact, there is no sharp, meaningful distinction between surface and groundwater. Instead, surface and groundwater form a continuum in the hydrologic cycle. Unfortunately, American groundwater law has never recovered from the contributions of Clesson Kinney. To this day, most states use the reasonable use doctrine to govern groundwater, and employ some other legal system for surface water. Arizona distinguishes "subflow" from percolating groundwater, and California recognizes "underflow" and "subterranean streams" flowing through "known" and "unknown" channels. Oklahoma refuses to acknowledge any connection between surface and groundwater. In 2000 the Oklahoma Supreme Court determined, "When the groundwater surfaces as a spring and forms a stream, it is at that point that the stream water statutes apply."

Although it is difficult to obtain new surface water rights in both the East and the West, it is relatively easy to secure groundwater rights. The law concerning groundwater rights varies from state to state but involves one of four rules. In most western states, groundwater rights are determined by a prior appropriation doctrine similar to the surface water prior appropriation system. This priority system will protect senior groundwater pumpers from harm caused by more junior pumpers. A second system, the reasonable use doctrine, in force in some western states and most eastern states, allows pumping for any beneficial use and offers no protection to more senior pumpers from the activities of more recent junior pumpers. Some states use the English rule of absolute ownership, which grants landowners complete autonomy to pump whatever quantity of groundwater can be extracted from beneath their property. The final system, the correlative rights doctrine of California and Vermont, provides for groundwater to be shared by all owners of land above the aquifer. Although some states require prospective groundwater pumpers to obtain a permit from a state regulatory agency, the upshot of these groundwater rules is that most states routinely allow the drilling of new wells.

In summary, thanks to new energy sources and developments in technology that made pumping more efficient and economical, and for added reasons of convenience, availability, quality, and permissive legal doctrine, groundwater has become a critical source of water throughout the nation. In 1995, the United States used 341 trillon gallons per day of freshwater, 22 percent of which was groundwater. Also in 1995, California alone pumped 14,500 billion gallons of groundwater per day. Groundwater withdrawals actually exceeded surface water diversions in Florida, Kansas, Nebraska, and Mississippi. In the United States, more than half of the population relies on groundwater for their drinking water supply. Two-thirds of the groundwater withdrawals occurred in the West, where 78 percent of the water (groundwater and surface water diversions) is for a single dominant use: agriculture.

FIGURE 2.2. Estimated percentage of state populations that used groundwater for drinking water in 1995. Figure courtesy of the U.S. Geological Survey.

This critical, historic consumption by agriculture has occasioned the creation of terms that define volumes of water by reference to irrigation standards. Thus, we speak of an acre-foot of water, that is, the amount of water needed to cover an acre of land with a foot of water, which turns out to be 325,851 gallons. It is a helpful measurement when referring to various crops with differing irrigation needs, but the acre-foot terminology is commonly used to describe water use by cities and mines as well. Not many urban residents, I suspect, think of their water consumption in terms of acre-feet, and the use of this term of art masks true levels of water use because people cannot easily equate acre-feet to any familiar terms of measurement.

The country cannot sustain even the current levels of groundwater use, never mind the projected increases in groundwater consumption over the next two decades. Our enormous expansion of groundwater pumping since the 1940s—a blink of an eye in geologic time—has caused a number of serious environmental problems. Throughout the country, water table levels are dropping as pumping exceeds recharge. Overdrafting or "mining" groundwater creates serious problems. Because water is heavy, about two pounds per quart or 1,358 tons per acre-foot, more energy is needed to lift water from lower levels. The drilling of new, deeper wells may be required, which is often a considerable expense. Poorer water quality may result because water pumped from lower levels frequently contains naturally occurring elements, such as arsenic, fluoride, and radon. At deeper levels, the earth's higher internal temperature dissolves more of these elements into solution. Along coastal areas, overdrafting may cause the intrusion of salt water into the aquifer, rendering the water no longer potable. This problem is quite serious in California, Florida, and South Carolina.

Overdrafting even raises the issue of running out of water. One commentator thinks that the irrigated acreage on the High Plains may drop from 7 million to 2 million in the next two decades. The Ogallala once held 3 billion acre-feet of water, but High Plains farmers pumped more than a half-billion acre-feet between 1960 and 1990. As much as half of the remaining water is too deep in the aquifer to justify the costs of recovery or is of poor quality. As the water table has plunged, some High Plains farms have already returned to dryland farming, and conservation districts have undertaken massive water conservation programs.

Another consequence of overdrafting is the prospect of land subsidence,

FIGURE 2.3. Land subsidence in the San Joaquin Valley of California. Signs on pole show approximate altitudes of land surface in 1925, 1955, and 1977. Photograph courtesy of the U.S. Geological Survey.

in which the land surface actually cracks or drops, in some cases dramatically (see figure 2.3). This phenomenon is a function of the amount of water withdrawn by pumping and the character of the subsurface geology. What geologists call the Basin and Range Province extends from western Texas through New Mexico, Arizona, Utah, Nevada, and up to southern Oregon. The topography consists of mountain ranges that border broad basins, called alluvial valleys, which consist of permeable, loosely compacted alluvial sand and gravel. The alluvium may be as much as 10,000 feet thick and may contain vast quantities of groundwater. The process of pumping water out of the aquifer can change the structural integrity of the surrounding soil.

Imagine a sand castle that you or your child has built with wet sand at the beach. When first constructed, the castle has great stability even up to the spires that adorn the turrets; with the passage of time, however, the effects of gravity, wind, and sun take their toll on the castle. As the water drains away from it, the castle slowly begins to crumble. The same thing can happen to an aquifer: the unconsolidated alluvial sand and gravel begins to settle. What happens at the surface depends on a number of vari-

FIGURE 2.4. Sign warning motorists of subsidence hazard was erected after an earth fissure damaged a road in Pima County, Arizona (left). Earth fissure near Picacho, Arizona (right). Photographs courtesy of the U.S. Geological Survey.

ables, but often, cracks in the earth's surface, called fissures, appear. In southern Arizona, some fissures measure ten feet wide, fifty feet deep, and several miles long.

Subsidence at the surface can damage homes and commercial structures and reduce property values. Underground, this settling process compacts the soil and reduces the storage capacity of the aquifer, impeding natural recharge. Land subsidence is a serious problem in Florida and coastal areas of east Texas, including the cities of Houston and Galveston, where groundwater pumping has caused significant subsidence that increases the risk of flooding and makes coastal areas more vulnerable to destructive tidal surges from hurricanes. Land subsidence caused by groundwater pumping is hardly a new phenomenon. That's what happened to Ubar.

The final consequence of groundwater pumping is its impact on surface water, including lakes, ponds, rivers, creeks, streams, springs, wetlands, and estuaries. These consequences range from minimal to catastrophic. As an example of a catastrophe, consider the Santa Cruz River.

Chapter 3

How Does a River Go Dry?

The Santa Cruz in Tucson

"All streams flow into the sea;
yet the sea is not full.
To the place the streams come from,
there they return again."
—Ecclesiastes 1:7

Driving west from Tucson, Arizona, toward the Tucson Mountains, you reach a bridge and a sign that reads "Santa Cruz River." As you glance at the fifty-yard-wide stream channel below the bridge, you're struck by an incongruous sight. There is no water in the Santa Cruz River. The channel is an expanse of dry sand. When tourists see the dry river, they chortle: "In Arizona, even rivers look like a desert!" However, the Santa Cruz through Tucson was not always a dry wash. Not too long ago, it had perennial flow in some sections and intermittent flow in others. In the uplands, adjacent to the river, stood enormous stands of mesquite trees and, along the banks, cottonwood and willow trees formed a lush riparian corridor that shaded the river and provided wonderful habitat for birds, small game, and even deer, coyote, bobcats, and an occasional mountain lion. But groundwater pumping has lowered the water table, drained the river of its flow, killed the cottonwood, willow, and mesquite trees, and driven much of the wildlife elsewhere. Today, the river flows only during spring snowmelt, during heavy rains such as the summer monsoon, or because of the release of effluent from the city's treatment plant. The Santa Cruz in Tucson is a dry river, an oxymoron.

Located in the Sonoran Desert, Tucson is approximately 2,500 feet above sea level and receives twelve inches of rain in a typical year (compared, for instance, to the state of Michigan, which receives thirty-five inches). Although the rainfall may seem modest, some southwestern deserts receive an average of three inches of rain per year. As a result, the habitat includes large numbers of mesquite and palo verde trees, shrubs, wildflowers, and animals, making the Sonoran the most diverse of North America's deserts.

Tucson sits in an alluvial valley rimmed by five mountain ranges that provide beautiful vistas, forests of pine and aspen trees, cool retreats from the summer heat, and even a ski resort. The higher mountains, particularly the Santa Catalinas, the Rincons, and the Santa Ritas, receive an average of thirty to forty inches of rain per year. During spring snowmelt, mountain creeks fill with water that tumbles down to the valley below, filling the Santa Cruz River that runs north through Tucson. The headwaters of the Santa Cruz River are in the Patagonia Mountains in southern Arizona, and the river first flows south into Mexico; it then loops back and reenters the United States. It continues north up a valley between the Sierrita Mountains to the west and the Santa Rita Mountains to the east. It passes through the San Xavier Indian Reservation, a division of the Tohono O'odham Nation, past an eighteenth-century mission, San Xavier del Bac, and then through the city of Tucson. North of Tucson, the river veers west and eventually flows into the Gila River near Phoenix.

The Santa Cruz River provided the impetus for original settlements in Tucson, first by Native Americans, then by Hispanic missionaries and settlers. Indeed, the word "Tucson" derives from a Tohono O'odham word, *stook-zone*, meaning "water at the foot of black mountain." The Santa Cruz River's perennial flows fostered self-sufficient agricultural communities whose principal crops included corn, beans, squash, and cotton. Recent archaeological discoveries have determined that Tucson was populated during the Late Archaic period—8,000 B.C. to 150 A.D.—by skilled farmers, not just hunters and gatherers. These prehistoric farmers were followed by the Hohokam, whose civilization thrived until about 1450 A.D. Their descendants, the Tohono O'odham, continued to live in the Santa Cruz valley, where they developed a quite clever farming technique known as *ak chin*. Immediately after the spring floods began to subside, Tohono

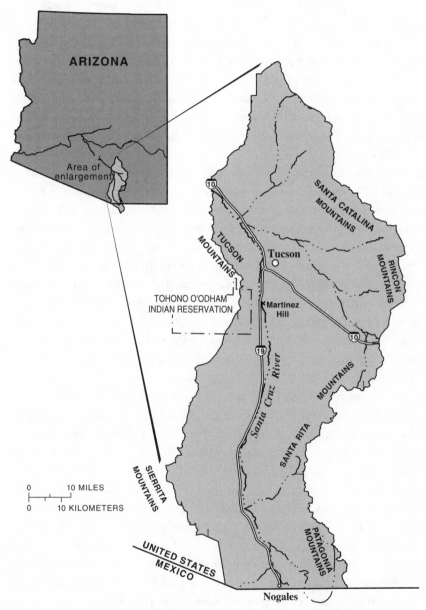

FIGURE 3.1. The upper Santa Cruz River basin in southern Arizona.

O'odham farmers would rush into the fertile floodplain and plant seeds of beans, squash, melon, and cat's claw (a vine used for weaving baskets).

In the late seventeenth century, the first Spanish settlers arrived, led by a Jesuit missionary, Father Eusebio Francisco Kino, who founded the mission at San Xavier del Bac. Father Kino introduced livestock grazing to the Santa Cruz valley, as well as new crops, including wheat, barley, oats, carrots, onions, and fruit trees. Unfortunately, the Europeans also brought with them diseases to which the Native Americans were vulnerable. The Indian population in the valley decreased by 95 percent between 1700 and 1800.

With the discovery of gold in California, the Old Pueblo, as Tucson came to be known, became a trading center and a stopping point for travelers heading west as well as north. Travelers entering Arizona from the east preferred this route, known as the southern route or the Gila Trail, because travel across northern Arizona meant confronting the Grand Canyon, while travelers across central Arizona encountered the rugged White Mountains and Mogollon Rim, areas controlled by Apaches, with whom there were increasing feuds. With the arrival of stagecoaches in the 1850s, the end of war with the Apaches in the 1870s, and finally, the completion of the Southern Pacific railroad system in the 1880s, most pioneers eventually opted to select one of the more northern routes. Tucson's era as a trading center had faded.

In the nineteenth century, giant cottonwood trees, smaller willow trees, and shrubs grew along the banks of the Santa Cruz River, creating a rich riparian environment that attracted myriad bird species and abundant wildlife. The diaries of early explorers describe a river full of "fish and tortoises of various kinds." Beaver, muskrat, and waterfowl were common. On the upland areas, mesquite bosques (near-river forests) covered vast areas. Nineteenth-century travelers described a valley covered with poplar, willow, ash, oak, and walnut trees. In the nineteenth century, two dams built across the river created Silver and Warner Lakes. The impounded water powered two gristmills to supply flour and a small stamping mill to process ore from nearby mines. The lakes became popular recreational spots, provided opportunities for waterfowl hunting, and sustained a commercial fishing venture.

Also in the late nineteenth century, new groundwater pump technology opened the way for more intensive use of water for agriculture in the Santa Cruz Valley. Alfalfa for cattle and wheat for human consumption grew well in the valley but demanded large-scale irrigation efforts. So too did pecan and citrus trees. The increased irrigation caused the water table to drop to a depth the technology could not reach. This decline, in turn, prompted farmers to dig crosscut ditches across the river in an attempt to collect more subsurface water. In the 1890s, heavy rains flooded the river and the ditches caused what hydrologists call entrenchment: the degradation of the river channel by a scouring process that lowers the river bottom and leaves steep or vertical banks along the sides. As the soil dries out, the banks collapse and the river channel becomes wider and deeper.

The European settlers contributed to the further degradation of the river when they cut trees to clear fields, build homes, fuel fires, and operate groundwater pumps. The removal of trees from a riparian zone severely impacts the river. Trees, shrubs, and grasses along rivers and creeks, as well as adjoining wetlands, slow the flow of water, which is particularly important during high flows or floods. Put simply, without trees, shrubs, grasses, and wetlands, rainwater enters the river channel more quickly and produces a more intense flood. The flooding process itself further abrades the river bottom, thus exacerbating the entrenchment process. Even though these human activities degraded the Santa Cruz River, the river remained relatively healthy and supported perennial flows until the 1940s; there were cottonwood-willow forests adjacent to the river and huge mesquite bosques on the upland areas. The Tohono O'odham still grew beans and corn in the fertile floodplain.

Today, the Santa Cruz River is but a sad mirage of a real river. The cottonwood and willow trees that once lined the river have died, as have the stands of mesquite, poplar, and oak. The birds and wildlife have gone away. The river has died. What happened? To answer this question and to understand the stories that follow, we must understand how water moves.

As the author of Ecclesiastes understood, water goes through a succession of different phases, called the hydrologic cycle. Fueled by the energy of the sun and the force of gravity, the hydrologic cycle continually moves water from the oceans to the land and back again. Oceans cover more than 70 percent of the earth's surface and absorb most of the sun's radiant energy. The sun's energy evaporates seawater, leaves behind the salts, and circulates the water into the atmosphere. Wind currents eventually carry the moisture-laden air over land, which sharply increases the relative humidity. As the relative humidity increases, the water vapor eventually

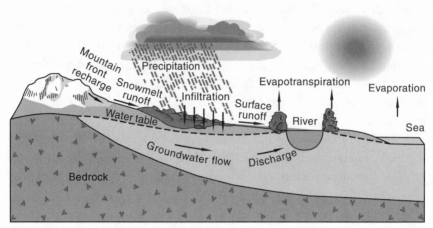

FIGURE 3.2. The hydrologic cycle.

condenses and becomes precipitation, in the form of rain, snow, or hail. As precipitation reaches land, the process of evaporation begins again and 50 percent of the precipitation returns directly to the atmosphere.

Three things happen to the other 50 percent. First, plants and trees absorb water from the soil through their roots but release water back into the atmosphere through their leaves, in a process known as transpiration. Second, the snowmelt or rain moves over the surface of the earth as gravity inevitably causes water to seek the lowest level. This surface runoff flows into creeks, streams, and rivers; eventually some water reaches the ocean, and the hydrologic cycle begins again. Third, and most importantly for our purposes, water percolates or infiltrates into the ground, in a process called recharge, where the water may remain for years, centuries, or even millennia. A portion of the groundwater near rivers and streams eventually emerges from the ground, in a process called discharge, to augment the surface flows of rivers or streams.

Less than 1 percent of the water in the hydrologic cycle is potable (drinkable). The oceans hold about 96.5 percent of the earth's water, though ocean water is clearly not potable because of its salinity. Of the remaining 3.5 percent, 1.7 percent is tied up in polar ice. Another 1 percent of freshwater is less saline than ocean water but still too salty to be drinkable. That leaves only 0.8 percent in lakes, marshes, and rivers, in the ground, and in the atmosphere. Equally surprising, most of this freshwater is not found in lakes, marshes, rivers, other surface water, or the atmosphere. It is groundwater! There is thirty times more potable water in the ground than there is in all the rivers and lakes on earth.

How does groundwater get into the ground? The movement of groundwater depends not only on gravity, but also on the particular geologic characteristics of what geologists call aquifers, subsurface geologic formations saturated with water. Most aquifers are composed of layers of fine sand and silt, larger gravel particles, fractured rock, and clay. In any particular geological setting, sediments or fractures produce interconnected voids that allow the transmission of water through the ground. Over the passage of millennia, water collects in aquifers—lots of water during wetter times such as the ice ages and less at other times. But aquifers are not static in their accumulation of water; their ability to accumulate water depends on recharge and discharge processes. Most recharge occurs when water from snowmelt and rainfall infiltrates the ground and percolates down to the aquifer. Over millions of years, recharge gradually added to the amount of water stored in aquifers. As the amount of water increased, some groundwater flowed from the aquifers toward rivers, creeks, or the ocean, where it discharged from the ground and joined the surface water. In the Santa Cruz River, water discharging from the aquifer sustained the river's perennial flow.

The character of an aquifer depends on the geologic history of the region. In the Santa Cruz River valley, a set of mountain ranges consisting of hard rock, such as granite, surrounds an alluvial valley. Beneath the valley floor is a hard rock formation called, reasonably enough, bedrock, which is impermeable to water flow. The alluvium—loose sediments hundreds of feet thick deposited on top of the bedrock—consists of sand and gravel eroded from the surrounding mountain ranges by wind and water. In the northern part of the United States, deposits associated with continental glaciers formed aquifers. With crushing force, glaciers moved south from the colder regions, grinding the bedrock over which they moved into sand, gravel, and even large boulders, only to leave this material in massive deposits called glacial till as the glaciers retreated in warmer millennia. In Texas, the Edwards Aquifer in the San Antonio region is an example of a large limestone aquifer. Water flowing through small limestone cracks over eons dissolved the limestone, and the cracks became fissures and even grew into caverns. Even harder rocks, such as granite and basalt (lava), can form aquifers if they are fractured.

An easy way to understand recharge and discharge from aquifers is to conduct an experiment with your bathtub. First, plug the bottom of the tub, then dump a couple of hundred pounds of sand into it. Your spouse may think that you have lost your mind but will come around once you announce that you are conducting an experiment in hydrology. If you haven't been committed to an institution by now, turn the water on and let it run for ten to fifteen minutes. This is the recharge. Now, let it alone for a day or so, telling your spouse to shower at the gym, and you will find that the sand at the top of the tub is virtually dry. Under the force of gravity, the molecules of water moved down through the sand and pooled up at the bottom, filling in all the spaces around the granules of sand. Every child who has ever played in beach sand as the tide receded knows that if you dig into moist or dry sand deep enough, you will "discover" water. If you take a kitchen spoon and dig into the sand in your tub, the level at which you hit water is the water table. Below the water table, the sand is completely saturated with water; above the water table, the sand contains air spaces or pockets. Water percolates through the sand in your bathtub in the same way that rain or snowmelt recharges an aquifer. Similarly, the water that drains from your tub resembles how an aquifer discharges water to a river. The bottom of the tub slopes gradually down toward the drain hole. If you remove the drain plug, the water will slowly move down the slope of the tub and out through the drain. The same thing happens when an aquifer discharges water. Where does that naturally discharged water go? To surface watercourses, such as the Santa Cruz River.

Groundwater and surface water are not separate categories of water any more than liquid water and ice are truly separate. The designations "groundwater" and "surface water" merely describe the *physical* location of the water in the hydrologic cycle. Indeed, ground- and surface water form a continuum. Groundwater may become surface water in some portions of a stream, and surface water may become groundwater in other portions. In most regions of the country, virtually all groundwater was once stream flow that seeped into the ground. The converse is also true but not obvious. Consider the following puzzle: where might water in a river come from if it has not rained in a while? No longer a puzzle to you: the water comes from groundwater that has seeped from the aquifer into the river, in what's known as baseflow.

Whether water flows from an aquifer to a stream or the other way around depends on the level of the water table adjacent to the stream. If the level of a stream is lower than the water table in the surrounding

(a) Gaining stream

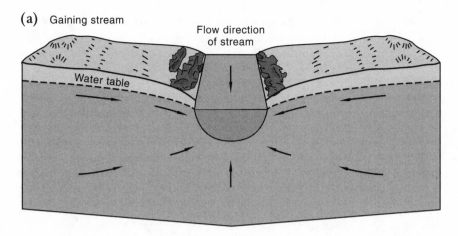

(b) Losing stream

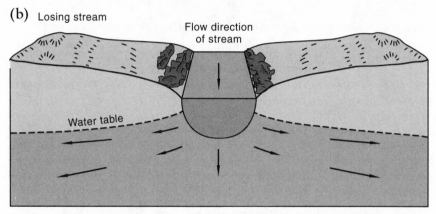

FIGURE 3.3. In a gaining stream (a), water discharges from the surrounding soil into the stream, but in a losing stream (b), water infiltrates the ground. Figures courtesy of the U.S. Geological Survey.

aquifer, water will flow from the aquifer into the stream. A stream that receives discharge from an aquifer is called a gaining stream. Conversely, if the level of a stream is higher than the water table in the surrounding aquifer, then water will flow from the stream toward the aquifer. A stream that recharges an aquifer is called a losing stream(figure 3.3).

To understand baseflow and gaining and losing streams, consider those times when the basement of your house has flooded. After a very heavy rainstorm, your lawn turned into a small pond. Then water began to pour into the basement window wells through casement window frames, or the trap door, and down the walls, where it formed another pond at the foot of your basement stairs. At this point, you had two choices. You could immediately begin to mop up the mess. Or you could turn on the TV and hope that the waters would recede. Sometimes, quite remarkably, they did. Where did they go? Because your basement pond was the equivalent of a losing river, water seeped from the basement through cracks in the foundation into the aquifer—well, actually just the ground below and adjacent to your home. It was possible for water to drain from your house because the water table was below the basement floor.

But now recall a time when you went to retrieve your tennis racquet from the basement, only to find a small puddle in the corner by the workbench. You were surprised because it had not rained recently. Yet the nearby wall was wet and, on closer inspection, water slowly seeped through a crack in the wall. You were very annoyed, so much so that the lesson in hydrology completely escaped you. Your basement was the equivalent of a gaining river with water discharging from the aquifer into the river (the basement). This process is continually occurring in almost every river, but we can't see it because it usually occurs below the surface of the water in the river. Water can discharge into your basement if the groundwater table is above the bottom of your foundation. Under the force of gravity, water flowed to the lowest spot, which, alas, was through a crack in your wall. It is no surprise that houses with such seepage problems are more likely to be found in Houston—a low-elevation region with abundant rainfall—than in Denver—a high-elevation arid region. Even in your neighborhood, your next-door neighbor will have a more severe basement flooding problem if he or she lives downhill closer to a wetland.

The hydrologic cycle teaches us that water exists in different phases and locations. It migrates through a continuous cycle of existence as ocean water, evaporation, condensation, precipitation, infiltration, recharge, discharge, and evaporation again, as the cycle begins anew. For humans, the inherent problem with the hydrologic cycle comes from the physical distribution of the amount of water in each stage, such as rivers, lakes, and aquifers. Water is often not where we want it when we want it. Sometimes it flows seemingly inexplicably where we don't want it, like our basements. More often, we can't get enough of it when we need it. Therefore, we spend billions of dollars on dams, canals, and groundwater wells to move water, thereby altering the hydrologic cycle.

As we now know, it takes energy to move water. For centuries, farmers used muscle power or machines to divert surface water into canals or ditches to irrigate their fields. On a larger scale, humans altered surface water flows by building dams, an effort that requires enormous energy. Using energy to pump groundwater and alter the hydrologic cycle eventually dried up the Santa Cruz River.

When a groundwater well begins to pump water, the withdrawal usually exceeds the rate at which groundwater flows into the vicinity of the well. The withdrawal lowers the surrounding water table, which begins to slope toward the well and creates a cone of depression that looks like the vortex in a drain (figure 3.4a). The shape of the cone depends on several factors, especially the rate at which water is pumped and the permeability of the soil. Water flows more quickly through more permeable soil. As a result, the shape of the cone in this soil will be flatter. If the soil is less permeable, water will flow more slowly, and the shape of the cone will be steeper. If this shape seems incongruous, consider that water enters a well not only at the bottom of the well but also through all points in the screened section of the well shaft below the water table. In permeable soil, water quickly flows laterally to replace the water pumped out of the well. As a result, the cone of depression is relatively flat. In less permeable soil, the water level in the well drops because the lateral flow is too slow to replace the pumped water. A sharp drop in the level of water in the wall produces a steep cone of depression that may resemble an ice cream cone. The initial cone of depression is in the immediate area of the well. As the pumping continues, the cone grows and expands until it intersects a source of water to capture, such as a river or a stream. At this point, the cone draws water directly from the river or stream (figure 3.4b). The pumping has lowered the water table so that less water discharges into the river, thus decreasing the river's flow.

What ultimately killed the Santa Cruz River was groundwater pumping. Recharge from rain and snowmelt typically adds 140,000 acre-feet per year (af/yr) to the aquifer. Before groundwater pumping commenced, the aquifer discharged water into the Santa Cruz River. However, between 1940 and 2000, groundwater pumping jumped from approximately 50,000 af/yr to 330,000 af/yr. What prompted the increase in pumping?

Municipal pumping skyrocketed as the city of Tucson water department and private water companies drilled new wells to supply a population that grew from 14,000 in 1912 to 900,000 in 2002. Mining also played a major role because open-pit copper mines pump large quantities of groundwater. The third major user of groundwater in the Santa Cruz val-

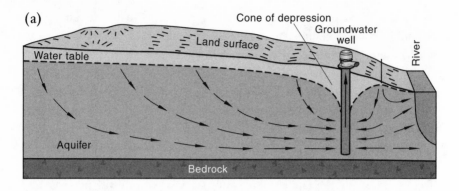

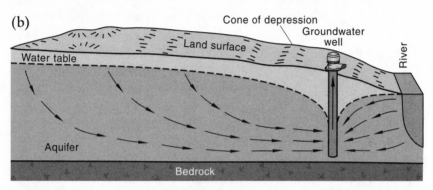

FIGURE 3.4. Under natural conditions, recharge to the water table is equal to discharge to the stream. In (a), the onset of groundwater pumping changes the equilibrium. Now recharge to the aquifer equals discharge to the stream *and* pumping from the well. Note the cone of depression created around the well by groundwater pumping. In (b), groundwater pumping has begun to draw water from the stream. Figures courtesy of the U.S. Geological Survey.

ley, as in every western state, is agriculture. Tucson provides a particularly hospitable climate for growing pecans, alfalfa, wheat, and especially Pima cotton, a soft, strong variety used in fine shirts and towels. As the population grew, the city, the mines, and the farmers collectively began to pump groundwater in an unsustainable fashion. In Arizona, groundwater pumping has dried up or degraded 90 percent of the state's once perennial desert streams, rivers, and riparian habitats.

When the city of Tucson, the mines, and the farmers began to pump groundwater, they introduced a new discharge process. The pumping captured water from the river, first indirectly, then directly. As illustrated in figure 3.4, the pumps intercepted water that had been moving toward the Santa Cruz River and, but for the pumping, would have discharged to the river. The pumping decreased discharge to the stream, increased the rate of recharge to the aquifer (by creating a partial vacuum that atmospheric pressure will refill), and drew on water stored in the aquifer. Note that the stream in figure 3.4a remained a gaining stream because it continued to receive discharge from the aquifer, but it receives less water than before the pumping commenced.

As Tucson's groundwater pumping increased exponentially, the water table plummeted 200 feet, creating significant land subsidence and damage to the foundations of homes and other buildings. As the water table dropped, groundwater pumping changed the relationship between the aquifer and the Santa Cruz River. As in figure 3.4b, groundwater pumping began to withdraw water from beneath and adjacent to the Santa Cruz River which, in turn, caused river water to infiltrate the ground. Once the water table declined below the level of the Santa Cruz River, water began to flow from the river to the aquifer. Groundwater pumping caused the annual flows of the river gradually to diminish and eventually to dry up completely. Groundwater pumping literally sucked the water out of the Santa Cruz River.

Another analogy may highlight the significance of this fact. Suppose you are a rational consumer (the science of economics, remarkably enough, is based on such assumptions). Second, I will assume that your income, on the average, is equal to your expenditures. I know this second assumption is equally unrealistic, as does anyone who knows anything about our national credit card debt. Nonetheless, suppose you crave a vacation on Maui. The vacation on Maui is the equivalent of groundwater pumping. What options do you have for paying for this little jaunt to Hawaii? You have three choices: (1) you can increase your income by moonlighting (increase recharge); (2) you can decrease your expenditures by forgoing fancy restaurants (decrease discharge); or (3) you can withdraw money from your savings account (draw from storage). Paying for the trip to Hawaii must result from some combination of an increase in income, a decrease in expenditures, and a reduction in savings. (I consider flashing plastic as a reduction in savings regardless of the number of frequent flyer miles that you receive.) Similarly, groundwater pumping must increase recharge, decrease discharge, or reduce the amount of water in storage. All three occurred in the Santa Cruz River valley.

FIGURE 3.5. Two photographs of the same section of the Santa Cruz River south of Tucson, Arizona, one taken in 1942, the other in 1989. Photographs courtesy of the U.S. Geological Survey.

In addition to drying up the Santa Cruz River, the pumping has had another horrible environmental consequence. The once vast stands of cottonwood, willow, and mesquite trees died as groundwater pumping lowered the water table below the root zone of the trees. A lush riparian zone of tens of thousands of acres became a dismal expanse of sandy soil. Figure 3.5 reproduces photographs of a reach of the Santa Cruz River. The one on the top, taken in 1942, shows a dense stand of mesquite and cottonwood trees. By 1989, when the photograph on the bottom was taken at the same location (notice the rock in the foreground of both photos), the deciduous trees had died of thirst, and the river had become nothing more than a barren bed of sand.

Riparian conditions were made worse by the efforts of the U.S. Army Corps of Engineers to channelize the banks for flood control purposes. Today, the banks of the Santa Cruz River are cement-lined, a process that involves, first, the removal of existing trees and shrubs in and along the sides of the arroyo and, then, application of a mixture of cement and river soil to the banks of the river channel. The soil-cementing process inflicts great harm on our rivers, streams, and arroyos in the name of flood control. Instead of preventing floods, it quite perversely makes them worse. The river channel, more constricted by soil cement, funnels floodwater downstream with greater velocity and force. At whatever point downstream that the soil cement ends is where greater erosion and flood damage will occur. The only winners are land speculators who purchased worthless land in a floodplain now made valuable because a wall of soil cement keeps the river's flood flows at bay.

Soil-cementing the banks sealed the fate of the riparian zones along the Santa Cruz River. Trees and shrubs don't grow through cement. The cement lining has also adversely affected birds and animals. Birds of course are attracted to both trees and water; take away both and you must say goodbye to the birds. In the Southwest, dry washes, called arroyos, serve as wildlife corridors for deer, coyotes, javelinas, mountain lions, bobcats, raccoons, and gray foxes, as well as smaller mammals such as cottontail and jackrabbits and ground squirrels. Think of arroyos as animal freeways: it is easier to move great distances in the washes than through higher land full of mesquite, ironwood, and acacia trees and opuntia and cholla cacti. Soil-cemented banks, because they are almost vertical and are bereft of vegetation, make it more difficult for animals to use arroyos as transportation corridors.

Metropolises of the American Southwest—Los Angeles, San Diego, Las Vegas, Phoenix, Tucson, to name just a few—exist only because we have altered the hydrologic cycle. We have created homes for tens of millions of people in areas with scarce water resources by building dams and canals that divert entire rivers out of their natural courses and by pumping groundwater in an unsustainable fashion.

In contrast, the Tohono O'odham's *ak chin* farming had a simple elegance that depended on the natural hydrologic cycle to maintain a high groundwater table that discharged groundwater to a gaining stream and that kept the floodplain moist after the spring floods receded. The moist soil provided enough water to sustain the beans and other crops until harvest. The Tohono O'odham learned this technique, one in harmony with nature, from their ancestors, the Hohokam, who may have learned it from even earlier inhabitants of the Santa Cruz River valley. The impact of groundwater pumping on the Santa Cruz River has had grievous consequences for the Tohono O'odham. The *ak chin* technique that endured for centuries, or even millennia, has been destroyed in mere decades by groundwater pumping. Recently, a Tohono O'odham elder was asked: "What happened to the Santa Cruz River?" He responded: "The city of Tucson took it."

Chapter 4

A River at Risk

The Upper San Pedro River in Arizona

"The well was dry beside the door,
And so we went with pail and can
Across the fields behind the house
To seek the brook if still it ran. . . ."
—Robert Frost

The headwaters of the San Pedro River rise in Mexico approximately twenty miles south of the Arizona border. The river flows north into Arizona, past the Huachuca Mountains, the cities of Sierra Vista and Benson, and the town of Mammoth, and joins the Gila River near the town of Winkelman. Runoff from the Huachuca Mountains has created streams, fragile oases in a harsh environment, that flow down the mountain canyons into the San Pedro River.

During the past two centuries, substantial geomorphic changes have occurred in the San Pedro River valley as the river washed sand downstream. Cienegas, or marshlands, were common along the San Pedro in the nineteenth century. So were beavers. In 1879, there was so much standing water that the *Arizona Daily Star* described the San Pedro as "the valley of the shadow of death," due to frequent outbreaks of malaria, dengue and yellow fever. Although it would be another two decades before the experience of building the Panama Canal confirmed the link between mosquitoes and malaria, suspicion in the 1880s that swamps caused disease led to

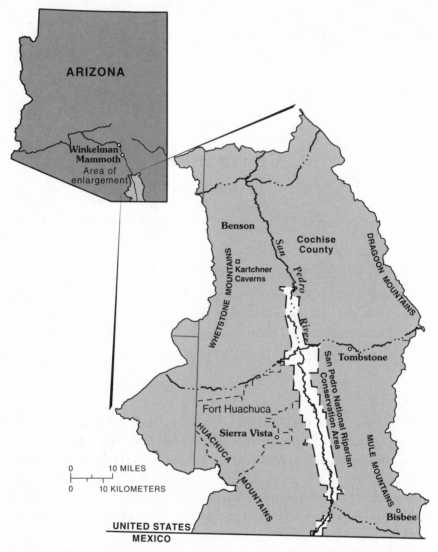

FIGURE 4.1. The upper San Pedro River in southern Arizona.

the extermination of the beaver and the removal of their dams, which significantly impacted the river. The river has also suffered from the introduction of cattle. Grazing, by destroying grassland and shrubs, has produced
quicker runoff and even greater erosion.

Nonetheless, the upper San Pedro still has an extraordinarily rich and
diverse riparian habitat, the largest surviving broadleaf riparian forest in the

Southwest. A ribbon of Freemont cottonwood/Gooding willow gallery forests, marshlands, and native Sacaton grasslands extends one-quarter-mile on each side of the river. This riparian habitat supports an estimated 390 species of birds (approximately half of *all* species seen in North America), eighty-three species of mammals (second in diversity only to rain forests in Costa Rica), and forty-seven species of amphibians and reptiles. The upper San Pedro is also home to at least three endangered species—the southwestern willow flycatcher, the Huachuca water-umbel, and the jaguar.

The enormous number of bird species comes from flyway patterns that make the area the southern limit for many northern species, and the northern limit for many Central and South American species, including fifteen varieties of hummingbirds. Approximately 220 species breed along the river, including the rare gray hawk and twenty other kinds of raptors. As many as 4 million migrating songbirds, including warblers and vireos, use the river on their annual trek between wintering grounds in Mexico and Central America and their breeding grounds in the United States and Canada. Many species, including the thick-billed kingbird, occur in the United States only in the upper San Pedro River basin. The area is so special that *Birder's Digest* named it *the* premier bird watching site in the United States. The Nature Conservancy placed the San Pedro River Basin on its list of "Last Great Places" in the western hemisphere. In 1995, the American Bird Conservancy, together with Partners in Flight and the National Audubon Society, designated the San Pedro a Globally Important Bird Area, the first such designation in the western hemisphere.

In 1999, the prospect of harm to the river from groundwater pumping prompted American Rivers, a national environmental group, to declare the San Pedro one of the ten most endangered rivers in the United States. The San Pedro plays an especially crucial role for the migrating birds. Paul Hardy, The Nature Conservancy's program manager for the San Pedro, has explained: "If you take the San Pedro out, you are jeopardizing a hemisphere's bird populations. It would be like trying to drive cross country if you took out all the gas stations and restaurants." The novelist Barbara Kingsolver, writing in *National Geographic* in April 2000, described the San Pedro as "a sparkling anomaly for sun struck eyes, a thread of blue-green relief."

On the other hand, not everyone appreciates the attention the river is receiving. The population of the city of Sierra Vista and Cochise County is exploding, and local politicians and developers fear that environmental issues may retard growth. One of them has been Harold Vangilder, a member of the Sierra Vista City Council, who has strong prodevelopment views. His priorities are clear: "If the San Pedro River is a national treasure, we are an impoverished nation. You can't drown a fish in it." The meaning of his odd assertion is elusive, but he is clearly unhappy with the attention the river is receiving.

The river is so special that Congress, in 1988, created the San Pedro Riparian Natural Conservation Area (Conservation Area), an area of 47,688 acres, which includes perennial reaches of the river. The legislation created a federal water right for the Conservation Area. Most water rights are creations of state law. When Congress sets aside (reserves) land for a particular purpose, say, an Indian reservation, military base, or national park, it may reserve water for the reservation. The Conservation Area legislation expressly reserved sufficient water to protect the riparian area and the aquatic and wildlife resources. As Senator Dale Bumpers, chair of the Senate Subcommittee on Public Lands, National Parks and Forests, put it: "[T]here is no point in having this legislation unless we are going to protect . . . the free flow of water year-round." Despite congressional intent to protect the flows in one of the last perennial, dam-free streams in the Southwest, the river is in jeopardy.

Thomas Maddock III, a professor of hydrology and water resources at The University of Arizona, is not the sort of individual to become involved in an environmental controversy. After attending the University of Houston on a baseball scholarship, he earned a Ph.D. in mathematics at Harvard and began teaching at The University of Arizona. He specializes in groundwater hydrology, which involves "building" elaborate computer models of how groundwater moves under various conditions. To understand this stuff, you need a Ph.D. in math because most models consist of an elaborate series of partial differential equations. Maddock is a scientist whose enthusiasm for his work is evident. Hydrology poses difficult puzzles, the type that mathematicians love to wrestle with. In 1988, when Cochise County asked him to examine the impact of groundwater pumping on the San Pedro River, Maddock jumped at the chance. The study allowed him to construct a hydrologic model to analyze "the relationship between the groundwater pumping and the surface water system, and how the cone of depression might be advancing or declining [in the area]." When I asked him whether he had ever hiked along the San Pedro River or was a bird watcher, he replied: "No, and I don't know a sparrow from a hawk." The scientific questions piqued his curiosity.

Maddock and a graduate student, Letitia Vionnet, prepared a groundwater flow model that varied from prior models by focusing on the interaction between the river and the floodplain aquifer. Earlier models had remarkably assumed that the river could never go dry! While this assumption might make hydrologic sense with respect to a river like the Mississippi, which in fact will never go dry because it contains such a huge volume of water, it made no sense with respect to a small river like the San Pedro. The assumption foreclosed any examination of whether groundwater pumping could dry up the river. Maddock's model at least allowed for the possibility that the river might go dry. When Maddock and Vionnet ran the model, they found that the river is fed, at least partly, by discharge from the aquifer. But they also found that nearly 40 percent of the groundwater pumped in 1988 was capture, water that would have discharged to the river. Even as of 1988, groundwater pumping significantly reduced the river's flow.

Maddock's model caused a problem for officials at Fort Huachuca, an army base just north of Sierra Vista, who were considering an expansion of the fort's activities. The fort's principal source of water is groundwater. Fort Huachuca, originally commissioned to protect white settlers from the Apaches after the Indian wars in 1877, has long been an economic engine for the town of Sierra Vista. In early 1993, the U.S. Base Realignment and Closure Commission (Closure Commission) proposed moving the Monterey, California, Defense Language Institute to Fort Huachuca, which would have increased the fort's population by approximately 5,000 and increased water use by approximately 2,500 acre-feet per year (af/yr). In discussions with the city of Sierra Vista, the Department of Defense raised the issue of water availability, but city officials assured them that the groundwater system contained enough water for "a thousand years." The city of Monterey naturally opposed the transfer, as did local environmental groups in Sierra Vista, who wished to protect the San Pedro River. Some opponents of the move characterized Sierra Vista as "a dusty cowboy town with inadequate water, insufficient housing, and scarce intellectual resources."

After the Closure Commission learned of the Maddock model, they asked Maddock and Bill Lord, an economics professor at The University of

Arizona, to comment on the proposed move. By letter, Maddock and Lord explained that the increased growth would exacerbate the adverse environmental impact on the San Pedro River and the Conservation Area. The letter set off a furor that has yet to subside. Sierra Vista officials blasted the letter, saying it was filled with "distortions and misstatements," and that Maddock and Lord were environmental extremists. An Arizona Department of Water Resources hydrologist criticized the letter as containing "erroneous and unsupported statements." The Closure Commission faxed the letter to Arizona Senator Dennis DeConcini, who relayed it to Manuel Pacheco, president of The University of Arizona. The University of Arizona administration, in the midst of negotiating a lucrative contract with the Army to supply instructors to the Defense Language Institute, was caught off guard. Dean of Engineering Ernie Smerdon, Maddock's boss, summoned Maddock into his office and told him "the president was pissed." Harold Vangilder and Bill Noyes, a University of Arizona vice president, took a different approach and offered Maddock space in Sierra Vista for an "Institute." People didn't want water problems to stand in the way of growth. But Maddock refused to recant.

The city of Sierra Vista decided to attack Maddock's model. In July 1994, the city requested proposals to evaluate it. In the world of consulting firms, requests to submit a bid on a particular contract are highly competitive. A successful proposal must convince the awarding agency that the bidding firm will produce what the agency needs. In most instances, it's fairly cut-and-dried: a municipality needs a certain study, and the consulting firm will generate it. In this case, the city sent an unambiguous message that it wanted the model trashed. The request for proposals claimed that "most people reviewing the [model], including some of those involved in producing it, do not have much confidence in its results."

The city awarded the contract to an engineering team that included R. Alan Freeze, a world-renowned groundwater hydrologist. After exhaustive study, however, the team found "inherent conflicts between groundwater pumping that accompanies economic development" and the survival of the riparian system in the San Pedro River valley. When the team released its evaluation of the model, an environmental newspaper, *High Country News*, observed that "it reads as if Maddock had written it."

In 1994, U.S. Secretary of the Interior and former governor of Arizona Bruce Babbitt entered the fray and declared that all parties involved in the San Pedro River controversy should enter into negotiation. Babbitt's emergence sparked an angry response from then-Arizona Governor Fife Symington, who grumbled, "Babbitt's problem is that he thinks he's still governor." A flurry of activity, with the appointment of committees and subcommittees, continued for several months, but all for naught. The issues were too complex, nobody was authorized to implement anything, and some water users weren't even at the table. Ultimately, the settlement group faded away. Through the settlement process, however, the hydrologists unanimously agreed on one thing: pumping was harming the river.

The political situation heated up again, in 1995, when the Center for Biological Diversity (then called the Southwest Center for Biological Diversity) initiated a lawsuit alleging violations of the Endangered Species Act and the National Environmental Policy Act. Under the leadership of Robin Silver, a Phoenix physician, the center had become known for its take-no-prisoners approach to environmental litigation. The lawsuit raised the hackles of Sierra Vista officials. In true Wild West fashion, the mayor declared: "We've been silent too long. Them days are gone." A headline in the local newspaper blared: "City officials declare war on enviro 'enemy.'" City councilman Harold Vangilder, in a particularly well-informed reaction, responded: "All right, there may be 500 species of wildlife found along the San Pedro. My response is, so what? What benefit do these animals have for humans? We are the ones who rule supreme, and if a plant or animal can't adapt to our needs, then it's too bad."

The feared growth in the fort's population never materialized. Instead, the fort's military and family member population, including those living off base, declined from 19,427 in 1994 to 16,393 in 1997. The fort's recent efforts to reduce its water use and to protect the river have been nothing short of remarkable. An aggressive water conservation program includes the reuse of treated effluent to irrigate the fort's parade field, golf course, and sports complex. The fort is replacing older, high-use plumbing fixtures and has designed projects to recharge treated effluent and storm runoff to the aquifer. The fort reduced its on-post water consumption by almost 50 percent, from 3,207 af/yr in 1989 to 1,655 af/yr in 2001. Its successful conservation program is partly due to the fact that it is a military facility. As Major General John D. Thomas, Jr., wryly observed: "If we tell people not to water their grass, they probably will not water their grass." Although the fort's population has declined, military personnel and their families, civilian employees, and military retirees made up 28 percent of Cochise

County's 1997 population. Fort Huachuca remains the driving force of the local economy with expenditures of $525 million in 1997. Yet the fort is no longer the principal threat to the San Pedro River.

— ~

For generations, Arizonans have been selling desert lots that lack water to folks from Illinois and other points back East. In Arizona, this is an honorable way to make a living. In 1973, after some particularly well-publicized scandals when the rubes showed up and discovered what they had purchased sight unseen, the state legislature began to require developers to obtain from the Arizona Department of Water Resources a determination regarding the availability of water for the development. If the supply of water is "inadequate," then the developer must disclose this fact in the promotional materials and sales documents. Although this red flag has put a real crimp in fraudulent land sales, marketing efforts now are directed toward selling land that is not subject to this subdivision development restriction. Though passing legal muster, land with inadequate water continues to be sold.

The most critical problem in Cochise County is to find water supplies for the expected increases in nonmilitary population. Between 1980 and 2000, the city of Sierra Vista's population increased 64 percent from 25,000 to 41,000. State of Arizona demographers predict that by 2025 the city's population will grow to nearly 70,000. Population growth in surrounding areas in Cochise County increased even faster, at an annual rate of 3.4 percent in recent years, rising from 108,225 to 123,750 over four years. Water demand to serve this projected population growth is likely to increase from 17,900 af/yr currently to 25,000 af/yr in 2025. Sierra Vista's historical dependence on Fort Huachuca for its economic growth is changing; to sustain growth, the city is relying on housing developments that target "snowbirds," a euphemism for winter visitors and retirees who flee northern climates for Arizona and other warm states.

One development, with the green-sounding name "Cottonwoods of the San Pedro," would have created a 90-lot subdivision immediately adjacent to the Conservation Area and served by groundwater. This development, perversely, would have contributed to killing the very trees after which it would be named. The same developer also proposed to build an additional 5,000 homes next to the "Cottonwoods" development. Fortunately for the San Pedro River, these projects got derailed when the developer was sent to prison in Nevada for fraud relating to his ownership of a water company in that state. But the "Cottonwoods" land is still being developed into four-acre parcels that are exempt from state regulation, a significant loophole in efforts to regulate development. Judy Anderson of the Cochise County Planning and Zoning Department believes that more growth is occurring through this unregulated splitting of properties than through platting of subdivisions, but no one knows the exact number of lots that are being split. There is another associated problem: water for platted subdivisions usually comes from a central supply, which makes it quite simple to monitor water use. However, when property is split, each parcel will have its own well. Arizona law, like that of almost all states, does not regulate these wells, known as "exempt wells," because they are deemed so small as not to be worth the trouble to regulate. Domestic wells present an enormous loophole in every state's water management system. Most states have tens of thousands, or even hundreds of thousands, of exempt wells. Making matters worse, most domestic wells are relatively shallow and usually located near rivers, streams, or wetlands; their cumulative impact on surface flows can be substantial.

The "Cottonwoods" development is not the only indicator of growth in the San Pedro River Basin. Another developer envisions a 7,500-home master-planned community within six miles of the Conservation Area. In 1999, a 400,000-square-foot, $60 million regional shopping mall opened, the first of its kind in the area. The mall created approximately 400 jobs. A new state park, Kartchner Caverns State Park, located just north of Sierra Vista, also opened in 1999. It may be the most remarkable cave in the country, with magnificent stalactites, stalagmites, helictites, soda straws, and especially "Kubla Khan," a massive 58-foot-tall column. Between 250,000 and 350,000 cave enthusiasts visit the park each year. A proposed industrial air park will encourage more in-migration. Richard Archer, mayor of Sierra Vista, welcomed this economic growth. "These [projects] will bring in new people, new growth. We should not be afraid of that."

Because of the growing demands on groundwater, a fight is brewing. The city's wells have cones of depression that have intersected those of Fort Huachuca, causing a drawdown of the water table. Under Arizona law, however, a landowner is not liable if his or her well interferes with the operation of another well. The reasonable use doctrine permits exactly such a result. As a consequence, both the fort and the municipal providers will need to drill deeper wells. The city's and the fort's wells significantly affect the river, because the cones of depression are intercepting water that is flowing underground from the Huachuca Mountains to the river. The cones of depression have reached the San Pedro River and are directly reducing the flow in the Conservation Area.

Frustrated by the failure of its litigation to produce effective reform, the Center for Biological Diversity used the river's international status to petition the Commission for Environmental Cooperation (CEC), set up as part of the North American Free Trade Agreement, to study the San Pedro River Basin. In 1999, the commission concluded that groundwater pumping has caused a steady decline in surface flows. Agricultural pumping near the river has "contributed significantly" to the reduction, and groundwater pumping by the city of Sierra Vista and Fort Huachuca has reduced groundwater discharge to the river by 70 percent. But the major long-term threat is "the creeping incremental demands on the groundwater that sustains [the river]."

What will happen if groundwater pumping continues to reduce flows in the river and to lower the water table? The riparian plant community will change. Aquatic plants require perennial flows; marsh plants require shallow groundwater. As the groundwater level drops, wetland plant species decline and upland species increase. Loss of perennial flow would collapse the aquatic ecosystem, killing fish, frogs, aquatic invertebrates, and terrestrial insects. The cottonwood-willow forest might initially survive, though it will undergo stress. The trees will die if the water table drops below nine to fifteen feet beneath the surface of the ground, which for trees on a bank next to the river leaves little margin for error. These changes will profoundly impact birds. Riparian species like the western yellow-billed cuckoo, green kingfisher, gray hawk, summer tanager, and Swainson's thrush will virtually disappear. Native, but exotic, bird species such as the vermilion flycatcher will sharply decline in numbers. Migrating songbirds would no longer stop there. Eventually, salt cedar trees will replace the cottonwoods and willows. They, in turn, will yield to mesquite woodlands, but even the mesquites will decline as the water table drops further.

Some local politicians, such as Harold Vangilder, expressed contempt for the CEC: "Our experience is that these guys are little more than new-age, feel-good thugs." Nothing will likely come from the CEC report, which is only a report of an advisory committee; it carries no force of law, nor is it the product of a politically powerful congressional committee. Nor does the CEC have any important local constituency to put political muscle into the report's findings. Instead, even before the release of the report, Sierra Vista interests persuaded the Arizona legislature to pass a resolution urging President Clinton not to declare any Arizona river an "American Heritage River," nor to allow international meddling in the affairs of local U.S. interests. According to the legislature, "The CEC study and report represent an unnecessary intrusion of an international environmental entity into state matters that excessively limits the use of both private and public lands in this state." The Arizona legislature managed to reach this conclusion *before* the CEC had released its report! Moreover, given that the San Pedro River crosses an international border as it flows from Mexico into the United States, it is difficult to understand how river issues are solely "local" or "state" matters.

Other heavy hitters soon weighed in to rail against the threat that the CEC represented to U.S. sovereignty. Lieutenant Colonel Oliver North (Ret.) circulated a petition claiming that the San Pedro River and the city of Sierra Vista "have come under attack from a new left-wing international commission. . . . " Sierra Vista officials were probably not happy with Mr. North's claim that the CEC was "trying to bully the town of Sierra Vista into cutting back on *water drawn from the San Pedro River.*" To combat this challenge to U.S. sovereignty, Mr. North asked recipients to sign the petition and to send him a check so he could continue his vigilant efforts to protect us from foreign threats.

In another attempt to resolve the issue, the CEC convened a thirteen-member Upper San Pedro Advisory Panel to consider public reactions to its report and to formulate recommendations for the future. Members of the advisory panel represented a spectrum of local interests, including environmental groups, civic organizations, and the ranching community, as well as regional and international perspectives. But the advisory panel achieved consensus by producing a report timid enough to secure the votes of its members from Cochise County and Sierra Vista who favored unrestrained growth.

Relations between local elected officials and University of Arizona hydrologists took a turn for the worse in 1999 when hydrologist Robert MacNish, at a meeting in Cochise County, proclaimed that the river was going to die due to elected officials whom he described as being members of a species called the "Cochise County ostrich, a noisy and flightless bird which does not see any problem because it buries its head in the sand."

MacNish thought that the ostrich should be put on the threatened or endangered species list "where it belongs." His comments were amusing to be sure, but they further annoyed local officials.

The San Pedro River reached the nation's radar screen in 1999 with the publication of a long piece in the *New York Times* that portrayed a bird oasis in peril. Once again, local officials responded defensively, insisting that the *Times* reporter did not comprehend the environmental efforts undertaken by Fort Huachuca and the city of Sierra Vista.

The U.S. Bureau of Land Management (BLM), which Congress entrusted with management of the Conservation Area, may hold a trump card. The federal water right that Congress created in 1988 when it reserved water for the Conservation Area supersedes subsequent state water rights. Those who initiated their water use *before* the creation of the Conservation Area may continue their activities. But newcomers stand in different shoes. Federal law protects the Conservation Area's water rights against interference by subsequent water users, whether these users rely on surface or groundwater.

Unfortunately, the Conservation Area's water rights are only theoretical at this point in time. Lawyers for BLM have asserted these water rights in the Gila River General Adjudication, a hideously complicated process that is attempting to quantify *all* water rights in two-thirds of the state of Arizona, including the San Pedro River. The special master, assigned by the Arizona Supreme Court to take a first crack at resolving the claims, is working watershed by watershed as he attempts to bring some semblance of sanity to this bizarre legal process. As of March 2002, there were no scheduled hearings concerning water rights for the Conservation Area. It will be years before BLM obtains a decision from the special master, and that decision would be subject to the normal process of appellate review.

The river cannot wait that long; incremental additional demands for water will have long since sealed its fate. BLM has another option. The special master has authority to issue a preliminary injunction in order to preserve the status quo for the duration of the judicial proceedings. In March 1999, Tom Maddock and I urged BLM to ask the special master to enjoin irrigation pumping that commenced after 1988. However, Michael Ferguson, deputy state director of the BLM office in Arizona, feared that such a request would undermine BLM's efforts to work with other agencies and landowners to achieve "community collaboration and cooperation" concerning the problems in the San Pedro River Basin. Consensus building is a wonderful process, but sometimes it just does not work. The most recent effort to achieve consensus is the Upper San Pedro Partnership, made up of federal, state, county, and city agencies and The Nature Conservancy, all of which own land, make land use policy, or have resource expertise in the upper San Pedro River Basin. Prior to the partnership came the Water Issues Group, the County Comprehensive Plan, and a federally sponsored water rights negotiation. Each failed to achieve consensus. The question is whether BLM's current effort will yield greater success.

The partnership began rather timidly by advocating for the preparation of additional studies and a new hydrologic model. The San Pedro River may give literal meaning to the phrase "studied to death." A September 1999 report by BLM and the Sonoran Institute identified various groups involved in conservation and research efforts concerning the San Pedro River. The results are staggering. They include four state of Arizona agencies; nine United States government agencies; seven universities, colleges, and foundations; eleven environmental organizations; two international organizations; one consulting firm; one unit of local government; and five coordinating committees and task forces. These are only the participants on the United States side of the border! There are also twenty-nine organizations and government agencies in Mexico. Despite the efforts of so many people and the expenditure of enormous sums of money, very little has occurred to halt the impact of groundwater pumping on the river. Every credible hydrologist understands this impact on the San Pedro River. A new hydrologic model might slightly improve the understanding of groundwater-surface water interactions, but the enhanced knowledge would come with a considerable delay and at a huge cost to the river.

In July 1999, Dale Pontius, associate solicitor in the Department of the Interior, along with Department of Justice lawyers and BLM officials, met with state, county, and city representatives in Sierra Vista. The meeting was cordial, but produced no concrete results. As soon as the federal officials left town, the Sierra Vista City Council approved a plan by California-based developer Castle & Cooke to build 7,000 new homes for 15,000–20,000 new residents on 2,000 acres near the San Pedro River. The mayor of Sierra Vista responded to criticism by arguing that the partnership would address water issues through a $6 million project to recharge treated sewage effluent in order to offset the effects of groundwater pumping on the river, and through conducting feasibility studies to capture and recharge floodwater from streams in the Huachuca Mountains. City councilman Harold Vangilder insisted that the only problem was outsiders who were stirring up trouble. He asked the city council to require citizens who might testify at future council meetings to indicate where they live.

The city council's action gave pause to BLM's hope of achieving consensus through "community collaboration and cooperation." When Secretary of the Interior Bruce Babbitt visited Sierra Vista in November 1999, he no longer offered an olive branch. Babbitt threatened to take management of the river away from city, county, and state officials unless they acted to curb growth. Babbitt asserted that it was his responsibility, as Interior Secretary, to "protect this extraordinary piece of God's creation." He placed special blame on the state, which, he stated, "has abdicated its responsibility to lead in the management of this resource." Babbitt deplored recent agricultural expansion as "an unimaginable abuse of the resource."

Rita Pearson, director of the Arizona Department of Water Resources, rose to defend her state and agency. Pointing to state funding for additional studies, the recharge project, and the Upper San Pedro Partnership, Pearson asserted that the state had a deep commitment to the San Pedro River ecosystem. She also claimed that no agricultural expansion was taking place. On this point, one wonders who advised her. Since 1988, her own agency had granted permits for four new large-capacity agricultural irrigation wells near the San Pedro. Director Pearson also claimed that hydrologic studies had concluded that the San Pedro River could withstand a 5,000-af/yr *increase* in groundwater pumping. The river would face a more promising future were she correct. In fact, every hydrologic model prepared by her own department since 1974 has concluded that the current level of pumping negatively affects the river. In the late 1990s, Ms. Pearson resisted pleas that she use her authority to bring about state regulation of pumping in the San Pedro River Basin. She apparently did not want to offend local officials by imposing state management on water use.

The efforts of the Center for Biological Diversity to use the Endangered Species Act (ESA) to restrict growth in Sierra Vista and Cochise County suddenly appeared to have merit in 1999, when a federal judge ordered the Fish and Wildlife Service (FWS) to designate critical habitat for the spikedace and loach minnow, both threatened species under the ESA. In April 2000, FWS designated hundreds of miles of streams and rivers in Arizona and New Mexico as critical habitat, including the San Pedro River. That same month, David J. Harlow, FWS field director in

Phoenix, expressed concern about development near the river. Under section 404 of the Clean Water Act, a developer must obtain a permit from the U.S. Army Corps of Engineers for the discharge of dredged or fill material into navigable waters, which include "intermittent streams," i.e., dry washes. Harlow argues that development on the floodplain of the San Pedro River requires a section 404 permit because the new construction, once operational, would rely on groundwater to the detriment of the San Pedro, the listed species, and their critical habitat. Section 7 of the ESA requires the Corps to consult with FWS in order to ensure that the final permit does not jeopardize a listed species or adversely modify or destroy its habitat. Under section 7, FWS must suggest "reasonable and prudent alternatives" that the Corps could take to avoid jeopardy to the listed species or its habitat. Because the threat comes from the impact of groundwater pumping on the San Pedro River, any alternative presumably must propose that the development *not* rely on groundwater. Unless there are other sources of water (and none come to mind), developers may be denied the necessary permits.

The ESA may also force the fort to reduce its water use even further. In April 2002, a federal judge found merit in the Center for Biological Diversity's attack on FWS and the fort's conclusion that its pumping would not jeopardize endangered species. He ruled that the biological opinion, required by section 7 of the ESA, did not contain adequate measures to mitigate the long-term impacts of the fort's pumping. FWS and the fort must prepare a new biological opinion.

The Endangered Species Act and the Clean Water Act have served as hammers to encourage the stakeholders to work with the Upper San Pedro Partnership. Indeed, Andy Laurenzi, The Nature Conservancy's Southern Arizona conservation manager, who has worked on San Pedro issues for twelve years, is "fairly optimistic" about the partnership. The process has created "a much more receptive environment" for discussing "amazing things like growth restrictions."

The fort, which is a partnership member, has committed substantial funds toward protecting the river. The fort spent $6 million on its effluent recharge project. It has also entered a partnership with The Nature Conservancy to spend $2.5 million over five years to purchase conservation easements from willing landowners to reduce agricultural water use. The jury is out on whether Sierra Vista and Cochise County will make the same commitment. Although the city and county historically looked to the fort for growth, city officials now admit—albeit not for attribution—that "we've already unhitched our wagon from the fort and are promoting Sierra Vista as a great place to come and live."

Can the situation be reversed? Options are limited. Reducing water consumption below current levels is a political nonstarter. Importing water from other basins would involve enormous costs and legal and environmental challenges. If new growth relies on groundwater, the impact on the river will become more severe. To protect the river, the city of Sierra Vista and Fort Huachuca have initiated an intriguing groundwater recharge project. Begun in 2000, this $7.5 million effort will construct a fifty-acre wetlands complex and thirty acres of groundwater recharge basins. Treated municipal wastewater will recharge the aquifer through these basins. The idea is to create a mound of water underground between the city's wells and the river, so that the city's pumping draws on this water rather than expanding the existing cone of depression. City officials initially hope to recharge between 800 million and one billion gallons per year, an amount that will increase as growth occurs and new development connects to the city's sewer system. This system will potentially reduce the impact of the city's pumping. However, by itself, it is not an adequate solution because recharge returns only a percentage of the total water used, and because significant pumping currently occurs throughout Cochise County at places other than the city's existing wells. The recharge project, according to a federal judge, "will mask and delay the effects of the groundwater pumping." It only postpones the inevitable if the quantity of pumping continues to increase.

After Congress created the Conservation Area in 1988, the BLM purchased and retired almost 20,000 af/yr of agricultural water rights. Since then, The Nature Conservancy (TNC) has purchased additional water rights, some in Ramsey Canyon, a tributary of the San Pedro River and a famous hummingbird observation site. However, irrigation outside the TNC-owned land and the Conservation Area presents a significant threat to the river. In the mid-1990s, BLM and TNC paid a nearby farmer to cease pumping on 500 acres. However, the farmer turned around and began to irrigate another 500-acre parcel. This irrigation unquestionably affected the river, yet the farmer's actions were perfectly legal under Arizona law. Some way must be found to prevent new large-scale pumping for low-value agriculture in areas near the river. Otherwise, the resolve of the city and fort may dissipate if a single landowner can undermine their efforts to conserve. A successful retirement program needs assurances that new irrigators will not undo the program. This raises the possibility of holding out for ransom; as water rights are purchased and retired, the value of the remaining private lands, and water rights, increases. Another option is to designate the region an active management area under Arizona law and inaugurate state regulation and control. This avenue requires state involvement, which is not likely to be forthcoming in the absence of support from the local stakeholders. The Cochise County board of supervisors has voted unanimously to oppose such a designation.

Water conservation is another option, but measures such as low-water-use landscaping requirements involve only modest amounts of water. Furthermore, it does not make sense to conserve a few gallons of water per household while increasing threefold the number of households.

One Rube Goldberg proposal is to pump more groundwater during periods of extreme drought and dump it into the river to offset lower surface flows. This is a kind of hydrologic Ponzi scheme. Increasing pumping would capture more water from the river. The whole process would produce an ever increasing cycle: more pumping, more capture, hence even more pumping, hence even more capture. This process would have to continue indefinitely.

The San Pedro River today has only a narrow ribbon of cottonwood and willow along its banks, so when rains come, the water flows quickly downstream through the Conservation Area. That may change if a 1999 program to reestablish beavers along the San Pedro River is successful. Beavers are truly remarkable environmental engineers who perform critical functions in maintaining healthy riparian ecosystems. Beaver dams slow the movement of water, encourage lateral percolation of water into the surrounding soil, and foster more diverse plant and animal species. As the water spreads out behind their dams, it saturates a wider band of soil, forming marshy backwaters favored by cattails, spiky bulrushes, and leafy veronica. During dry periods of the summer, the water stored in the riverbanks and marshes discharges into the river, assuring a continuous flow over a longer period of the year. Beaver dams also discourage flooding. During significant storms, rainwater fills the beaver ponds rather than flooding the river, which would scour out the channel and cause further erosion. Beavers contribute to a healthier river because the water, as it tumbles over the top of the beaver dams, gets aerated and provides more favorable habitat for native fishes, such as the longfin dace. Riffles that form below the dams also attract a wider variety of insects which, in turn, attract a wider variety of bird species, such as the endangered willow flycatcher.

Early reports from BLM and the Arizona Game and Fish Department suggest a successful restoration program. Officials hope a self-sustaining population of twenty to thirty beaver colonies will eventually inhabit the Conservation Area. A robust beaver population would produce, in the long term, marshy areas next to the river, with a swath of willows and other shrubs behind the marshes. The cottonwood gallery would be farther back from the river because cottonwood seeds would land on moist soil behind the marsh and willow areas. The net effect would be a larger riparian habitat with a greater variety and number of plants, animals, insects, and birds.

If the San Pedro River is not to suffer the same fate as the Santa Cruz, dramatic changes must occur. Even if all the good ideas are implemented— retiring agricultural irrigation, recharging effluent, installing low-flow fixtures, mandating water conservation, and repopulating beavers—they will not bring the present rate of overdraft to zero. Saving the San Pedro demands the *will* to save the river, and the local community may lack the necessary resolve. The river does not play an important part in the life and culture of Sierra Vista. Lying eight or ten miles east of the city, off a road traveled mostly by tourists on their way to Bisbee, the San Pedro River is a small river of interest mostly to bird watchers. One suspects that many people in Sierra Vista are puzzled by the claim that the city's water supply affects a river ten miles away. It takes a rather sophisticated understanding of hydrology to grasp how the pumping is intercepting water that would otherwise reach the river. A 1994 poll revealed that approximately one-half of Sierra Vistans did not know there was a problem with the river.

The saga of the San Pedro River offers a number of lessons, each of them useful for those trying to protect other rivers and streams. First, population growth is driving the increased demand for groundwater. Real estate developers and local politicians are unreceptive to claims that controls on growth are necessary to protect rivers and streams. It is often said that the "engine of the American economy" is growth, and challengers to this mantra may expect a hostile audience. Second, the complicated nature of hydrology and of capture processes creates a serious information problem. It takes considerable time and resources to document the hydrologic connection between pumping and surface flows. It takes little effort to obfuscate the issue by claiming that the science is uncertain. Truth will eventually win out, as declines in river flows confirm that pumping has caused a reduction in flows. Third, time passes to the disadvantage of the resource. Capture processes may occur over decades and be hidden from view. Each new subdivision and irrigation well places additional stresses on the system and enlists new advocates for permissive pumping rules. As time goes by, it becomes increasingly difficult to reverse direction.

Chapter 5

Tampa Bay's Avarice

Cypress Groves, Wetlands, Springs, and Lakes in Florida

"And it never failed that during the dry years the people forgot about the rich years, and during the wet years they lost all memory of the dry years. It was always that way."
—John Steinbeck, *East of Eden*

In the late 1980s, Cathy and Steve Monsees lived near Tampa Bay, Florida, while Steve was stationed at MacDill Air Force Base. Steve was a colonel assigned to the U.S. Central Command, Special Forces branch. His immediate supervisor was General H. Norman Schwarzkopf. Although Cathy and Steve grew up in Kansas City, Missouri, they enjoyed living in Florida and decided to retire there after returning to the United States from Steve's last posting in the Sudan (from which they were evacuated during the Gulf War in 1991). In 1988, they purchased a beautiful seven-acre parcel of land about forty miles north of Tampa Bay on which they built their dream home. At the front of the lot was Prairie Lake, about 100 acres in size. At the rear of the property was a five-acre pond. Cathy and Steve looked forward to fishing for bass, watching birds and wildlife, and enjoying the amenities of lakefront living. What they did not anticipate was that Prairie Lake and the pond would both dry up.

Although Florida is one of the wettest states in the country—it averages over fifty-four inches of rain a year—it has always had a problem with water. Historically, the problem was too much water. In a state surrounded on three sides by ocean and with enormous aquifers and extremely high water tables, the problem was how to get rid of the water. In 1850, Congress passed the Swamp and Overflow Act, which deeded the state of Florida 20 million acres of land that the state would attempt to dry up. The state constructed canals, ditches, and drains to move the water away and filled wetlands to create dry land suitable for building. Such policies wreaked havoc on the environment, especially Everglades National Park, and have now been abandoned. Indeed, the Clinton administration initiated an $8 billion effort to restore flows to that "river of grass."

Although that story is relatively well known, another version of Florida's water woes is not. In 1950, Florida had a population of 2.7 million people. By 2000, the population was almost 16 million, making Florida the fourth most populous state (after California, New York, and Texas). Demographers project Florida's population to exceed 20 million by the year 2020. A region that is experiencing particularly explosive growth is Tampa Bay, located in the Southwest Florida Water Management District, affectionately known as "Swiftmud," from its initials. Although Swiftmud's boundaries encompass sixteen counties, the population boom has been in the metropolitan region of Tampa and St. Petersburg. The district's population grew from 2.5 million people in 1980 to 3.3 million by 1990, an increase of 33 percent, and is projected to reach 4.6 million, an additional 37 percent increase, by 2010. To put this growth in perspective, the district has 1,179 new residents every week. And Florida has the highest per capita consumption of water in the world.

Most of the area is flat—typical Florida land. Although the highest elevation is hardly 300 feet above sea level, the area has several different ecosystems. An upland environment of well-drained sandy soil supports drought-tolerant vegetation, including various oak and other hardwood trees. Low-lying areas consist of freshwater swamps and marshes, wetlands with lush plant growth, and an abundance of epiphytes. Hardwood-cypress swamps are wetland forests of tall trees with a canopy that partly closes out the sky. The trees stand in still-water pools for six to twelve months of the year, an interval known as a wetland's hydroperiod. Sawgrass, flag, and cattail marshes are treeless wetlands with vegetation consisting of grasses, sedges, and forbs, and having hydroperiods seven to ten months a year. Swamps and marshes profoundly depend on water table levels.

The geology of the northern Tampa Bay region consists of limestone deposits, particularly a region of karst. Because limestone is water soluble, as water moves through fractures in the rock, it dissolves the underlying limestone, thus progressively enlarging the fractures. As a result, the land surface may eventually collapse, producing sinkholes that then fill with water. Accordingly, surface water and groundwater in the region are very closely interrelated.

The cities of Tampa and St. Petersburg, the two population centers of the region, sit on peninsulas a few miles apart, which creates problems with their water supplies. First, as a result of urban development, there is less permeable land into which rainwater can percolate and recharge the aquifers. Rainwater readily infiltrates most soils but runs off buildings, concrete, and asphalt. Second, extensive groundwater pumping from beneath a small peninsula may cause saltwater intrusion into the underlying aquifer.

In search of additional supplies during the 1970s, Tampa Bay Water (then known as West Coast Regional Water Supply Authority) purchased large tracts of rural areas in Hillsborough, Pinellas, and Pasco Counties. In the late 1970s and early 1980s, Tampa Bay Water developed three major well fields: Cypress Creek, Starkey, and Cross Bar Ranch. By 1996, ground-

FIGURE 5.1. Sinkhole created by groundwater pumping in west-central Florida. Note person standing on edge. Photograph courtesy of the U.S. Geological Survey.

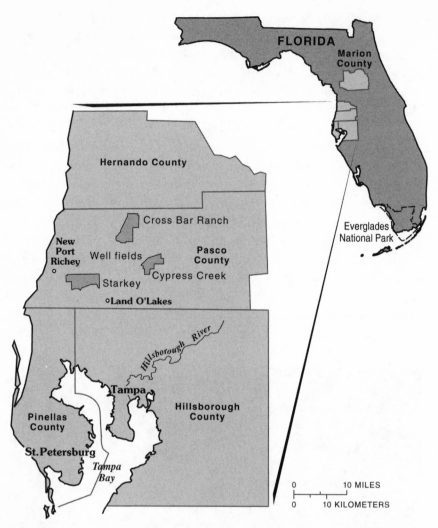

FIGURE 5.2. Tampa Bay, Florida, region.

water withdrawal in Hillsborough, Pinellas, and Pasco Counties had risen to approximately 255 million gallons per day (mgd), a 400 percent increase over 1960 levels. In Pasco County alone, over 20 billion gallons per year are exported via pipeline to Pinellas County. Projections for the year 2020 anticipate an increase to 425 mgd, a nearly 170 percent increase over 1996 pumping levels.

When Prairie Lake dried up in the early 1990s, Cathy and Steve Monsees were at a loss for an explanation. They reacted calmly at first because

Tampa Bay Water officials assured them that the region's lakes were drying up due to a prolonged drought. That answer made sense to Cathy and Steve until they found out that rainfall had actually been above average. When they pointed this out, officials shifted tacks. First, they blamed development, then irrigation. Eventually, Steve and Cathy found out that Tampa Bay Water had drilled the Cross Bar well field less than three-quarters of a mile from their home, a field that pumped 45 million gallons per day. Cathy and Steve were shocked. Together with some neighbors and homeowners' associations, they tried to bring the issue to Swiftmud's attention. Beginning in 1992, they wrote letters, made phone calls, addressed Swiftmud's governing board, and did everything else you're supposed to do to resolve grievances in a democratic society.

In some areas of the country, ongoing debate and uncertainty cloud the extent of the hydrologic connection between groundwater pumping and surface flows. This is not the case with the northern Tampa Bay region. An exhaustive 1996 Swiftmud study found a "significant connection between streams, lakes, wetlands and the . . . aquifers." Of the 153 lakes in the region, it found that fewer than ten functioned as healthy lakes and over half were seriously impacted or even dry. For example, consider the photographs of Crooked Lake in figure 5.3. A reduction in the water level of a lake causes a decline in dissolved oxygen, nutrient enrichment (i.e., algae blooms), an accelerated buildup of bottom sediments, changes in vegetation, and a reduction in fish and wildlife. A lake that dries up obviously cannot support any fish.

Northern Tampa Bay has a number of creeks and springs, including Cypress Creek, Jumping Gully, Brooker Creek, and Crystal and Sulfur Springs, that are located near major well fields and have suffered declining flows. Reductions in spring and creek flow may ultimately harm major rivers such as the Hillsborough and Withlacoochee, which depend on flows from springs and creeks. Reduced river flows, in turn, will alter the coastal estuary ecosystems, which depend not only on the quantity but also on the timing and quality of freshwater. Some northern Tampa Bay estuaries are already suffering environmental degradation.

Groundwater pumping has also had a catastrophic impact on the region's wetlands. Florida's wetlands, once 54 percent of its land surface, now cover only 30 percent of the state. Cypress wetlands support substantial fish and amphibian populations. To remain healthy, cypress trees need standing water for more than six months a year, and as water levels decline

FIGURE 5.3. Contrasting photographs from the 1970s and 1990 of Crooked Lake in central Florida. Photographs courtesy of the *Florida Water Resources Journal*.

and the hydroperiod shortens, the cypress dome undergoes a profound transformation. It begins with a decline in wetland vegetation species and an invasion by competing upland species. Declining water levels encourage land subsidence and the loss of what biologists call overstory and what the rest of us call "big trees." In some areas, centuries-old cypress trees have recently died. The loss of water produces severe oxidation of the soils, encourages fire damage, and results in a loss of wildlife.

The decline in wetlands is critical not only because of the loss of trees and vegetation that are wetland-dependent but also because wetlands perform other valuable functions. They enhance water quality, store water, recharge water to the aquifer, and buffer adjoining regions during flood surges. Swiftmud's 1996 analysis of almost 350 wetlands concluded that the overwhelming number had suffered low water levels, the intrusion of upland plants, and dying trees. Pumping for well fields was the primary cause.

Ninety-five percent of the area's lakes have been degraded by *current* groundwater pumping rates. Additional environmental degradation will occur but is not yet apparent because the processes of groundwater movement occur slowly and the effects of capture are not always immediately visible. Just imagine the added environmental harm that Tampa Bay Water can inflict on its rural neighbors when its groundwater pumping increases from 250 mgd to 425 mgd, as is projected to occur by the year 2020. In addition to the predictable impact on the region's lakes, streams, rivers, estuaries, and wetlands, the pumping may create a significant problem of saltwater intrusion, resulting in a serious water quality problem for domestic water supplies.

Swiftmud, one of five regional water management districts created under Florida law, is governed by an eleven-member board appointed by the governor and subject to confirmation by the state senate. It has regulatory authority over institutions that supply wholesale or retail water, and these institutions must obtain permits from Swiftmud to divert surface water or pump groundwater. The state legislature has mandated that Swiftmud establish minimum water levels and flows for lakes, streams, and aquifers. The 300-pound gorilla among water suppliers is Tampa Bay Water (TBW). As the largest provider of wholesale water, it serves Hillsborough, Pasco, and Pinellas Counties, including the cities of Tampa, St. Petersburg, and New Port Richey.

In the mid-1990s, relations between Swiftmud and TBW turned frosty when Swiftmud attempted to restrict the amount of water TBW could pump from wells in Pasco and Hillsborough Counties. At one late-night meeting, after Swiftmud officials suggested that Tampa and St. Petersburg might have to shut down some wells, a water utility manager banged his fist on the table and threatened: "The day you try to stop me from pumping the well fields is the day you pry my cold dead fingers off the on switch!" Swiftmud was reluctant to renew groundwater well permits because the pumping would violate the minimum flow levels that Swiftmud set pursuant to state law. Pinellas County (the home of St. Petersburg) and TBW officials claim that there is no valid scientific evidence that their groundwater pumping is hurting the environment. They accused Swiftmud of manipulating the media, wasting taxpayer dollars, and risking the health and public safety of Tampa Bay area residents. In 1996, Pinellas County spent $800,000 on a campaign to convince the public that a drought rather than groundwater pumping was responsible for the environmental harm to lakes and wetlands. The drought surely exacerbated the problem.

In 1996, Pinellas County chose to play hardball. When Gilliam Clarke, Judy Leonard, and other lakefront property owners created a coalition and began to speak out against the impacts of groundwater pumping, Pinellas County promptly sued them in a type of lawsuit known as strategic litigation against public participation, or SLAPP, suit. SLAPP suits aim to muzzle the protests of citizens by threatening them with the hassle involved in litigation. The SLAPP message is clear: stop your protests and we'll dismiss the suit; but if you continue to threaten our objectives, you can look forward to prolonged, expensive litigation and a claim for damages that you have caused us. Several of the SLAPP defendants quickly settled, but other intrepid critics of TBW countersued and demanded damages. In 1999, Pinellas County settled, offering $341,000 and an apology. A Pinellas County commissioner, Robert Stewart, described the suit as a "public relations nightmare."

But TBW faced a bigger public relations disaster as more lakes and wetlands began to dry up. Big Fish Lake, famous for its large bass, once was thirty feet deep and covered 287 acres. It went dry in 1990. Pasco Lake once held eight feet of water and entertained recreational boaters. It, too, went dry, thanks to groundwater pumping. To offset these effects, TBW for years has periodically augmented the quantities of water in various lakes. Where did TBW get this additional water? From groundwater pumping. The lakes went dry because the water table supporting the water level in the lakes dropped as a consequence of groundwater pumping. To remedy that, TBW pumped additional groundwater back into the lake, where much of it would inevitably drain back into the ground in search of the water table. Refilling the lakes is like bouncing a check and, when the merchant seeks payment, writing her a second check drawn on the same account. This "solution," which requires an endless loop of pumping to mask the environmental consequences of groundwater pumping, remains a core, yet flawed element in TBW's vision of the future. Were he alive, Rube Goldberg would have been chagrined—complicated as his inventions were, at least they worked.

In 1996, TBW spent $300,000 to pump 372,000 gallons per day (gpd) that were poured back into Lake Loyce, Triangle Lake, and Monsees Pond. If the name Monsees rings a bell, it should. TBW decided to name the previously unnamed pond on Cathy and Steve's property after them. A nice gesture, don't you think? In the mid-1990s, TBW drilled four 700-foot wells into the Floridan Aquifer adjacent to Prairie Lake and the pond. According to Cathy and Steve, the pumping initially replenished Monsees Pond, so Cathy and Steve stocked it with bass and channel catfish. But as TBW continued to pump, the water table continued to fall. In the end, even 150,000 gpd could not keep up with the drainage from the pond into the soil. Monsees Pond went dry again.

TBW engineers did not take the fact that the water drained from the pond as a sign that the idea was flawed. They thought the execution just needed tweaking. In 1997, TBW engineers devised a project that would have made Rube Goldberg smile. To make the bed of the pond leak less, TBW considered bringing in truckloads of clay to create an impermeable liner on the bottom of the pond. TBW eventually decided not to execute this plan.

In addition to the harm that TBW's pumping has inflicted on lakes, ponds, rivers, creeks, wetlands, and estuaries, it has cracked the foundations, walls, and ceilings of local residents' homes. By lowering the water table, pumping causes rainwater to infiltrate more deeply into the ground. The downward movement of water gradually dissolves the limestone, which supports the surface soil. It may take decades, but eventually land subsidence and sinkholes occur, destroying buildings and causing property values to plummet.

In 1998, attorney David Smolker, on behalf of Benny Guy and Terry Sims, who live in the town of Wesley Chapel about an hour north of Tampa Bay, filed suit for damages against Tampa Bay Water. The suit alleged that TBW's pumping destroyed a 2.5-acre cypress wetland on Guy and Sims' property adjacent to the Cypress Creek well field, dried up their domestic well, caused subsidence, and produced cracks and fissures in the concrete driveway, sidewalk, and block walls of their residence. In 2001, TBW settled the case by buying Guy and Sims' property and paying them damages and attorneys' fees. Smolker is considering representing a group of Guy and Sims' neighbors, including Gilliam Clarke, Paul and Cynthia Firmani, and Nancy and Kerry Boatwright, who have suffered similar harm. The neighborhood's large lots range up to eleven acres. The homes, built in the late 1980s, are dream houses, designed and built to accent the vast stands of cypress trees and wetlands.

Although the stories vary in details, they share common threads. Consider, for example, the situation of Nancy and Kerry Boatwright, whose eleven acres included hundreds of mature cypress, oak, and pine trees, bay head wetlands, and a small creek frequented by alligators. They cleared an area for the house, which they designed and had built in the late 1980s. Then their well dried up. Tampa Bay Water, under its "good neighbor policy," determined that the municipal well field's cone of depression had interfered with the Boatwrights' well, so TBW paid the costs for drilling a deeper well. Next, the creek dried up, and the alligators departed. As the wetland dried up, the cypress trees began to die; then the upland oak and pine trees died. Old-growth trees with four- to five-foot-diameter trunks literally toppled over. When sinkholes appeared in the yard, the foundations on the Boatwrights' porch and garage slab cracked, and the stucco walls of the house began to chip. TBW disclaimed responsibility and blamed the cracks on faulty construction.

The Boatwrights contacted their homeowner's insurance agent at Nationwide Insurance. Nationwide arranged to conduct tests, which revealed sinkholes beneath the Boatwrights' home, a condition covered by their policy. Nationwide's contractor began repair work in September 1999, a process that continued for three years. The contractor drilled thirty-two holes around the perimeter of the home and began to pour concrete into the holes to fill up the sinkholes. He poured and poured, ultimately 108 cubic yards of concrete, or enough concrete to fill a three-foot by three-foot ditch longer than a football field. In July 2000, Nationwide arranged to replace the front porch slab and the garage slab. After completing the exterior work, Nationwide fixed the interior stucco, tile, and paint, spending $80,000–$85,000 in the process. Alas, the repairs to the back porch have not held up. The land is still sinking.

Although the Boatwrights were fortunate that insurance covered the damage to their home, anyone who has endured a home remodeling project knows it is about as welcome as a trip to the dentist for a root canal. Plus, the home repair did not bring back the trees, the wetland, the creek, or the alligators, which were desirable reasons for the home to be there in the first place. The Boatwrights fell in love with the property because of the special environment created by the cypress bay head. Even with a substantial reduction in pumping by TBW, it would take decades to restore that environment. Plus, the subsidence may continue. Every rainstorm causes a little more erosion of the limestone. There is no assurance that the walls won't chip again. That happened to the Boatwrights' neighbor, Gilliam Clarke. Subsidence caused her ceilings to buckle, which the insurance company repaired. But the ceilings are buckling again. Clarke thinks that all the homes in the neighborhood are unsellable. She asks rhetorically: "Who would buy a house sitting in a yard where all the trees are falling down because of sinkholes?"

In May 1998, Swiftmud and TBW entered into an agreement that called for developing eighty-five mgd of new water supplies by 2007 and for reducing pumping from eleven existing well fields. The agreement called for a maximum withdrawal of 158 mgd through the year 2002, 121 mgd between 2003 and 2007, and not more than 90 mgd beginning in 2008. These reductions will present significant challenges to TBW. Swiftmud has committed itself to providing financial assistance to help TBW achieve these objectives. But the plan also anticipated some short-term *increases* in pumping from the Cypress Creek well field and even bringing new wells on line. The agreement to achieve significant reductions in pumping has put increased pressure on TBW to produce alternative supplies of water.

For one alternative, TBW decided in late 1999 to build the largest saltwater desalinization plant in the western hemisphere, a $120 million project capable of providing 25 mgd. The desalinization proposal has run into its own environmental problem. Although the process of desalinization generates a substantial amount of potable water, it is also very costly because it requires considerable energy to run the plants and expensive synthetic membranes to filter out the salt. It also produces as a waste product highly saline water, representing 3 to 12 percent of the total volume of desalted water. Most desalinization plants simply dump this waste stream back into the ocean. In the case of the west coast of Florida with its sensitive estuaries, environmentalists fear the long-term impact of this particular "fix." Florida's top environmental official, David Struhs, initially withheld approval of the desalinization project. At a public meeting, protesters confronted Struhs with signs that objected: "If I wanted the Dead Sea, I'd live in Israel." On the other hand, Pasco County officials think that this plant may finally provide a way for TBW to reduce its groundwater pumping. Steve Simon, a Pasco County commissioner, reasoned: "Has Pinellas County done anything to control growth? No. So the question is how to provide the water, and as I see it, desal is the only answer." TBW eventually received approval and began construction of the desalinization plant in August 2001.

Another threat has surfaced recently. Robert Thomas' family has been ranching in Florida for generations. They own 14,000 acres in Pasco and Hillsborough Counties, including Crystal Springs, an area that Thomas kept open to the public for recreation until 1996. Thomas has granted access to the property to Zephyrhills Spring Water Co., a wholly owned subsidiary of The Perrier Group of America. Since 1989, a permit from Swiftmud has allowed Perrier to pump 301,000 gpd from Crystal Springs just before it discharges at the surface. Perrier transports the water by stainless steel pipe three miles to its bottling plant. In 1997, Thomas proposed to increase pumping to 2.6 mgd, or 949 million gallons per year, to allow Perrier to meet an expected increase in demand for Zephyrhills bottled water. As we've seen, as Perrier's bottled water business has boomed, it has acquired a number of independent spring water companies, including Zephyrhills, Calistoga, Poland Spring, and Arrowhead. To satisfy demand, Perrier has sought new sources of water around the country; these efforts have led to conflicts with other water users and environmentalists in Maine, Texas, Wisconsin, Michigan, and Pennsylvania.

In Florida, reaction to Thomas' proposed increase in pumping was swift and negative. Environmentalists objected to pumping huge amounts of water that would otherwise discharge to a beautiful stream, although the project would pump less than 10 percent of the flow in Crystal Springs. Led by Terri Wolfe, local citizens created a new organization, Save Our Springs, dedicated to the preservation of Florida's springs. They also commenced a consumer boycott of Perrier and its parent, Nestle. Nearby residents feared that the pumping would lower the water table in the aquifer, threaten private wells, and drain lakes. TBW also opposed the increase in pumping because Crystal Springs flows into the Hillsborough River, the principal water supply for the city of Tampa. At a time when TBW must reduce its groundwater pumping pursuant to its agreement with Swiftmud, TBW strenuously opposes new pumping that would reduce the flow in the Hillsborough River.

Before Thomas and Perrier could increase pumping, they had to obtain a permit from Swiftmud. In January 1999, Swiftmud's staff recommended that its governing board deny the permit request, which the

board did. The staff's recommendation rested on concern over environmental impacts, the effect on TBW's existing water rights, and the failure
of Perrier to demonstrate that it needed the water it was seeking. Thomas
and Perrier subsequently scaled back their request to 1.8 mgd, enlisted a
professional mediator to facilitate a compromise (which was not reached),
and filed suit in state court challenging the staff's recommendation.
Thomas and Perrier funded a hydrologic study that concluded that the
increase in pumping would not adversely affect groundwater, surface
water, or the environment. At a September 1999 hearing, James Wayne
Mercer, Jr., a hydrologist for Thomas and Perrier, testified that the augmented pumping would not change the flow in the Hillsborough River:
"You will not be able to detect this withdrawal in the Hillsborough
River." Robert Thomas made the same point: "Our proposal causes no
measurable or noticeable impact."

Let's see, now. Pumping 1.8 mgd multiplied by 365 days equals 657
million gallons per year. Yet Mercer claimed that science could not "detect"
a change in flow. Mercer blamed reduced flows in the Hillsborough River
and in Crystal Springs on nearby groundwater pumping, which is assuredly
correct, but just because one culprit has been found doesn't mean there
can't be two. Swiftmud hydrologists naturally challenged Mercer's conclusions. They reasoned that the Hillsborough River is already inadequate to
meet the city of Tampa's needs and that diverting more water from the
springs would further reduce the river's flow. In January 2000, the judge
agreed with Swiftmud that the increased pumping would reduce the flow
in the Hillsborough River, which would be "an adverse impact on the city
of Tampa." In February 2001, the Florida Court of Appeal unanimously
affirmed the decision. However, that did not end the matter, because while
the case was on appeal, Thomas filed a scaled-down application for a permit to pump 603,000 gpd.

The Swiftmud governing board granted Thomas a permit in April
2001 but limited the increase to 30,000 gpd and required that he replace
every gallon he pumps with an equal amount obtained from outside the
Hillsborough River basin. Thomas and Perrier have increased their pumping by that amount. In February 2002, Thomas contracted with a Pasco
County farmer to supply 30,000 gpd of groundwater, which is loaded on
tanker trucks and then dumped into the Hillsborough River. The farmer's
neighbors are unhappy, for they fear the pumping will cause sinkholes and
dry up their wells. Jeff Hupp, a local firefighter, commented bitterly: "It's

pretty ridiculous that I can't water my lawn but this guy can pump five tanker trucks of water out of the ground every day."

Crystal Springs is not the only place in Florida where Perrier is seeking additional groundwater. In 2001, Joe Priest of Ocola in Marion County sought a permit to lease rights to Zephyrhills to tap spring water from his land on the Rainbow River. In July 2001, owners of the Blue Grotto Diving Resort in Williston received permission from Swiftmud to pump 99,000 gpd from the spring, which they will sell to an unnamed bottled-water company. Finally, Three Sisters Springs Water Company sought, in February 2001, permission to bottle water pumped from the Three Sisters Spring in Crystal River. This last proposal led Al Coogler, chair of Swiftmud's regulation committee, to propose in June 2001 a ban on new permits to pump spring water for bottled water.

It is puzzling why the state of Florida, or any other state for that matter, would allow a private company to obtain control over the state's water. For some natural resources, this might be understandable. Mining oil, for example, requires an enormous investment of time, effort, and money. Even with this effort, there is no assurance that oil will be found in sufficient quantity to make the effort financially successful. Hence, it makes some sense to reward those who risk labor and capital, or else people will be reluctant to undertake the effort. But pumping spring water is a no-brainer. The spring makes its presence known by bubbling to the surface. The bottler merely needs to drill a well, bottle the water, and deposit the checks. It is hard to justify windfall profits to Perrier, especially when the increased pumping threatens the water supply of others and harms the environment.

The critical situation in Florida has become worse due to drought. El Niño winds produce heavy rains, but La Niña winds create dry conditions, as occurred in 1999 when area lakes dropped two to three feet during the year, and the Floridan Aquifer dropped 5.5 feet. In April 2000, Swiftmud declared a water shortage emergency that triggered restrictions on watering lawns and plants. The drought continued. By February 2001, it had become the worst recorded drought in west Florida history. Swiftmud officials estimated that the Hillsborough River was running at a third of its normal flow. The water table dropped an additional ten feet, and 29,000 acres of wetlands in the Tampa Bay area turned to sand. Between 1999 and 2001, rainfall in the region plummeted sixty-two inches below average.

Pressures on TBW come from a variety of directions. For example, one controversy focuses on the amount of water needed to maintain the natural ecosystem both in the river and in the estuary where the river flows into Tampa Bay. Ten miles upstream from the mouth of the river, the city of Tampa has a dam that creates a public water supply reservoir. Downstream of the dam, the river flows through a highly developed section of the city of Tampa before flowing into Tampa Bay. In this reach, the river is a pale imitation of its former self; two miles of the channel are frequently bone dry. Trees and vegetation have given way to concrete-lined banks constructed in the name of flood control. City of Tampa assistant city attorney Kathy Fry asks rhetorically: "Which is more valuable: saving 2.5 miles of river [badly degraded over the last 100 years] or lakes and pristine wetlands yet to be altered?"

Yet memories die hard. Restoring the river to its former state remains a goal of many environmentalists, who pushed for higher minimum flows while the city argued for lower flows. In the end, the city agreed, in what was clearly a political settlement, to provide minimum flows of ten cubic feet per second or forty-five hundred gallons per minute to the lower reach of the river. This translates into 6.5 mgd or 2.37 billion gallons of water per year that the city will allow to flow into Tampa Bay. For the river and the estuary, the positive environmental consequences represent a trade-off against other environmental harms.

As a result of the settlement, TBW will continue to supply its customers, including the city of Tampa, by relying on groundwater pumped from Hillsborough and Pasco Counties. The visible flows in the river will be offset by capture, the hidden consequences of groundwater pumping. The settlement, a Solomon-like effort to divide the bay, appeased neither side. Local residents sued, claiming that the proposal will not adequately protect the brackish section of the Hillsborough River below TBW's reservoir. Robert Thomas also sued because he considered the proposal a devious attempt to prevent him from pumping Crystal Springs water.

In April 2001, an engineering firm hired by TBW released a list of the most feasible future water sources for TBW. It included Weeki Wachee Spring in Hernando County. Legislators who represent Hernando County voters went ballistic. Senator Ginny Brown-Waite threatened that "the previous water wars of the 1990s will be [viewed] as tame," and Florida legislator David Russell warned that "my cold dead body will be lying in the right-of-way before they put the pipe in." Even discounting for political hyperbole, TBW will have its hands full if it goes after Hernando County water.

TBW's pledge to reduce groundwater pumping and to construct the desalinization plant was too little, too late to help Cathy and Steve Mon-sees. As they came to understand the hydrologic principle of capture, that TBW's groundwater pumping dried up their lake, they reacted angrily. Said Cathy: "We've been cheated out of our retirement. It's more than upsetting. My husband wanted to kick back and fish, but we'll never see water in that lake." Cathy and Steve's efforts to save their pond came to naught. In 2000, after spending seven years and $30,000 struggling to regain "Monsees Pond," they gave up and moved away.

Chapter 6

The Tourist's Mirage

San Antonio's River Walk,
the Edwards Aquifer, and Endangered Species

"All water has a perfect memory and is forever trying to get
back to where it was."
—Toni Morrison

In 1836, Mexican general Antonio Lopez de Santa Anna defeated an army
of Texas patriots, including Davy Crockett, who fought for Texas' independence at the Alamo. For most of the twentieth century, the Alamo
occupied the top niche as the city of San Antonio's most popular tourist
attraction. Not anymore. In 1995, Paseo del Rio, or River Walk, moved
into first place. A 2.5-mile section of the San Antonio River that flows
through the heart of downtown, River Walk anchors a $3.5-billion-a-year
tourist industry. River Walk offers tourists cobblestone streets lined with
flowering shrubs and elm, sycamore, and cypress trees, shopping in elegant
boutiques, food and drink in forty cafés, numerous Mexican restaurants,
flashy nightspots such as Planet Hollywood and the Hard Rock Cafe,
strolling mariachi bands, sight-seeing cruises on the river, and upscale
accommodations in new Sheraton, Westin, and Adam's Mark San Antonio
hotels.

Most tourists would be surprised to learn that the river they enjoy is
the creation of dams, floodgates, and, above all, groundwater pumped from
the Edwards Aquifer and dumped into the San Antonio River above River

Walk. The San Antonio River was once navigable through the River Walk stretch, but it dried up due to groundwater pumping. Since 1911, the city of San Antonio has been pumping water from the Edwards Aquifer into the river to make it flow. Up to 10 million gallons a day of groundwater are fed into it for no other reason than to create an economically useful illusion—that of a real river. Once a year, the city drains the river and cleans the channel of debris, mostly silverware, bottles, cans, and coins. This occurs in January because there are fewer conventions in town. As the owner of a River Walk restaurant put it, "[Tourists] think San Antonio is safe and clean. They like it being natural." Now that River Walk has evolved into a major source of tourist dollars, the city wants to maintain its appearance.

The headwaters of the San Antonio River rise north of the city in the San Pedro and San Antonio springs that discharge from the Edwards Aquifer, a limestone formation that gives the water a rich blue cast. In the downtown area, the river flows through the "great bend," an oxbow formation, before turning south on its way to the Gulf of Mexico. Thousands of years ago, the Payaya Indians camped on the banks of the San Antonio River, which they called Yanaguana Creek. Each year, during springtime, the creek would overflow its banks. When the Spanish arrived in the early eighteenth century, they renamed the creek Rio San Antonio and began to divert it into irrigation ditches, called acequias. An elaborate system of acequias harnessed the river's water and created a thriving agricultural community. San Antonio remained a quiet outpost until after the end of the Mexican War in 1848. The presence of the river encouraged European settlers to flock to the area. But the river was still prone to severe flooding; some sixty square miles of land north of the city drain into normally dry creeks that funnel floodwaters into the San Antonio River.

The river anchored the city's growth to the end of the nineteenth century, but by then, the river had suffered a serious decline in flows. The settlers had drilled artesian wells for domestic water supplies that drew on the same Edwards Aquifer water that sustained the river. Eventually, the river became an eyesore filled with refuse and raw sewage. In the last half of the nineteenth century, periodic epidemics of cholera killed thousands of people.

A prolonged drought in 1900 completely dried up the river. In 1911, a study commissioned by downtown businessmen proposed filling in the river and building an underground conduit to transport floodwater safely past downtown. But public support to save and restore the river led to the formation of the San Antonio River Improvement Association. In 1911, Mayor Bryan Callaghan approved installation of a shallow groundwater pump at the northern end of the city. Soon, 1,500 gallons of water per minute were being pumped into the river. As the water revived trees and vegetation, support grew for a major effort to save the river.

Between 1913 and 1921, six disastrous floods ripped through San Antonio. The worst flood, in 1921, killed fifty people and destroyed thirteen of the city's twenty-seven bridges. The new flooding occasioned considerable debate over the future of the river. Some business interests favored a major diversion project that would take the waters away from downtown. The river channel could then be filled in and developed as prime commercial real estate. However, thanks to the efforts of the newly formed San Antonio Conservation Society, the city moved instead to build a dam and a cutoff channel on the great bend that would reduce the risk of flooding. The city then moved aggressively to develop River Walk along the great bend section.

The Edwards Aquifer plays a critical economic role in the life of south-central Texas. The aquifer and its drainage region include approximately 8,000 square miles. Over the last forty years, agricultural expansion and population growth have dramatically increased the demand for water from the Edwards Aquifer. With a metropolitan population of 1.4 million, San Antonio is the eighth-largest city in the nation. The population of the area is expected to double by the year 2020. The city relies on groundwater from the Edwards Aquifer for over 99 percent of its municipal supply, giving San Antonio the dubious distinction of being the largest city in the country to rely so heavily on groundwater.

As in most other states, water law in Texas fails to recognize the hydrologic connection between ground- and surface water. The prior appropriation doctrine governs the right to divert water from rivers and streams, while the rule of capture controls rights to groundwater. In a 1904 decision, *Houston & Texas Central Railway v. East*, the Texas Supreme Court adopted the English rule of capture, which grants landowners an absolute right to pump as much water as they wish, even if the pumping causes a neighbor's well to go dry. The court refused to protect adjoining landowners because it thought that the principles that control the movement of groundwater

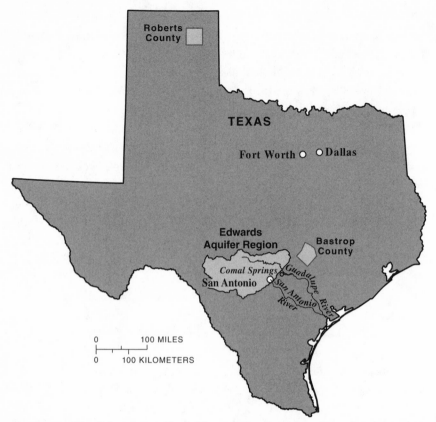

FIGURE 6.1. The Edwards Aquifer in Texas. T. Boone Pickens's ranch is located in Roberts County.

were "so secret, occult, and concealed that an attempt to administer any set of legal rules [would result] in hopeless uncertainty, and would, therefore, be practically impossible." Texas law has also immunized well owners against claims by surface water users. In Texas, the prior appropriation doctrine applies to spring waters only after they have emerged from the ground. Before that point in time, the rule of capture allows unlimited groundwater pumping, even if the result is to dry up the spring. The consequence of this harsh rule is that thousands of small springs have ceased flowing.

Today, the science of hydrology offers answers to the secret and occult movement of groundwater, so it was inevitable that parties would try to persuade the Texas Supreme Court to overturn the rule of capture. The most recent challenge came in a dispute involving the Ozarka Natural Spring Water Company, a subsidiary of Perrier, which in 1996 began pumping water for its bottling plant from an area around Roher Spring, northeast of Dallas. Within a few days, Ozarka's pumping of 90,000 gpd began to deplete the water in neighboring wells. The local residents sued, but the trial judge, though sympathetic to their claim, dismissed their suit. "The job of [a trial judge] is to rule on the law, not change the law. I don't understand the common sense of it, but it is not my job to rule on what the law should be, but what the law is." Quite so, agreed Lauren Cargill, a spokeswoman for Ozarka, who stated that the company was complying with Texas' rule of capture. "You can do with groundwater what you want, regardless of your neighbors." Not a very neighborly attitude, but she accurately described the rule of capture, known in Texas as "the rule of the biggest pump."

The residents appealed to the Texas Supreme Court, which in May 1999 reaffirmed the rule of capture. In *Sipriano v. Great Spring Waters of America*, the court conceded that there are "compelling reasons for groundwater use to be regulated" but refused to do so. The Texas legislature has broad power to regulate groundwater use and in 1997 enacted Senate Bill 1, which created local conservation districts to manage groundwater. But like many such efforts, it is heavy on planning and light on sanctions and penalties. In light of Senate Bill 1, the Texas Supreme Court decided not to abandon the rule of capture. Though the potential for sweeping change remains, Senate Bill 1 has thus far achieved little. The consequence of the *Sipriano* decision for San Antonio and the Edwards Aquifer is significant. The doctrine of capture prevails.

The Edwards Aquifer holds a huge amount of water (estimates range up to 250 million acre-feet, or twenty times the capacity of Lake Livingston and Lake Travis, two of Texas's largest lakes). Annual recharge to the Edwards Aquifer is quite substantial, averaging 650,000 acre-feet per year, but, given the hydrology of the aquifer, certain problems have arisen. The Edwards Aquifer sits in a limestone formation that is highly transmissive: water moves quickly through it. The water level in the aquifer changes rapidly depending on pumping or drought conditions. Movement of water in the aquifer is generally toward the Gulf Coast, where there is an extraordinarily productive artesian zone in which the pressure of the water moving southeast produces springs and artesian wells. Some wells produce as much as 6,000–7,000 gpm. One remarkable well drilled in 1991 hit a pressurized area 1,600 feet deep and produced a thirty-inch column of groundwater that gushed forty feet into the air. An adjoining neighbor remembered that "the ground rumbled like a freight train." This one artesian well produces 43 million gallons per day, or 48,000 acre-feet per year—about one-quarter of the amount of water used annually in San Antonio. The owners, Ronnie Pucek, Jr., a thirty-two-year-old entrepreneur from Alvin, Texas, and Louis Blumberg, a New Jersey developer of tract housing, thankful for their blessings, named the well "Avé Maria No. 1" and promptly searched for a use for all this water. They decided to raise catfish. No joke. Well, it became a joke, but that's the story.

Pucek and Blumberg formed Living Waters Artesian Springs Ltd. and started their catfish farm. They hoped to raise 750,000 catfish on the amount of water that San Antonio uses to raise 250,000 human beings. They built concrete tanks, called raceways, and began to flow Edwards Aquifer groundwater over thousands of catfish. After they installed an aerator to reduce the level of hydrogen sulfide, netting above the tanks to keep preying birds out, and a feeding system that automatically dumped pellets into the tanks, they were in business. With one problem. That many catfish in a closely confined space excreted an enormous volume of waste, which ultimately reached the Medina River. After the catfish farmers refused to reduce their water use, two water agencies brought suit, claiming that they had failed to obtain permits to discharge polluted wastewater into the river. A state court judge issued a temporary injunction that shut down the catfish operation pending trial. Even in the state that has given us "the rule of the biggest pump," the catfish farm seemed a grotesque waste of water.

Even though the Edwards Aquifer contains a large volume of water, a modest decline in the water table will dramatically affect the discharge to the springs. Groundwater pumping has lowered water levels in Comal and San Marcos springs (the two largest springs in Texas), home to five endangered or threatened species: the fountain darter, the Texas blind salamander, the San Marcos gambusia, Texas wild rice, and the San Marcos salamander.

The Endangered Species Act (ESA) protects threatened or endangered species and their habitats. A person violates the ESA by "taking" an endangered species, which includes not only killing an animal but also "harming" it indirectly by "significant habitat modification or degradation." The ESA has spawned complex litigation, initiated in 1991 by the Sierra Club, over San Antonio's groundwater pumping. U.S. District Judge Lucius Bunton found that continued groundwater pumping, by lowering the water level in the springs, violated the ESA. He directed the Texas Water Commission to submit a plan to ensure that Comal and San Marcos springs do not drop below certain critical levels. He also announced that unless the Texas legislature enacted, by May 31, 1993, a regulatory plan to limit groundwater withdrawals, he would develop and implement his own plan. The legislature got the message and, one day before Judge Bunton's deadline, enacted Senate Bill 1477. The legislation established the Edwards Aquifer Authority, a conservation district that has the power to issue groundwater withdrawal permits, which are readily transferable. The act attempted to create a market in groundwater rights that would encourage voluntary transfers and transactions between willing buyers and sellers. During times of drought or particularly high water use, the Authority is required to adopt a management plan to reduce pumping.

Procedural wrangling and litigation slowed the authority's adoption of rules and regulations for issuing permits for pumping. In 2000, the authority began to quantify the rights of pumpers, including those of the catfish farmers, who ultimately received a withdrawal right to 17,000 acre-feet. Though this was only a fraction of the 48,000 acre-feet they originally pumped, with the permit the farmers had a marketable commodity that the city of San Antonio was happy to purchase. The farmers received $9 million for 10,000 acre-feet, or about $700 per acre-foot, and almost $200,000 per year for a lease of the remainder. When the news broke about San Antonio's buyout of the catfish farmers, the blood pressure of local editorial writers went through the roof. One protested that the farmers' message to the city was: "Stick 'em up! I've got a pump!" This, I suppose, is a reasonable characterization of the rule of capture.

Metropolitan San Antonio also has an unusual blend of community activists who oppose measures that elsewhere would seem progressive. For example, until recently, community opposition kept San Antonio from fluoridating its public water supply. Good news for dentists, I guess. San Antonio voters have also refused to support water projects that would create alternatives to pumping from the Edwards Aquifer. In 1991 and 1994, San Antonio voters defeated a proposal to build the Applewhite Reservoir on the Medina River south of the city to provide surface water. They were convinced that water shortage problems were created by political interests or were judicially imposed and not due to an actual physical shortage of water. Allowing catfish farmers to use billions of gallons a year gave some credibility to this perception.

In 1992, the San Antonio City Council created the San Antonio Water System (SAWS), a single utility that has responsibility for water, wastewater, storm water, and reuse. Since then, SAWS has moved aggressively to secure new water supplies, to implement a municipal effluent treatment program, to recycle water in River Walk, and to reduce pumping from the Edwards Aquifer.

Where will new water supplies come from? In December 1998, SAWS's board of directors approved the purchase of 55,000 acre-feet per year (af/yr) of groundwater from the Aluminum Company of America (ALCOA) and City Public Service (CPS), both of which own land with deposits of lignite, a form of coal. To mine the lignite, water located beneath the deposit must be pumped out, in a process called "depressurization." Although the water is high quality, the mining company has no use for it. San Antonio surely does. But there is one big problem: the mines are 100–120 miles north of San Antonio. When cities and states begin to think about high-cost water delivery systems, their minds soon focus on the federal treasury. Pork barrel spending occupies a sacred place in funding water projects. In this case, however, San Antonio is going it alone. A consultant's report explored the feasibility of five different water delivery options, most involving a sixty-six-inch diameter pipeline. Projected construction costs range from $280 to $457 million, or $688 to $840 per acre-foot. San Antonio ratepayers are in for a rude awakening.

The additional 55,000 af/yr will surely help SAWS reduce its demand on the Edwards Aquifer and thereby reduce the impact of pumping on Comal and San Marcos springs. While helping to solve one surface water/groundwater problem, however, it will create another. The water will be pumped from the Carrizo-Wilcox Aquifer in Bastrop County. A number of streams and springs overlie the aquifer. According to Gunnar Brune, author of *Springs of Texas*, most springs above neighboring aquifers have suffered reduced flows from heavy groundwater pumping. The city's consultant conceded that new pumping for San Antonio would affect the streams and reduce spring flow but concluded that the volume would not "produce any reasonably discernable changes in either physical habitat or biological communities." The Houston toad, a federally listed endangered species, inhabits the area.

Environmentalists from Bastrop County and San Antonio oppose the proposed pumping. Ann Mesrobian, conservation chair of the Bastrop County Environmental Network, fears that the pumping will dry up seeps and springs and reduce flow in the Brazos and Colorado Rivers. Local neighbors believe it will impact their own wells. In May 2000, a newly formed citizens group, Neighbors for Neighbors, organized a protest march from Elgin to San Antonio, a distance of 120 miles. Eighty women took turns walking five-mile shifts in a three-day, round-the-clock march. One of the marchers, Sherry Webb, a retired Air Force lieutenant colonel, wore a sign that read: "Stop Water Rustling." Despite the protests, San Antonio probably will get its newly purchased groundwater because Texas' doctrine of the biggest pump does not restrict use of the water to land directly above the aquifer.

Where else is San Antonio looking for water? To its wastewater treatment system. SAWS has begun to dump effluent into River Walk as a substitute for groundwater. In July 2000, the city completed construction of a $125 million water treatment and reuse system. With four treatment plants, euphemistically called "water recycling centers," and seventy-three miles of pipelines, the city has the capacity to treat and deliver 140,000 acre-feet per year of effluent, making San Antonio one of the largest reusers of water in the country. The city has stopped pumping groundwater directly into River Walk and has begun to rely entirely on effluent, which is treated to an advanced secondary level, "suitable for incidental human contact." River Walk still consists entirely of groundwater, but it's been used before. When SAWS announced its plan to substitute effluent for groundwater in River Walk, one local news story proclaimed: "Don't tell the tourists!" My bet is that they won't care.

San Antonio is exploring dozens of other possibilities for its future water supply. One alternative would purchase Guadalupe River water rights from agricultural irrigators. If done properly, this has potential to produce water for San Antonio and not harm the environment. The project would divert water at the mouth of the Guadalupe below the confluence with the San Antonio River. A network of pipes would transport the water to the city, where, after use, it would be treated and then released into the San Antonio River to flow back into the Guadalupe and then into the Gulf of Mexico. Before the project moves forward, years of feasibility studies are necessary to assess the impact on the Guadalupe River estuary, but the potential is intriguing. As San Antonio's water treatment system expands, it will produce more effluent—for reuse for River Walk, golf courses, and parks, or discharge into the San Antonio River. According to Susan Butler, SAWS water resources director, their preliminary modeling suggests that "flows into the bay and estuary might actually be improved." An attractive feature of this proposal, according to Butler, is that the water "gets used by the river, it gets used by us, and then it gets used by the river again."

San Antonio has available another source of water. In 2000, T. Boone Pickens, a well-known corporate raider of the 1980s, proposed to pump groundwater from the Ogallala Aquifer beneath his own and neighboring ranches in Roberts County in Texas's Panhandle and sell it to San Antonio. Mr. Pickens is apparently taking a page out of the book of two Texas oilmen, Ed and Lee Bass, who, in the mid-1990s, purchased 45,000 acres in the Imperial Irrigation District in southern California, intending to sell the water to thirsty California cities. In 1997, they sold their interests to U.S. Filter Corporation, owners of Culligan water filtration systems, for 8 million shares of U.S. Filter, worth approximately $350 million. This is a nice return on real estate that cost the Bass brothers less than $100 million.

If one wants a glimpse of the future, the Pickens scheme may provide it. In addition to his 24,000-acre ranch, Pickens has purchased or leased 125,000 additional acres of land and, as of April 2001, wanted to acquire an additional 50,000 acres. He could pump more than 60 billion gallons per year, and the doctrine of capture would allow him to sell the water to distant cities. In May 2000, a consultant retained by Pickens concluded that "this project is doable," even though San Antonio is 535 miles away from Pickens's ranch and he will need to build a pipeline at an estimated cost of $1 billion. Pickens pitched the deal to San Antonio, at a cost ranging between $1,007 and $1,200 per acre-foot. The city gave the project serious consideration but declined his offer, at least for now. The letter from Michael F. Thuss, president and CEO of SAWS, stressed "the high range of costs" of Pickens's proposal and concern over "the rate of water level declines in the project area." Therefore, he stated, "the San Antonio Water System is not ready to pursue this proposal at this time."

The Pickens offer is another in the annals of bizarre water projects. As Pickens's proposal to San Antonio noted: "Water extracted from this portion of the Ogallala is replenished at almost imperceptible rates." Groundwater does not sit quietly in one place; it moves laterally in response to pumping and the resulting cone of depression. So, although Pickens is proposing to sell groundwater initially located under his property, the water he sells later on will have been legally drawn to his pumps from beneath neighboring lands. His proposed sale to San Antonio is like trying to sell the sleeves out of his vest.

Chapter 7

Suburban Development
and Watershed Initiatives

Massachusetts' Ipswich River Basin

"The watershed is the first and last nation whose boundaries,
though subtly shifting, are unalterable."

—Gary Snyder

The Commonwealth of Massachusetts consists of 351 separate cities and
towns, many established during the seventeenth century. Most towns
conduct business at town meetings, a curious form of government that
traces to the colonial era. All residents may participate, speak their minds,
and offer their opinions to an appointed town administrator, who serves
at the pleasure of a board of selectmen. Religion, ethnicity, and race were
once important variables in settling these discrete communities. Though
these factors are less critical today than in times past, many Massachusetts
towns and cities remain highly stratified in terms of income, ethnicity,
religion, and race, even though they no longer banish religious dissidents,
as they did in the seventeenth century when Roger Williams fled to
found Rhode Island, or burn suspected witches at the stake, as the Town
of Salem did in the 1690s. In October 2001, the Commonwealth of
Massachusetts enacted legislation exonerating five accused witches who
were hanged in 1692 and 1693; the governor signed the bill on Hal-
loween. Communities cherish local control and mistrust outsiders. New
Englanders take enormous pride in the character and attractiveness of the

region. Many adults live within a stone's throw of the homes where they grew up and could not imagine moving very far. Residents of metropolitan Boston regularly praise the area as the best region in the United States, even if they have never traveled west of Worcester, in the middle of the state.

In an earlier chapter, I expressed my fear that the San Pedro River in Arizona might go dry due to groundwater pumping. Southern Arizona

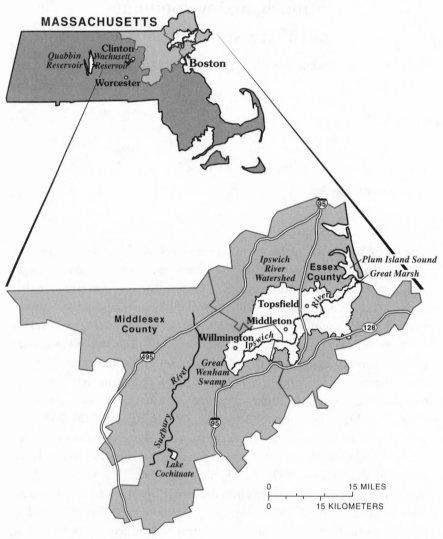

FIGURE 7.1. Ipswich River watershed in eastern Massachusetts.

receives only twelve inches of rain per year. Could a similar fate beset a river in Massachusetts, which receives on average forty-five inches of rain per year, or four inches more than Seattle? It not only could, it has. In 1995, 1997, and 1999, the Ipswich River dried up.

Centuries before the Puritans and other Europeans arrived, American Indians called the Ipswich River "Agawam . . . place of the fishes of passage." The river contained herring, alewives, salmon, bass, and brook trout. Enormous clam beds grew in the estuary at the mouth of the Ipswich River, and today, the Town of Ipswich remains famous for its clams. In 1638, Chief Masconomet sold both land and fishing rights to John Winthrop, son of one of the state's early colonial governors. Puritans began to settle the region, and by the mid-eighteenth century, the river hosted a tannery and a shipbuilding yard. The river suffered during the Industrial Revolution of the nineteenth century, when the Ipswich was dammed for paper and textile mills and additional tanneries. Although many New England rivers ran red, blue, or green, depending on the color of the dye used at the textile mills, the Ipswich escaped this fate only to suffer an ironic one. Because it was not as badly polluted as some other rivers, communities began to rely on the Ipswich for their public water supply.

More recently, the Ipswich River has become a popular recreational spot for swimming, canoeing, and bird watching. When Kerry Mackin moved to a house in Topsfield within walking distance of the Ipswich River in the early 1970s, she "knew nothing about the river then, except that it was beautiful." Many evenings, she would wander down to the river, sit on a big rock, and enjoy "the peacefulness of that quiet, wonderful place." Later, she began to canoe the river after work or on weekends and thus began a "personal sort of love affair" with the river. She purchased a house overlooking the last bend of the river before it empties into the ocean. After graduate school in natural resource management, she began in the late 1980s to work on wetlands issues for the Conservation Commission of Topsfield. In 1993, she became executive director of the Ipswich River Watershed Association (IRWA), a nonprofit environmental group. Under her leadership, IRWA has played a critical role in efforts to protect the river. After organizing a forum with state officials and local residents, Mackin concluded that the state officials did not understand that Massachusetts' water permitting process profoundly impacts the river.

From its headwaters in Wilmington, the Ipswich River meanders northeast for thirty-five miles to its mouth in Plum Island Sound. Because it lies within the Atlantic Coastal Plain, the Ipswich has a low gradient of only 2.5 feet per mile. Adjacent to a section of the river in Middleton and Topsfield lies a silver maple floodplain forest. As the name suggests, floodplain forests depend on regular flooding for their survival. Most of this habitat in Massachusetts was long ago cleared for agriculture. The silver maple floodplain forest survives as a rare example of this habitat. In another reach of the river, the Massachusetts Audubon Society owns and manages the Ipswich River Wildlife Sanctuary, part of the 2,500-acre Great Wenham Swamp. Eight miles of the Ipswich run through the sanctuary, affording visitors glimpses of river otter, mink, weasels, beaver, painted turtles, great blue herons, and other birds. The swamp has a critical role in maintaining the river's flow—it stores water during flood conditions and then slowly filters the water back into the river. Finally, at the estuary of the Ipswich is the Great Marsh, a key stopover for migrating birds on the Atlantic Flyway and home to commercially important shellfish beds.

The health of the sanctuary, swamp, floodplain forest, marsh, and estuary depends on a high groundwater table to discharge water and provide perennial flows. When flows are low or nonexistent, the river banks become undercut, thus exposing tree root masses and causing overhanging vegetation to dry out. The low flows in the Ipswich have devastated the fish population, virtually extirpating river species, such as brook trout, creek chubsuckers, and fallfish. In the sections of the river that dried up, the fish died or migrated elsewhere. Even in sections that retain water, the environment is significantly degraded. A healthy river has quick-moving water with deep pools and ripples that cause oxygen to dissolve in the water as it tumbles over the rocks. A slow-moving stream has low levels of dissolved oxygen that are conducive to algae blooms but not to the good health of fish. Low flows in the river also create problems for the Great Marsh and the estuary by slowing down the rate of "flushing," the time it takes for a drop of water to enter and exit the river. Flushing times are critical to water pollution. A short flushing time means that pollutants in the river move rapidly downstream and out into the ocean, where large volumes of seawater dilute their concentration. Low flows lengthen the flushing time and permit pollutants, such as fecal coliform bacteria, to settle in the estuary and shellfish beds.

Why has the Ipswich River dried up? In 1995, Massachusetts experienced a very dry summer. After an IRWA volunteer reported "river in sad shape, no sign of life," Kerry Mackin grabbed her camera and drove upstream to the monitoring station. Adjacent to the river, she drove past emerald green lawns being watered by lawn sprinklers and found a completely dry riverbed and thousands of dead fish. The correlation was obvious, as was the cause, Mackin believed. After she made a few telephone calls, television news crews arrived to film the river and bring the plight of the Ipswich into the homes of Massachusetts viewers. In 1997, the environmental organization American Rivers declared the Ipswich one of the "20 most threatened rivers" in the United States, the only East Coast river to receive such an ominous designation. Public awareness of the low-flow problem grew, especially when the river went dry again that summer.

The Hub, as Boston is known, first began to import water from outside its boundaries in 1795. It took water from Jamaica Pond, then part of

FIGURE 7.2. Dead fish, Ipswich River. Photograph courtesy of Kerry Mackin, Ipswich River Watershed Association.

Roxbury, through wooden pipes. In the nineteenth century, Boston began to rely on water from Lake Cochituate and the Sudbury River. Early in the twentieth century, it constructed Wachusett Reservoir in Clinton as an additional source, but even these supplies would prove inadequate for Boston's future. In 1939, the Metropolitan District Commission constructed Quabbin Reservoir, sixty-five miles west of Boston, by diverting water from the Ware and Swift Rivers and submerging four towns. With a storage capacity of 412 billion gallons of water, Quabbin provides most Boston-area cities with their public water supply, under the auspices of the Massachusetts Water Resources Authority (MWRA). MWRA supplies 250 million gallons of water per day to 2.5 million people in forty-six communities. Because Quabbin is such a large reservoir, towns that receive water from the MWRA have access to adequate, even abundant, supplies of water. However, communities that do not receive water from MWRA must depend on local surface supplies or groundwater wells. These are the communities in the Ipswich River basin. The major demand on the Ipswich River has old roots. In the early twentieth century, the cities of Beverly, Salem, Lynn, and Peabody received permission from the legislature to divert surface water from the Ipswich River. The Salem-Beverly Water Supply Board dug a two-mile-long canal through the Wenham Swamp in Topsfield to the Ipswich River, and the cities of Peabody and Lynn diverted water from the river upstream in North Reading (and later from Peabody). These communities may divert over 50 million gallons a day during the winter and early spring from the Ipswich River to Wenham Lake and other reservoirs, where they store the water for use year-round. These older communities have vested rights to divert water from the Ipswich and other rivers; newer communities have generally turned to groundwater to supply municipal needs.

As Ipswich River basin towns search for future water supplies, two Massachusetts laws will restrict their options. The 1985 Watershed Management Act requires state approval for any new water withdrawal greater than 100,000 gallons per day. A permitting process allows for extensive state regulation concerning stream flow depletions, review of rare species, and consideration of other environmental concerns. Agencies or water suppliers that receive permits are subject to a variety of conservation standards, including the detection of leaks, the calibration of water meters, and the mandated use of low-flow fixtures. On the other hand, the act exempted existing diversions and pumping and, as a benchmark to quantify existing rights, used a period of dry years and inefficient water use, one in which large quantities of water were diverted, thus resulting in anomalously large rights.

Kerry Mackin has been quite critical of how the Watershed Management Act has operated. When she asked officials at the state's Department of Environmental Protection (DEP) why they chose to give cities and towns more water when the river was already being pumped dry, a state bureaucrat responded: "Water suppliers demanded more, and you were the weaker constituency." Such remarkable candor from state regulators is unusual, even though the justification is quite outrageous. Mackin dismisses the new permit allocations as creating rights to "phantom water . . . water that doesn't exist." Instead of encouraging conservation during dry periods, the state has allowed water use to increase. Duane LeVangie, director of a water management program at the Massachusetts DEP, agrees with Mackin. "When streams and rivers are the most distressed naturally, that's when humans use the most water. It's a double threat to the river."

A second law, the Interbasin Transfer Act, requires approval of the Massachusetts Water Resources Commission for any increase in the amount of water transferred between basins in the Commonwealth. The community requesting such a transfer must demonstrate not only that it has a real need but also that it has explored all other alternatives, including conservation. Withdrawals must also ensure reasonable in-stream flow in the river from which the water is diverted. However, the act applies only to new transfers. Existing pipelines have been grandfathered in.

There has been considerable debate over whether diversions through the existing pipelines have caused the Ipswich River to dry up. Tom Knowlton, executive director of the Salem-Beverly Water Supply Board, thinks not. He defends the diversions because under state law the board can pump only between December and May, when the river is full. Knowlton points the finger at small towns whose water supply has come from recently installed groundwater pumps located adjacent to the river. Although the lion's share of Ipswich River surface water is diverted by the older, established communities of Beverly, Salem, Lynn, and Peabody, newer communities such as Hamilton, Wenham, Ipswich, Reading, North Reading, Wilmington, Topsfield, and Lynnfield have sunk wells along the banks of the river for municipal supplies. Robert Zimmerman, Jr., executive director of the Charles River Watershed Association, notes: "Very few people understand the dynamic connection between groundwater and surface water. Somehow, people think that the water that flows underground is disconnected from surface water, and nothing could be further from the truth." In the case of the Ipswich River, understanding this relationship is critical, as is establishing a forum for debating, discussing, and resolving water use conflicts in the basin. Unfortunately, in the United States we rarely manage water resources in an integrated fashion. The politically stronger constituency usually ends up with the water.

━ ━

Although we, as a nation, rejected John Wesley Powell's nineteenth-century plea to take a watershed approach to managing various rivers, some recent, remarkably inventive efforts are trying to recapture Powell's original insight. The last ten years have seen the creation of perhaps 400 watershed groups around the country. Watershed initiatives involve local stakeholders and decision makers trying to forge consensus about how to manage a watershed's natural resources. Watershed initiatives seek a significant shift in decision making from federal agencies to local interests and from elected or appointed officials to a self-appointed group of local stakeholders. Most watershed groups operate on the principle that collaboration must achieve consensus and not on the principle that the majority rules. Although some environmentalists have criticized watershed groups as heavy on process and meetings and light on achieving significant protection for the resource, watershed initiatives may produce true reform. Massachusetts, with its cen-turies-old tradition of local control, offers an interesting case study for watershed management.

In 1993, the Massachusetts Executive Office of Environmental Affairs, the umbrella organization for the Commonwealth's environmental agen-cies, established the Massachusetts Watershed Initiative, which created mul-tidisciplinary watershed teams for each of the twenty-seven watersheds in the state. Operating under the auspices of the Executive Office of Envi-ronmental Affairs, the Massachusetts Watershed Initiative aims to integrate the activities of state environmental programs with federal and local gov-ernments, nongovernmental organizations, businesses, and environmental groups. The key element is to focus financial and other resources on build-ing grassroots watershed organizations in each of the twenty-seven water-sheds. The aim is to develop, through consensus, watershed work plans that will protect the resource. This initiative has impressed even environmental-ists who are otherwise critical of government programs. Kerry Mackin describes the watershed initiative as "by far the best thing that happened in Massachusetts regarding water management in decades."

Mackin and the IRWA assembled a group of stakeholders that includes representatives of water user groups, environmental organizations, and state and local governments. The group morphed into the initiative's Ipswich River Watershed Team. Led by Rich Tomczyk, the team is attempting to identify the factors that have caused the low flow in the Ipswich and to work with local communities that depend on the river to develop a watershed plan that will permit sustainable development while restoring the river's health.

In 1997, under the auspices of the Ipswich River Task Force (formed by IRWA), the Massachusetts Departments of Environmental Management and Environmental Protection funded a study by the U.S. Geological Survey (USGS) of the impact of both diversions and groundwater pumping on the river. The USGS employs a talented group of scientists but, as a government agency, is not inclined to get out in front on controversial issues. Yet its Ipswich River study, released in April 2000, was quite dramatic. It concluded that the blame did not lie with surface water diversions by the older towns because their diversions occur during the winter or high-flow season. Instead, the USGS determined that "ground-water withdrawals have a large effect on the magnitude, duration, and frequency of the low flows." Pumping from wells immediately adjacent to the river during the summer months is the real cause of the problem, said the USGS.

To understand the Ipswich River, one must understand both the historical and projected demands for water in the region and the environmental context of the river. As noted above, thanks to the historic allocation of surface water rights in the river, some communities that rely on the Ipswich are water-rich, while others are water-poor. The consequence is a dramatic difference in water rates and water conservation programs. In communities with lower water rates and modest sewer charges, one finds, not surprisingly, that water consumption is greater. As the price for water increases, so does the interest of residents in conserving water. In Salem, Beverly, Lynn, and Peabody, the four largest cities served by the river, town officials have been reluctant to ask residents to engage in water conservation because they believe that they have an ample supply.

The jury is out on whether communities and residents will be able to put aside what Tom Knowlton describes as the "New England penchant for knee-jerk parochialism," and work cooperatively to save the Ipswich

River. Some people mistrust the motivation of environmentalists. Richard Dawe, superintendent of Lynn Water and Sewer, has remarked, "A lot of these [environmentalists] would rather have people not drink water."

None of the problems facing the Ipswich River would have become so contentious were it not for suburban sprawl. Metropolitan Boston now extends north into New Hampshire, west to Worcester, and south into Rhode Island. Interstate Highway 495, dismissed as "the road to nowhere" by critics when it was built, has become the main highway through fast-growing suburbs. The 155-square-mile Ipswich River basin serves as the water supply for 335,000 people who live in twenty-two remarkably diverse municipalities. The town of Boxford, an upscale homogeneous community with a 2001 median household income of $78,562, requires house lots to be a minimum of two acres. Many residents travel the hour or so to Boston by commuter rail service. Andover, located at the intersection of I-93 and I-495, offers easy commuter access to Boston. It is also home to high-technology firms that include Hewlett-Packard, Raytheon, Digital, Gillette, and Genetics Institute. Ipswich, once a thriving mill town, has become culturally and economically diverse, with substantial populations of Greek, Polish, Irish, and English immigrants. It became largely a bedroom community for Boston during the 1950s, with easy access provided by both highways and commuter rail. The town of North Reading had an economy based on subsistence farming during the seventeenth and eighteenth centuries. It has sustained its agricultural heritage and retains its historic character with many well-preserved eighteenth-century homes and buildings. The town of Wilmington, once a quiet agricultural community, boomed as the population quadrupled after the completion of Route 128 in the 1950s. Suburban residential development has had a major impact on the town. The city of Beverly, founded in 1626, has a rich history as the birthplace of the U.S. Navy, as the home of the first cotton mill, and as an important industrial site for shoe factories. More recently, it has become predominantly a residential community with relatively easy access to Boston. Finally, the city of Peabody, an important leather producer in the nineteenth century with more than 100 tanneries, remains a regional employment center for communities on the North Shore of Massachusetts.

This growth has fueled high summer water use. New trophy homes are often accompanied by Olympic-sized swimming pools and enormous lawns watered by automatic in-ground sprinkler systems. Thousands of gallons of water evaporate from a single swimming pool each summer. Elaborate landscaping uses even more water. Indeed, new developments consume 50 percent more water than older ones; and communities use two to three times as much water in summer as during the rest of the year. Along with increased consumption by these sprawling communities, residential and commercial development has created impermeable surfaces, such as rooftops, roads, and parking lots, that inhibit natural recharge into the aquifer. Rainwater hits the rooftops, roads, and parking lots and runs quickly off into watercourses. In the past, this water would have slowly infiltrated the ground and raised the water table.

The Metropolitan Water Resources Authority plays another significant role in eastern Massachusetts' water resources. For decades, municipalities dumped raw sewer water into rivers and streams that eventually emptied into Boston Harbor or related bays, making the region one of the most polluted areas in the United States. Swimming in the ocean around Boston was something to avoid. Over the last twenty years, Boston Harbor has had a remarkable recovery in water quality, thanks to the hammer of the federal Clean Water Act, the jurisdiction of a courageous and persistent federal judge, and $4 billion generated from some of the highest sewer fees in the United States. Today, most Boston-area communities export their municipal wastewater to MWRA's regional treatment plants, especially one at Deer Island in Boston Harbor, which treats the water and then releases it to the ocean through a 9.5-mile tunnel.

In acting aggressively to solve its water *quality* problem, the Commonwealth of Massachusetts has inadvertently created a water *quantity* problem. Eighty percent of Ipswich River water is ultimately, after various uses, transported out of the watershed and discharged elsewhere through inter-basin pipelines and sewer systems. Approximately 25 million gallons of water per day leave the watershed, headed for treatment at MWRA's Deer Island facility or other wastewater treatment plants that discharge to the ocean. Anything that goes into the regional sewer system leaves the basin and is not available for recharge. Regional water treatment plants, once seen as the solution to Boston Harbor's water quality problem, are now viewed by environmentalists as the cause of low flows in the Ipswich River. As a consequence, Kerry Mackin and others advocate construction of a sewage treatment plant located in the Ipswich River basin. Knowledge of the hydrologic cycle has taught us that potable water, wastewater, and storm water runoff are all part of one system. Water supplies are dependent on water treatment and disposal. In Massachusetts, this insight has led to a new principle of water management: "Keep water local." Residential septic systems, local municipal treatment of effluent, and storm water retention facilities can effectively clean wastewater, which can be released to recharge groundwater supplies. In Wilmington, where a sewage treatment plant is proposed, town officials have balked at the $10 million price tag. The town already pays $1.5 million annually to MWRA to use MWRA's Deer Island facility to treat its sewage. However, state officials are joining the crusade to keep water local. The head of the Massachusetts Water Resources Commission, Mark Smith, has commented: "The Ipswich River is the most egregious example of what can happen when you don't take a comprehensive view of water supply issues."

A critical part of any solution is to stop treating water as a free resource—in other words, to recognize its market value. Until recently, many Massachusetts communities did not charge individual users for either the amount of water used or the actual cost to the town of providing the water. Instead, municipalities charged a discounted fee for the water, and the balance of the cost of providing it came from the town's general fund. Somewhat perversely, towns occasionally granted discounts to the largest users, particularly businesses. That culture is changing as towns begin to recognize that ascending block rates (charging higher rates for higher water use) make better financial and environmental sense because they create an incentive to consumers to reduce consumption.

Still, higher rates will not completely solve the problem. A *Boston Globe* report found that some residential customers had used more than 500,000 gallons during a six-month summer billing period, even during times when towns banned certain kinds of water use. Even $3,000 water bills for single-family houses have not deterred such profligate consumption. There is a perceived need to "keep up with the Joneses" in upscale newer neighborhoods with large lawns. A sales manager for a company that installs private wells noted that neighbors "feel embarrassed if they have a brown lawn. That's emotion, and emotion sells." Apparently it does, as well-drilling businesses in Massachusetts are booming. One company in Tewksbury digs about 160 wells a year at an average cost of between $5,000 and $7,000 per well. Cities and towns have attempted to deal with water shortages by imposing various kinds of conservation restrictions, ranging from a ban on in-ground irrigation systems to odd-day or specified-hour water use regulations. In the town of Randolph, one resident, Paul King, was so concerned about his flower and vegetable garden that he decided not to comply with the town's summertime outdoor water use ban. Instead, he had a well dug and thus avoided the legal requirement. At the time, Mr. King was a member of the town's Conservation Commission.

The plight of the Ipswich River is a warning to Massachusetts about the health of its rivers and streams, just as the death of a canary was once a warning to miners. Similar problems exist in the upper Taunton River basin, the upper Neponset River basin, the upper Assabet River basin, the North Coastal Watershed, which stretches between Saugus and Rockport, the Parker River basin, the Jones River basin, and the upper Charles River basin. For the Ipswich, a January 2002 USGS hydrologic model predicted that a combination of shutting down groundwater wells seasonally, from May to October, and returning treated wastewater to groundwater discharge locations in the Ipswich River basin would actually result in river flows that exceeded the historic average. So, is there reason to be optimistic? In January 2002, when I asked Kerry Mackin whether the Ipswich River can be saved, she replied: "It is possible. Nevertheless, the politics and the economics of making the changes to achieve that result are still formidable."

Chapter 8

A Game of Inches for
Endangered Chinook Salmon

*California's Cosumnes River, the Army Corps
of Engineers, and Sacramento Sprawl*

"When the river is dry, water always returns in the spring."
—Afghan proverb

The most majestic of Pacific Ocean salmon, chinook or king salmon typically weigh between ten and fifty pounds. Chinook may travel 2,000 miles during their ocean migration, yet miraculously find their way back to spawn in the river where they were born. A beautiful fish prized by anglers as well as chefs, chinook are silver, slender, and muscular. As they navigate upriver, they may jump waterfalls as high as ten feet. In the spawning process, their silvery bodies gradually turn a deep red.

In California's Cosumnes (kuh-SOOM-ness) River, chinook face such enormous obstacles to survival when they hatch that it's a wonder any survive to spawn. Droughts can dry up spawning beds, and floods may wipe out beds or deposit silt that deprives the eggs of needed oxygen. Only a small percentage of eggs become young salmon fry—each about an inch long—and 90 percent die as they move downstream to the ocean. On the downriver voyage, young chinook undergo a transformation in their bodies that enables them to survive in salt water. If low flows delay the journey, the smolt process may reverse itself. Along the way, the young salmon encounter osprey and other fish-eating birds, as well as largemouth and striped bass, voracious predators of baby salmon. They may also lose their way by going into irrigation canals—mazes from which they may never return. Once in the ocean, they migrate as far north as Alaska but may encounter commercial fishing nets along the way. Chinook find their way home to the Cosumnes from the Pacific by swimming under San Francisco's Golden Gate Bridge, heading north in San Francisco Bay, then past San Pablo Bay and Suisun Bay, where they risk predation by sea lions and other marine mammals. At the delta, where the Sacramento and San Joaquin Rivers converge, chinook need to pick up a Cosumnes River odor trail if they are to head south up the San Joaquin, into the Mokelumne River and, finally, into the Cosumnes. Chinook enter the river in September and October and then face the cruelest fate of all, one from which there is no escape. As they swim upriver, they arrive at a section that is bone-dry. They must wait for the fall rains and hope that the river begins to flow.

Historically, two or three million chinook annually returned to spawn in California's Central Valley rivers. Commercial chinook fishing in California started in about 1850; most salmon were destined for canneries, some for export to Australia. Today, only 200,000 return, and some of them are hatchery hybrids. Spawning by wild chinook is minimal; many species of chinook have become extinct. The decline of Central Valley chinook is the result of overfishing, mining activities that degraded the streams, and dams and water diversions that reduced salmon habitat.

The Cosumnes River, northern California's last major river without a dam, flows out of the lower Sierra Nevada foothills west into the great Central Valley, just south of Sacramento. The Cosumnes is a small, unassuming river compared to the American River to the north and the Mokelumne River to the south; it carries a modest volume of 365,100 acre-feet of water per year (af/yr), or 505 cubic feet per second (cfs), about one-seventh of the flow of the American and one-half of the flow of the Mokelumne. In September and October, at the end of California's dry season, the Cosumnes' flow drops to a measly twenty-five or thirty cfs. Ironically, the Cosumnes' low flow is its salvation; otherwise it would surely have been dammed. The Cosumnes once supported a large fall run of chinook, but dwindling numbers resulted in the U.S. Fish and Wildlife Service's listing Cosumnes chinook as an endangered species. In recent years, fewer than 1,000 chinook have returned annually to spawn in the river.

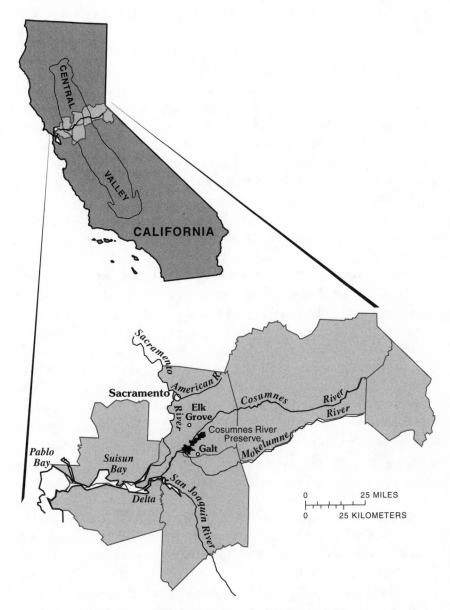

FIGURE 8.1. The Cosumnes River in north-central California.

To describe California's great Central Valley as a valley does not do it justice. It stretches from Shasta County in the north to Kern County in the south—some 450 miles, or the distance between Boston and Washington, D.C. The valley varies between forty and sixty miles wide, with mountain ranges on either side: the snow capped Sierra Nevada to the east and the Coastal Ranges to the west. Covering over 42,000 square miles, an area larger than the state of Ohio, the Central Valley has remarkably fertile soil from massive alluvial deposits washed down over millennia from the Sierra Nevada in snowmelt and floodwaters. The nation's most productive agricultural region, the Central Valley generated more than $15 billion in 1997. Although valley farmlands constitute only 1 percent of all farmland in the United States, they produce 8 percent of the nation's total agricultural output. Valley farmers grow over 350 different crops and commodities, especially wine grapes, almonds, rice, cotton, tomatoes, strawberries, oranges, and pears.

The Central Valley before development was an American Serengeti, according to Marc Reisner, author of *Cadillac Desert*. It had blond grasslands during summer, California's dry season, and a vast marsh during the winter and spring, California's rainy season. The winter rains prompted millions of ducks, geese, and cranes to migrate to the Central Valley from Alaska, Washington, British Columbia, and Alberta. Thousands of grizzly bears and perhaps a million antelope and tule elk lived year-round in the Central Valley. This rich environment had much more water on the land—and immediately below the surface—than today. At the end of the nineteenth century, settlers transformed the Central Valley by draining wetlands, logging thousands of acres of valley oak forests, and planting crops. What has changed since the end of World War I is the advent of irrigation. Lots of it. By the end of the 1930s, irrigation farming had expanded from a few thousand acres to millions of acres, much of it relying on groundwater. The Central Valley changed from a Serengeti to a desert with irrigation, as groundwater pumping lowered the water table and the baseflow of rivers.

The farmers were helped immensely by the U.S. Bureau of Reclamation (Bureau) and the U.S. Army Corps of Engineers (Corps). In the 1930s and 1940s, the two agencies engaged in a legendary bureaucratic squabble, elegantly chronicled by Marc Reisner, over the right to dam Central Valley rivers. When the fur settled, only the Cosumnes remained undammed, and powerful California farming interests received huge quantities of heavily subsidized irrigation water.

A common thread in our efforts to alter the hydrologic cycle—to deliver water to farmers at times other than when Mother Nature would supply it—is our belief in the capacity of technology to tame nature. The science of engineering allows us, we think, to overcome the limits of nature. Nowhere is this philosophy more evident than in the Corps, an agency run by engineers—military men and women with large budgets, accountable only to members of Congress, who could not care less how the money is spent, just as long as it is spent in their districts. The Corps enjoys a formidable reputation as an effective advocate before Congress. Members of Congress may expect Corps support for projects in their districts in exchange for their support for other Corps projects. For generations, senators and representatives have been reelected by constituents grateful for the construction projects they brought home.

A Department of Defense agency, the Corps undertakes military construction projects; but, since its creation in 1802, its civilian branch has had a greater impact on rivers and coastal areas than any other agency in the world. From its initial modest role of dredging harbors for ships, the Corps in the late nineteenth century began to alter rivers to accommodate barges and large ships. Beyond this navigation role, the Corps also found a niche in flood control, for which it is justly famous or infamous. The Corps built levees, dikes, and dams to force water to stay within the banks of rivers. Many Corps activities, undertaken in the name of flood control, actually worsened flooding. A deepened, straightened river, lined with concrete or soil cement, moves floodwater downstream faster and more dangerously than a river with meanders and wetlands that can absorb much of a flood's energy. By damming, deepening, straightening, bridging, reversing, and riprapping the country's rivers, the Corps has destroyed millions of acres of wetlands and riparian habitat.

The Corps has begun to change in response to recent proposals that have come, surprisingly, from within the Corps itself. In the aftermath of disastrous flooding in the Mississippi and Missouri River basins in 1993, President Clinton established a committee to make recommendations on how to prevent a reoccurrence. The committee report, *Sharing the Challenge: Floodplain Management into the 21st Century*, became known as the Galloway Report after the head of the committee, the Corps' Brigadier General Gerald E. Galloway. The report signaled a significant change in policy by calling for greater emphasis on nonstructural solutions, including the acquisition and restoration of wetlands. It also called for stricter limits on development in floodplains and changes in federal farm policy that would discourage converting wetlands into cropland.

Despite the Galloway Report, the Corps' entrenched bureaucracy adheres to the traditional idea that the Corps' mission is to build things. A recent Corps flood control study is illustrative. At the base of the Tortolita Mountains north of Tucson, Arizona, is a broad alluvial fan. Although the area is a floodplain, some development is occurring, thanks to the Federal Emergency Management Agency, which provides flood insurance to property owners who import fill and build above specified flood elevation stages. The Corps study analyzed the costs and benefits of various flood control options, and concluded that "[t]he most significant benefit category is savings from reduced flood-proofing costs which generated 99 percent of all potential benefits." Translated into English, this language means that Corps flood control measures would save developers the expense of undertaking drainage improvements or importing fill. The benefits would flow entirely to a specific group of private property owners, while the costs would be borne by the public tax coffers.

The study considered both "structural and non-structural alternatives" for controlling floods. The structural flood control options were typical of those advocated by the Corps: concrete-lined channels, culvert crossings, bridge crossings, soil-cement embankments, and detention basins. Most revealing of its mentality was one of the Corps' "non-structural alternatives," namely "raising existing structures above the flood hazard level or removing homes and other structures from the flood zones." This alternative offers insight into the Corps' lexicon. It is breathtaking that the Corps thinks a nonstructural alternative is to elevate or move homes and structures. However, to the Corps, its mission is to control the flow of water by building levees and dams and dredging waterways. Therefore, measures that regulate the flow of water are structural, while measures that elevate or move the homes are "non-structural."

A more bizarre example of the Corps' capacity to rationalize comes from another portion of the study. One solution to the flooding problem was for the Corps to purchase and set aside the land in the floodplain. The Corps dismissed this option because

> [n]o flood control benefits would result. There would be no bene-
> fits derived . . . because no flood proofing would take place. . . .
> The cost to purchase all lands in the flood zones may be less than

the structural alternatives available. However, no flood control benefits would result, therefore [this option] was eliminated from further consideration.

The logic was unimpeachable, at least if one assumed that something had to be engineered and built. Purchasing and setting aside the land would have eliminated the flooding problem entirely. But the Corps dismissed this option because it would not produce "flood control benefits." The Corps conveniently ignored the fact that there would be no need for "flood control benefits" if the land were not developed! The tail wagged the dog. Of course, if the Corps could not engage in construction activity that altered the natural drainage of the floodplain, it would have brought into question its own purpose. The study ultimately recommended an option that cost considerably more than the option of purchasing the land in the floodplain to remove it from development.

However, Congress now expects the Corps to depart from its overwhelming emphasis on construction projects. In 1999, Congress passed legislation (known as Challenge 21) declaring that the Corps should rely on wetlands and floodplains to retain and store excess floodwater, rather than build dams, flood walls, and levees. Challenge 21 aims to reduce flood hazards by restoring "the natural functions and values of rivers," and by authorizing projects that "emphasize, to the maximum extent practicable and appropriate, nonstructural approaches to preventing or reducing flood damages."

In an almost perverse reversal of course, the Corps has begun to position itself as the lead federal agency to supervise and undertake environmental restoration. The new generation of Corps engineers, in an ironic about-face, will have an opportunity to devise construction projects that remedy the harmful environmental consequences of the Corps' projects from an earlier generation. For example, Congress has given the Corps responsibility for overseeing an $8 billion effort to restore the Florida Everglades, a move akin to placing the fox in charge of the chicken coop. It's a perfect solution for an agency that engages in serial engineering; every problem created by tampering with nature requires an engineering solution that begets one or more additional engineering fixes. At this rate, the Corps will never lack construction projects.

The Cosumnes River may have escaped being dammed, but it has felt the weight of the Corps' flood control program. In the 1930s, the Corps financed an extensive network of levees that confined the river to its main channel so that farmers could grow crops in the floodplain. Over time, levees wreak havoc with a river. A floodplain's riparian vegetation, once deprived of water and nutrients, gradually dies. The levees allow the river to transport more water and, with it, more sediment, which comes from the channel bed. This erosion of the channel bed deepens the river, further isolating it from the floodplain. In the 1950s, the Corps embarked on a "river improvement project" for the Cosumnes. Back then, the Corps preferred straight rivers with deep, narrow channels, so it bulldozed the Cosumnes, cleared the channel, and ripped out the trees and vegetation. The Corps used a template that conceived rivers as arteries of commerce. Never mind that freighters had no need for access to the Cosumnes. The "improvement project" produced ungodly amounts of sediment, which moved downstream and scoured out the river's channel, causing what hydrologists call incisement (or entrenchment), and what the rest of us call "steep banks." An incised river channel, by making it more difficult for water to flow over the banks, reduces the amount of water stored in a river's floodplain.

Corps-financed levees and its "improvement project," combined with farmers' groundwater pumping and surface water diversions, have left the Cosumnes in a precarious state. Until the 1940s, the Cosumnes flowed year-round because it received baseflow (discharge) from the extensive floodplain aquifer. But the network of levees has constricted the river's flow and sharply reduced the amount of water that the floodplain can recharge to the aquifer and, in turn, that the floodplain aquifer can slowly discharge to the Cosumnes. Increased groundwater pumping, especially since the 1950s, has lowered the groundwater table to fifty-five feet below the river channel and converted the river from a gaining to a losing stream. The river now recharges the aquifer. A five- to ten-mile section of the river (between Meiss Road and Highway 99) actually dries up in the fall at the end of California's dry season.

Until quite recently, little was known about the Cosumnes River and its chinook; that has changed thanks to the CALFED Bay-Delta Program. Created in 1995, CALFED is a cooperative partnership among federal and state agencies (which accounts for the name), urban and agricultural interests, and environmental organizations that seeks to restore the ecological health of the largest estuary on the west coast of North America—the San Francisco Bay/Sacramento–San Joaquin Delta. Along with the Packard

Foundation, CALFED funded Jeff Mount, a geologist at the University of California at Davis, and his colleagues to establish an interdisciplinary research program to monitor the Cosumnes River watershed. The U.C. Davis scientists have found that groundwater pumping is "at least partly responsible" for the decline in fall flows and the reduction in the number of fall-run chinook. As flow in the Cosumnes declined, some farmers stopped using diversion canals and sunk groundwater wells next to the river. Local anecdotes suggest that some farmers even drilled wells at a slant, thereby putting the bottom of the well closer to the river to suck greater amounts of water from beneath it.

Groundwater pumping has lengthened the interval during which the Cosumnes is dry. In the past, the onset of the fall rainy season in November would immediately produce flows in the dry section of the river. Because of the lowered water table, the initial fall rains percolate into the ground. So now, fall rainstorms must completely saturate the dry streambed before the river will flow. As a consequence, the river stays dry well into November. By then, chinook have already entered the river and are waiting downstream for the intermittent section to fill so that they can dash upstream to spawn. The flow pattern in the Cosumnes is no longer in sync with the genetics of the fish. If it takes too long for the river to open up, the chinook will die before reaching the spawning beds. Their fate is a cruel one. Having endured long odds and numerous obstacles during their ocean voyage, they arrive in their natal river only to find it dry. An equally pathetic end came to some chinook during fall 2001. A November rainstorm opened up the Cosumnes and a couple hundred chinook raced upstream, only to have the river abruptly stop flowing. The stranded salmon died. Saving the chinook from extinction, according to Jeff Mount, involves "a game of inches," as the salmon need only seven inches of water to get upriver.

Scientists, environmental organizations, and government agencies have enormous interest in saving the Cosumnes because it *is* the last undammed river, it has endangered chinook, and it supports the largest surviving valley oak forest. The search for solutions has led to innovative partnerships and unorthodox tactics. In the 1980s, The Nature Conservancy (TNC) embarked on a major effort to preserve and expand the remnants of valley oak forests, the craggy trees once found throughout the Central Valley. Valley oaks, or swamp oaks, as they are also known, thrive in the Cosumnes River basin because it has a natural cycle of seasonal flooding, at least in those sections without levees. Periodic flooding deposits nutrient-rich silt on the floodplain, which encourages oaks to reproduce and discourages nonnative species from developing. In 1987, TNC purchased an 800-acre parcel, now called the Cosumnes River Preserve.

TNC's traditional long-term strategy for protecting the environment involved identifying a parcel of land that contained rare habitat, fauna, or flora and then raising funds to purchase the parcel and preserve it from development. However, TNC has come to realize, reluctantly, that this strategy does not necessarily protect the parcel from the effects of nearby development. TNC ecologists have recently formulated a much broader strategy for conservation at some seventy-five sites, known as the "Last Great Places," including the Cosumnes River valley. In 1993, TNC initiated a program to protect the entire Cosumnes watershed, a 1,200-square-mile area, by developing partnerships with nonprofit organizations and state and federal agencies. Nurturing those partnerships has required some flexibility. Its first partner, Ducks Unlimited, desired to protect a robust population of waterfowl that rely on the Cosumnes in their migration along the Pacific Flyway. TNC, on the other hand, cared more about maintaining and restoring the valley oak forest. But both organizations came to understand that the two objectives shared a common element: seasonal flooding created both oak seedlings *and* the wetlands that ducks love.

Other partnerships soon developed, including ones with the California Departments of Fish and Game, and of Water Resources; the state's Wildlife Conservation Board; and the Sacramento County Department of Parks and Recreation. The Cosumnes River Preserve now consists of 14,000 acres of wetlands, grasslands, and forests, including 700 acres of valley oaks—the largest stand in California. TNC has turned day-to-day management of the preserve over to the U.S. Bureau of Land Management.

As a vehicle for protecting more land—some 40,000 acres—TNC entered into conservation easements with neighboring farmers that impose specific limitations on how the farmers may use or develop their lands. These conservation easements—restrictions placed on deeds—prohibit large-scale residential development and the planting of perennial crops that require intensive agriculture, such as orchards and vineyards. The easements allow agricultural uses that are more compatible with wildlife use, such as the cultivation of rice or corn. Major funding ($18 million) for TNC's land acquisition and conservation easement program has come from CALFED.

Although it may take decades, levees eventually succumb to the power of nature. On the Cosumnes, this happened in 1985 when floodwaters breached a levee and created a sandbar across neighboring farmland. Soon, willow and cottonwood seedlings began to sprout from the sandbar. Then the seedlings attracted scrub jays, which deposited acorns in the soil. Within five years, valley oaks began to flourish. The lesson was clear: left to itself, the Cosumnes would begin to recover. Scientists from TNC wondered if they could hasten the recovery. In winter 1995–96, TNC bulldozed fifty feet of levee. The winter rains flowed through the breach onto the floodplain and, as predicted, a new forest began. What was unpredicted was that juvenile chinook would swim from the main channel onto the flooded fields. Fishery biologists think that this seemingly odd behavior is actually a genetically developed method of survival. Chinook use the nutrient-rich floodplain (Peter Moyle of U.C. Davis calls it "a soup of invertebrates") to fatten up before they travel in the spring downstream to the ocean, a fact previously unknown to science and therefore overlooked in other salmon restoration efforts. Funding for TNC's breaching of the levee came from the Corps, whose engineers were directly involved in planning and oversight, and TNC is exploring with preserve partners and neighboring farmers the possibility of breaching other levees. Environmental restoration often involves nothing more elaborate than tearing down things we have built in the past. It's an exciting development for Jeff Mount, who notes: "We are finally going to get a chance to evaluate the ecological and economic benefits of promoting floods on the floodplain."

Despite the efforts of TNC, its preserve partners, and the U.C. Davis scientists, the Cosumnes faces an uncertain future because of groundwater pumping that supports continuing suburban sprawl. In the last twenty years, a large portion of the Central Valley has began to support a new crop—subdivisions. The valley's population, currently about 5 million, is expected to double by 2020, partly from folks fleeing the San Francisco Bay region in search of affordable housing. The Cosumnes lies between Elk Grove and Galt, cities that are experiencing rapid growth as bedroom communities twenty or twenty-five miles south of Sacramento, off Interstate 5. Municipal pumping has created two major cones of depression that already capture water from the Cosumnes. In addition, the Cosumnes faces threats from three proposed developments: a huge regional shopping mall, a planned community, and a destination resort. In June 2001, the Elk Grove City Council gave its approval to Lent Ranch Marketplace, a 295-acre,

$500 million, 1.3-million-square-foot mall, to be surrounded by 1.8 million square feet of commercial space and 280 multifamily homes. The mall would border undeveloped farmland on the southern tip of Elk Grove. Wells to supply groundwater for the development would unquestionably reduce flow in the Cosumnes. The mall's parking lots would practically abut the Cosumnes River floodplain.

A second threat comes from a proposed 29,000-home, 6,000-acre Sunrise-Douglas development, part of a proposed new city called Rancho Cordova northeast of Elk Grove. Developers would like to pump water from beneath the project, but the California Department of Health Services (DHS), which has jurisdiction over polluted groundwater, has refused to allow pumping. The reckless disposal of defense industry waste from the Aerojet Rocket Testing Facility and Mather Air Force Base in the 1950s poisoned the groundwater with perchlorate and other nasty stuff. DHS has concluded that the proposed wells are too close to the current edge of the plume of pollution; pumping would draw that plume more quickly toward the wells. The contamination plume might migrate into the taps of tens of thousands of new residents. Sacramento County was relying on these wells to serve the next tier of growth.

DHS's decision has forced Sacramento County and the developers to consider developing a well field farther south, nearer the Cosumnes River. Sacramento County officials have concluded that this well field could supply the Sunrise-Douglas development without harming the Cosumnes River. According to Mike Eaton, director of TNC's Cosumnes River Project, they reached this conclusion "without any analysis of ongoing or cumulative impacts or potential future impacts on surface water systems. They literally ignored it." The environmental impact report, California's equivalent of a federal environmental impact statement, considered the possible detrimental impacts of increased groundwater pumping on practically everything, except stream flow in the Cosumnes River. According to U.C. Davis hydrology professor Graham Fogg, "I can't say for sure that this development will have a significant impact. I'm saying that the developers and county planners haven't done their homework to find out."

The third threat comes from Omo Ranch Resort, which sought approval from the California Water Resources Control Board to divert surface water from the middle fork of the Cosumnes River for a golf course. Jeff Mount's research team reviewed the proposal and concluded that the diversion would significantly increase the number of low-flow days, double the number of days that the river was dry, impede fall-run chinook salmon passage to the spawning grounds, and adversely affect salmon survivorship. The low flows would expose eggs buried in spawning gravels. The low-oxygen and high-temperature conditions would kill many of the developing eggs. Low-flow periods in the spring might retard fingerlings from migrating to the ocean; lower flows would certainly increase the time needed for fingerlings to move from the spawning beds to the estuary, which would increase their vulnerability to predators.

The most critical problem facing the Cosumnes is that California law for the most part fails to regulate groundwater pumping. Existing pumping has already lowered the water table beneath and adjacent to the Cosumnes. Lent Ranch Marketplace and the Sunrise-Douglas development will worsen the situation. Think of the Cosumnes River basin as a gigantic milkshake glass, with each well representing a straw in the glass. California law allows new straws to be added without requiring new development to remove (or pinch) existing ones. So it is likely that Lent Ranch Marketplace and the Sunrise-Douglas development will go forward because they would pump groundwater, and California law is indifferent to groundwater pumping. Omo Ranch Resort, on the other hand, poses less of a threat because, as it would rely on surface water, the developers must obtain permission from the California Water Resources Control Board.

According to a hydrologic model prepared by Jeff Mount and his U.C. Davis colleagues, restoring flows in the Cosumnes would require a reduction in *current* levels of pumping by approximately 190,000 acre-feet per year. No one thinks that will ever happen. But a glimmer of hope comes from a fall 2001 proposal by the U.C. Davis team to divert surface water, as little as fifty cfs (12,000 af) between September and December, from the American River through the Folsom South Canal, which crosses the Cosumnes, and discharge it to the Cosumnes itself. This modest amount of water would significantly improve flow. Although more than one-half of this augmented flow would seep into the ground, it would prewet the channel before the fall rains, thus increasing the amount of precious rainwater retained within the river's channel. It might provide just enough water for the chinook, thereby winning the "game of inches."

Chapter 9

Wild Blueberries and Atlantic Salmon

Down East Maine

"We forget that the water cycle and the life cycle are one."
—Jacques Cousteau

Any reasonable person who looked at a map of the state of Maine would conclude that the state does not have a shortage of water. A large chunk of Maine consists of lakes, ponds, rivers, streams, and wetlands. But the state has water problems. Ski resorts in the mountains increasingly rely on artificial snow, which consumes large quantities of water, to augment the natural supply. A burgeoning population in southern Maine, mostly transplants from farther south, has created a demand for more golf courses, which also require large quantities of water to keep the greens and fairways lush. Poland Spring Water, a subsidiary of Perrier, has opened a new bottling plant in Hollis, Maine, that uses 50 million gallons of water per year. Nearby residents fear the impact on their domestic wells and on local streams and ponds. Finally, a recent conflict concerns wild blueberry growers who irrigate their fields with water diverted from rivers with populations of endangered Atlantic salmon.

When we think of salmon and water issues, we usually think of the Pacific Northwest. Three major factors have caused stocks of wild salmon in the Pacific Ocean to decline precipitously in recent decades. First, hydroelectric power dams blocked returning salmon from their spawning habitats and exposed juvenile smolts to high mortality during their migration to the ocean. Second, clear-cut logging operations increased muddy

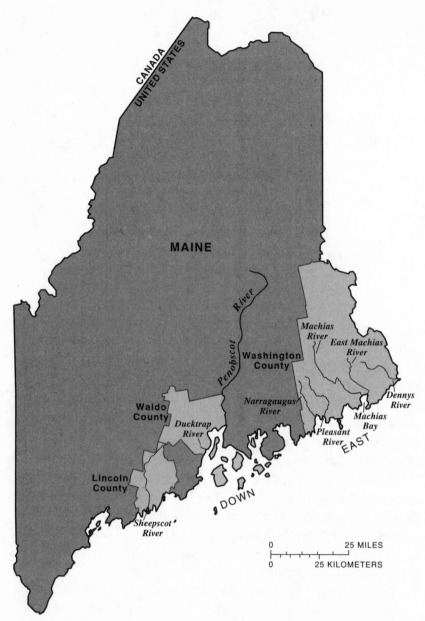

FIGURE 9.1. Blueberry-growing regions of Maine and rivers with wild Atlantic salmon.

runoff into rivers and streams, thereby depositing silt and other fine sediments in spawning beds, thus impeding reproduction. Finally, commercial fishing interests around the world are harvesting fish at unsustainable levels. As a consequence, the U.S. Fish and Wildlife Service (FWS) and the National Marine Fisheries Service (NMFS) have declared many species of Pacific Ocean salmon either endangered or threatened under the Endangered Species Act. These federal actions produced sharp controversy but often received support from elected officials who, although mindful of the powerful hydroelectric interests, are sensitive to other concerns, including those of commercial fishing interests, Native Americans who rely heavily on salmon as a staple food source, and sport anglers who enjoy fishing for salmon.

A less well-known story involves Atlantic Ocean salmon, a species that faces grave threats but has received less popular and political support. Like their Pacific Ocean cousins, Atlantic salmon are anadromous, meaning they spend a portion of their life in freshwater and a portion in the ocean. Pacific salmon, as we know from the chinook, are born in freshwater but soon migrate to the ocean, where they remain until they return to the same river where they were born to spawn and then to die. In contrast, Atlantic salmon spend their first three years in freshwater as smolts, then migrate to the sea, returning the next year to the river, as grilse, where they remain for a season but do not spawn. At the end of the season, fully mature, they return to the ocean. As adults, Atlantic salmon return to the river to spawn but do not die. Instead, they may go back and forth several times, spawning each time in their natal river before eventually dying there. During each spawning season, a female Atlantic salmon produces about 7,200 eggs. Every salmon, therefore, has the potential to contribute significantly to the population of its native river. Although Atlantic salmon enter the river between June and August, they do not spawn until October or November. During this interim, they need deep, cool pools in which to rest.

Historically, Atlantic salmon inhabited practically every coastal river between the Hudson River in New York and New Brunswick, Canada. In the nineteenth century, with the onset of the Industrial Revolution, dams blocked access to spawning habitat and textile factories spewed wastewater directly into rivers. As a result, salmon runs in southern New England disappeared by the end of the nineteenth century. Despite efforts to reestablish runs by artificial propagation of fertilized eggs, Atlantic salmon continued to decline. Today, Atlantic salmon are found only in small numbers in a handful of rivers in eastern Maine. A 1999 FWS and NMFS report estimated that the number of returning adult salmon in all Maine rivers was between 1,592 and 3,216.

The principal cause for the decline in the number of Atlantic salmon is the presence of numerous hydroelectric dams that obstruct salmon migration. But these dams have been in place for decades, and the numbers of salmon have continued to diminish. What accounts for the recent decline? Historically, overfishing was partly responsible; yet today, neither commercial nor recreational fishing constitutes a significant threat to Atlantic salmon. International agreements, negotiated among the United States, Canada, and European countries, have either ended or significantly restricted commercial fishing for salmon. In Maine, recreational fishing for salmon is strictly catch-and-release.

A new and growing threat comes from the aquaculture industry. The worldwide appetite for salmon has recently exploded. In the United States, salmon consumption increased 20 percent in 1999, making salmon the third most popular seafood, behind tuna and shrimp. In addition to its rich, buttery flavor, salmon is high in protein, the antioxidant vitamin E, and omega-3 fatty acids, which reduce both cholesterol and blood pressure levels and strengthen the immune system. With this surge in demand, it became clear that harvesting wild salmon could not produce an adequate supply. Various companies around the world have begun to cultivate certain strains of salmon in cages or pens located in the ocean off the coast near historic salmon rivers. The industry has expanded dramatically. The Maine industry involves twelve companies that raise salmon at thirty-three sites in cages that cover 800 acres of ocean. In 1998, six million salmon were raised in pens off the coast of Maine. The Canadian industry, just over the Maine border, is twice the size of Maine's. Aquaculture, as the practice of farm-raising fish is called, now accounts for more than half the salmon consumed in the United States.

The cultivated salmon threaten wild Atlantic salmon in several ways. If they escape the pens, which happens regularly, they may (1) compete with wild salmon for spawning grounds and food; (2) transfer diseases or parasites to wild salmon; and (3) produce genetic contamination though interbreeding. Even in cages, farm-raised salmon may affect the wild salmon as they migrate past the cages. According to recent studies, wild salmon are exposed to danger from seals and other predators that congregate near the cages. Aquaculture poses a real threat to wild salmon, yet it is not the most severe potential harm they face.

If it's not dams, overfishing, or aquaculture, what is the most significant threat to wild Atlantic salmon? A 1999 FWS and NMFS status report on the salmon concluded that the "most obvious and immediate threat" is the extraction of water from critical rivers where salmon still return to spawn, especially the Dennys, East Machias, Machias, Pleasant, and Narragaugus Rivers in Washington and Hancock Counties; the Ducktrap River in Waldo County; and the Sheepscot River in Lincoln County.

Why is the water being diverted? To irrigate blueberry fields.

Down East Maine, so named for prevailing winds that required sailing ships from Boston to sail downwind to Maine, which is east of Massachusetts, was shaped by the advancement and withdrawal of glaciers. During the Pleistocene Ice Age, which ended about 10,000 years ago, glaciers covered the state. As the glaciers advanced, they changed the landscape by carving the bedrock, scraping the land, and transporting rock debris from mountain ranges into the valleys. As the glaciers receded, the melting ice washed huge quantities of sediment into the valleys and ocean, forming deltas of glacial sand and gravel, called outwash. The melting process left large ridges, known as eskers, kames, or moraines, which formed at the edges of the retreating glaciers. With the glaciers gone, and as the climate continued to warm, tundra vegetation developed in peat bogs, marshes, and swamps. These, in turn, gave way to forests in much of Maine but not on long stretches of Down East coastline, where the glaciers left behind a rocky, treeless terrain, called the "barrens," that does not retain water. The glacial sand and gravel deposits are unconsolidated (not compressed over time), so water moves fairly easily through these porous deposits. The plant communities, such as wild blueberry bushes, that developed on the barrens had to adapt to these harsh circumstances.

Succulent and flavorful, wild blueberries grow nicely along Maine's barrens. They grow even better, Maine farmers have discovered, if you give them more water than Mother Nature provides. Growers harvest berries every other year. During the harvest season, an additional twelve inches of irrigation water will dramatically improve yield. Compared with natural yields of 2,000–4,000 pounds per acre, irrigated blueberry fields produce 8,000–12,000 pounds per acre. Maine has 60,000 acres of wild blueberries, and thanks largely to irrigation, the harvest jumped from 65 million pounds in 1995 to 110 million in 2000. Maine farmers currently irrigate only 6,000 acres of blueberries but expect to double that area by the year 2005.

Growers developed their fields from native plants first harvested by Native Americans. Because Down East Maine's rocky terrain prevents mechanized harvesting, gathering wild blueberries involves backbreaking labor. These "lowbush" wild blueberries, in contrast to the "highbush" plants cultivated elsewhere, never exceed one foot in height. Yet farmers continue to irrigate new acreage to grow them, as demand for them has grown. Wild blueberries may become even more popular as the baby boomer generation seeks to ward off aging and disease. Recent U.S. Department of Agriculture studies ranked blueberries first among fruits and vegetables in antioxidants, which neutralize free radicals, the molecules suspected to promote aging, cancer, and heart disease. *Martha Stewart Living* recently touted the "more concentrated and complex flavor" of wild blueberries.

The conflict with the salmon occurs because the prime growing season for blueberries, when supplemental irrigation is needed, comes precisely in the months when salmon are moving into the rivers—June, July, and August. Salmon need adequate water flows to trigger their genetic instincts to reenter their natal rivers and for spawning, the survival of eggs, the emergence of fry, and the migration of smolt. Reduced water flows may also degrade water quality by reducing the dilution of contaminants. If a pesticide or fertilizer runs off into a river and subsequent water diversions reduce the flow, the concentration of the pesticide or fertilizer will increase. In many Maine blueberry fields, water diverted for irrigation mixes with pesticides and fertilizers and a portion finds its way back into the river, carrying with it some concentration of pollutants. Reduced water flows also may degrade water quality by increasing the ambient water temperature. Because they are cold water fish, Atlantic salmon are very sensitive to changes in water temperature. Significant water diversions may raise the temperature of a river by several degrees, an amount that may profoundly change a salmon's behavior and adversely affect reproduction. During summer 1999, low precipitation levels in New Brunswick produced higher river temperatures and discouraged salmon migration into the Miramichi River, the most famous Atlantic salmon river in North America.

A state such as Maine, which has abundant water resources and is blessed with rainfall that exceeds four feet annually, is ill-equipped to deal

with water controversy. Maine law leaves most water uses entirely unregulated. Under the doctrine of riparian water rights, any person who owns
property on a river or lake has a right to make a reasonable use of the
water. Traditionally, reasonable use encompassed all domestic purposes,
which might include a modest garden. Recently, some eastern states have
expanded the riparian doctrine to allow large-scale agricultural irrigation
projects.

On the other hand, Maine does have some means of curbing irrigation.
Maine law divides the state into organized and unorganized regions,
depending on whether local residents have chosen an incorporated form
of government. The state allocates environmental responsibility for the
organized sections to the Maine Department of Environmental Regulation
(DER) and, for the unorganized regions, to the Maine Land Use Regulation Commission (LURC). LURC requires permits for both surface water
diversions and groundwater wells, but DER does not. In 1999, LURC limited the amount of water that could be diverted from the Pleasant, Narragaugus, and Machias Rivers, pursuant to a state law that sets minimum flow
levels. DER is developing a rule that will eventually address diversions on
a statewide basis. At the moment, however, the state does not have an accurate picture of how much water is being used by whom and from what
source.

In 1993, an environmental organization, RESTORE: The North
Woods, filed a petition with FWS and NMFS to have the Atlantic salmon
listed under the Endangered Species Act (ESA). Maine's business community and political leaders, especially Governor Angus King, quickly
mounted an effort to prevent the listing. Concerned about the impact on
Maine's $65 million blueberry industry, its logging industry, and its nascent
aquaculture industry, they developed a conservation plan that aimed to
protect salmon in seven critical rivers. In 1995, federal agency biologists
wanted Interior Secretary Bruce Babbitt to list the salmon, but U.S. Senator William Cohen of Maine threatened to rethink his position against gut-
ting the ESA unless Babbitt backed off, which he did. In 1997, the federal
government accepted the state's conservation plan as an alternative to listing the fish. In April and May 1999, LURC reduced the amounts of water
that blueberry growers could divert from critical rivers.

In August 1999, the Atlantic Salmon Federation and Trout Unlimited,
two of the country's leading salmon conservation groups, unhappy because
they considered the state's plan inadequate, sued FWS and NMFS to force

them to list the salmon under the ESA. According to Jeff Reardon of Trout Unlimited, the state's plan hoped to save the salmon "with Band-Aids, bailing wire and a few volunteers." Three months later, FWS and NMFS proposed listing Maine's Atlantic salmon as a distinct species in danger of extinction. After reviewing recent biological studies and efforts under Maine's conservation plan to protect the species, FWS and NMFS concluded that the species' status had deteriorated. They found (1) a continuing decline in the number of returning adults; (2) lower than expected smolt survival rates; (3) a disease affecting the Canadian aquaculture industry had now spread toward the U.S. border; (4) an increase in aquaculture's use of non-American strains of Atlantic salmon; (5) continued escape of farm-raised fish into the wild; and (6) habitat degradation by water diversions and sedimentation. The report stated that "[t]he most obvious and immediate threat is posed by water extraction" from rivers where Atlantic salmon spawn. FWS and NMFS concluded that Maine has to ensure that water diversions for agriculture do not adversely affect salmon habitat. They also advocated significant changes in the aquaculture industry, including using sterile fish, developing secure pens to prevent fish from escaping, and moving cages twelve miles offshore from the mouths of the eight rivers where wild fish spawn. The effect of listing the salmon would be to require significant conservation efforts for wild salmon.

The reaction from Maine's political leaders to the proposed listing was swift and critical. Governor Angus King accused the federal government of an "abuse and miscarriage of the Endangered Species Act." He pledged "all the resources we can muster" to resist the federal government's use of the ESA. Governor King was particularly critical about efforts to protect a species that has mated with various strains of hatchery stock over the last century. The governor complained: "[Atlantic salmon] are no more genetically pure than I am a purebred Scot, with my English, German, and God-knows-what-else ancestors." U.S. Senator Olympia Snowe, who chaired a Senate committee with jurisdiction over oceans and fishing, called for an independent study of the government's research. The study backfired on Snowe, as it led FWS and NMFS to conclude that the Atlantic salmon comprise a genetically distinct species and, therefore, warrant protection under the ESA. In January 2002, a National Academy of Sciences panel also concluded that wild Atlantic salmon are a distinct species. The panel found "surprisingly strong evidence" that hatchery and farmed salmon do not dilute the genes of wild Maine salmon. King and Snowe were not alone among Maine's political leaders in their contempt for the listing. As the *Bangor Daily News* put it: "If there is an elected official in the state who supports [the listing], they've been very quiet about it."

The reaction of Governor King and other officials created a huge problem for Ed Baum, senior fisheries biologist for Maine's Atlantic Salmon Commission. Baum is the author of *Maine Atlantic Salmon: A National Treasure* and is widely recognized as the foremost authority on Atlantic salmon. As early as 1992, Baum had published papers and reports that detailed the salmon's decline and outlined the steps necessary to restore salmon stocks. He had also helped craft the state's conservation plan. As a state employee whose boss was Governor King, he was squarely in the middle between the federal government's decision to list the species under the ESA and Governor King's attack on that decision. An attorney for the state of Maine employees' association cautioned Baum against speaking out. Yet Baum had dedicated his entire career—thirty-two years—to working on Atlantic salmon issues. Although he "felt like the lone ranger," excluded from meetings and ignored by the governor's office, Baum "felt [he] really needed to stand up and be counted and really did-n't care what the consequences would be." Speak out he did, describing Governor King's claim that there are no wild Atlantic salmon left as "absolutely, totally 100 percent false."

In November 2000, after a public comment period, FWS and NMFS decided to list Atlantic salmon as endangered. Despite the state of Maine's conservation plan, FWS and NMFS concluded that withdrawals of water for blueberry production created "a danger of extinction" for wild Atlantic salmon. FWS and NMFS must develop a recovery plan for Atlantic salmon that will assure the salmon's survival.

The aquaculture industry and Maine's political leadership responded angrily to the decision to list the Atlantic salmon. A lobbyist for Atlantic Salmon of Maine, an aquaculture company, testified before a U.S. Senate committee that the listing decision was "a dangerous backslide into an inflexible interpretation of the ESA" and "a political listing that had noth-ing to do . . . with the best science available."

Governor King had the Maine attorney general file a federal court law-suit challenging the conclusion that wild Atlantic salmon are a "distinct population segment" under the ESA. The Wild Blueberry Commission of Maine spent $50,000 funding research to criticize the science behind the decision by FWS and NMFS to list the species. A coalition of agricultural interests, blueberry growers, and the timber industry raised $600,000 to challenge the listing. Des FitzGerald, chief executive officer of Atlantic Salmon of Maine, described the fear of farm-raised salmon escaping and interbreeding as overblown. He contended that new practices by the company had reduced the number of escapees to zero. However, in December 2000, a severe northeaster slammed into Machias Bay, collapsing steel cages and releasing more than 100,000 hatchery fish into the ocean. Word of this potential ecological disaster did not become public until February 2001 because a state of Maine employee "forgot" to report it. A FWS biologist who had been roundly condemned for bad science dryly observed: "It looks like the feds were right. Salmon do escape."

In fall 2001, disaster struck the Maine aquaculture industry in the form of infectious salmon anemia, a nasty virus that spread from Norway to Canada to Maine. Highly contagious and incurable, the virus kills salmon but is not dangerous to humans. In September 2001, fish farmers destroyed 700,000 salmon in hopes of halting the disease's spread. However, the tactic did not succeed. In January 2002, at the order of the Maine Department of Marine Resources, the aquaculture industry destroyed *all* of the remaining salmon, some 2.5 million in total. As a result, the pens are bare and the industry on hold while it determines whether it can sanitize the pens and gradually start over. The U.S. Department of Agriculture has pledged $17 million to fight the virus and to compensate fish farmers for the destroyed fish. Whether the virus will spread to wild Atlantic salmon is unclear, but Mike Hendrix, director of the U.S. Fish and Wildlife Service's Northeast Fisheries Center, noted that "we see this as potentially a very big threat to our salmon."

The decision to list Atlantic salmon places enormous pressures on blueberry growers to change their irrigation practices. Under the ESA, once a species is listed, FWS and NMFS must designate "critical habitat" of the species, which will obviously include the eight rivers in Maine where wild Atlantic salmon spawn. The ESA makes it unlawful for anyone to "take" a listed species, which includes not only such obvious activities as shooting or killing but also activities that cause "significant habitat modification or degradation" that impairs breeding patterns. Even though threats to the fish come from many directions, the FWS and NMFS have identified water diversions as "the most obvious and immediate threat."

What choices are available to the blueberry growers? A dramatic reduction in the amount of water diverted from the critical rivers would obviously solve the problem but at the cost of greatly diminished yields of blueberries. At a time when wild blueberry growers in Maine are struggling to compete with domestic blueberry producers in the mid–Atlantic states, the Maine growers fear that a smaller crop will not give large commercial consumers of blueberries, such as the baking industry, the assurance of a stable, continuous supply.

Three other options are under consideration. First, growers could build impoundments, otherwise known as dams, on small tributaries or ephemeral washes that would retain water behind them during the spring thaw, a time when river flows are at their highest. In the summer months, growers would rely on these stored waters to irrigate their fields. The beauty of this system is that it involves no diversions during the summer months, which are most critical for the salmon. New dams would create new ponds that would attract waterfowl. This plan has the endorsement of Ducks Unlimited, among other organizations. But there are some significant complications. An impoundment on a tributary to a river triggers the Clean Water Act requirement of a National Pollution Discharge Elimination System (NPDES) permit from the U.S. Army Corps of Engineers. Many tributaries are adjacent to wetlands, and a dam would change the function and structure of the wetland. The problem is that federal agencies have conflicting mandates. FWS is charged with protecting salmon and the Corps with permitting wetland development. Dams would impound water and allow the growers to remove their diversion pipes from the critical rivers. But the dams, by creating ponds, would inundate wetlands. Perhaps the Corps will permit impoundments; perhaps not. Growers face an uncertain regulatory nightmare in trying to obtain permits to flood wetlands.

Impoundments create another problem. Scientists who study river channels have a fancy-sounding specialty, called fluvial geomorphology, that focuses on how water flows alter the characteristics of a river: its width, shape, depth, direction, and slope. Holding back the peak flows in springtime may provide water to maintain summer month flows. Yet reduced peak flows may profoundly alter the very river itself. River channels are dynamic. Peak flows are critical to moving sediment downstream, to cleansing the spawning redds, and to maintaining the general health of a river. A reduction in peak flows may move less sediment downstream. As a consequence, the river channel may become clogged with sediment, prompting the river to create a wider channel, or even to spill over its banks. Over time, reduced peak flows may produce a wider, slower river with lower water flows. These alterations in the river's physical character-istics would surely change the biological processes in the river and on its margin. Scientists are uncertain how impoundments would affect Atlantic salmon or other fish and wildlife.

The second option, a groundwater recharge project, would divert water from the rivers during the spring peak flows, and store the water in natu-ral depressions in the topography where there are no wetlands. The water would percolate into the ground, recharging the area beneath the depres-sion. This option would avoid the requirements of the Clean Water Act because there would be no construction and hence no need for an NPDES permit. Indeed, the Corps might support such projects because they would create new wetlands. The growers would install groundwater pumps and, during summer months, pump the water that had been recharged beneath the depressions during the previous spring. However, this plan raises the same unanswered question as the idea of constructing an impoundment: what is the long-term impact on the river from reducing the peak flows?

The first two options involve diversions of surface water from the sen-sitive rivers, thus creating one problem while solving another. To escape this catch-22, some growers have turned to a third possibility, "alternative supplies" of water. What might that be? Groundwater. It is available when needed, requires no expensive impoundment facility, and ostensibly solves the problem of reducing water flows in the critical rivers. Maybe. Under the best-case scenario, groundwater pumping *could* provide a win–win sit-uation. Under less than ideal circumstances, pumping could harm the salmon's habitat just as surely as does direct withdrawal of water from the river, but it would do so indirectly and more discretely though the processes of capture. Many aquifers surrounding the eight critical rivers are composed of unconsolidated sand and gravel left behind as glacial outwash. Pumping from this highly permeable material will result fairly quickly in capturing water that would normally flow to the river. However, *if* the blueberry growers pump from the wells only during the key summer months when flows are already low and *if* the impact on the rivers from capture does not occur until the autumn, then a reduction in the river's flow would not harm the salmon. At the end of August, after the growing season, the blueberry farmers would turn off the pumps, and the cone of depression would gradually fill up as precipitation recharged the aquifer. By the following summer, discharge to the river would have returned to normal. Under this scenario, pumping would not affect river levels during the critical summer months, and a moderate reduction in flows during the fall or winter months would pose no problem for the salmon, which migrate in June, July, and August.

For this rosy scenario to be realized, good science must be done using pumping tests that evaluate how the location of the wells, the timing of the pumping, and the quantity of water pumped influence the river. Wells located too close to the river, for example, will quickly reduce surface flows, and too many wells pumping large quantities of water may have the same effect, even if located farther away.

Another significant concern is the water level in the rivers during the fall and winter. Atlantic salmon have minimum water level requirements at all seasons of the year, not just during the summer months when they return from the ocean. Because salmon spawn during October and November, flow levels are crucial if the eggs are to survive. During the winter, low flows present two dangers to the immature salmon and their habitat. Low water temperatures slow a salmon's metabolic rate, which reduces the ability of a salmon to transform food into usable energy. Salmon seek refuge in deep pools to stay out of the higher flow velocities that would require them to expend more energy to avoid being swept downstream. But low flows may produce a thick ice cap of surface and subsurface ice, called anchor ice, that traps fish and kills eggs deposited on redds. Anchor ice, so-called because the ice forms from the bottom up, rather than from the surface down, may profoundly alter the river itself. When spring thaw arrives, instead of ice floes that move gradually downstream and cause some superficial scraping of the channel and banks, anchor ice will scour the channel bottom, moving larger rocks, trees, and debris downstream as the melting occurs. When this happens, the effect is like dredging the channel. The channel becomes deeper (more incised), causing changes to the biological processes in the river and damaging the salmon redds. Finally, low flows during spring months may change the sediment flow and cause other problems, as noted above. It is essential that groundwater pumping not interfere with the minimum levels needed for the health of both the river and the fish. Despite these caveats, the situation in Maine may prove to be one for which groundwater pumping provides a real solution, not just a band-aid. As of 2001, no one really knew if this complicated balancing act could be performed, but there are positive signs.

Cherryfield Foods, one of the largest wild blueberry producers, farms on 8,500 acres in Washington County. In 1998 and 1999, it received permits from the Maine Land Use Regulation Commission (LURC) to divert water from the Narragaugus, Machias, and Pleasant Rivers, which have Atlantic salmon runs. LURC conditioned the permit on maintaining minimum flows in those rivers during the 1999 growing season. For the 2000 growing season, Cherryfield Foods sought a permit to pump groundwater from a well located on a wetland adjacent to Sam Hill Brook, a tributary to the Machias River. Drilled forty-eight feet into a sand and gravel aquifer approximately 300 feet from Sam Hill Brook, the well would pump between 1,500 and 3,000 gallons per minute (gpm). For 912 acres of blueberry barrens, Cherryfield Foods would pump as much as 143 million gallons during the growing season.

In October 1998, Brad Caswell, a hydrologist retained by Cherryfield Foods, conducted a pumping test of the irrigation well and nine surrounding monitor wells to assess the impact of the pumping on flows in Sam Hill Brook and on the adjacent wetlands. He pumped 1,210 gpm continuously for five days, then checked the monitor wells for five more days. He concluded that there is little, if any, hydrologic connection between the aquifer and Sam Hill Brook or between the aquifer and the wetlands above the aquifer.

LURC staff, the Maine Department of Inland Fisheries and Wildlife, and the Maine Atlantic Salmon Commission raised doubts about these conclusions. They were dubious about Cherryfield Foods' claim that pumping 143 million gallons from a shallow well located only 300 feet from a brook in a sand and gravel aquifer would not significantly affect the brook. The problem is that the hydrologic testing did not last long enough, nor was a sufficient quantity of water pumped, to allow a confident prediction of the effects of the proposed irrigation pumping at that location. Pumping 1,210 gpm for five days is quite different from pumping 3,000 gpm for sixty days. Pumping at a higher rate over a longer period of time would create a cone of depression that would surely capture water from the brook.

Cherryfield Foods' assertion that the overlying wetlands would not suffer from the pumping is also puzzling. The report prepared by Cherryfield Foods' hydrologist identified a confining layer of impermeable sediments that ostensibly prevents a hydraulic connection between the wetlands and the aquifer. However, the report also claims that precipitation during the fall and winter would recharge the aquifer and replenish the water pumped during the summer. But if an impermeable barrier underlies the wetlands, how is rainfall going to percolate through this barrier? Cherryfield Foods can't have it both ways. Pumping millions of gallons from beneath the wetlands must increase the recharge to the aquifer, thus reducing the water in the wetlands, or it must capture water from Sam Hill Brook.

In response to criticism, Cherryfield designed a plan to use monitor wells and stream gauges to evaluate the impact on the river and wetlands before, during, and after the irrigation season. In January 2000, on the recommendation of its staff, LURC granted the permit with a number of conditions. Pumping may not exceed 3,000 gpm; monitoring of the wells and gauges will be weekly or twice weekly; and, if the monitoring data reveal that the wells are affecting Sam Hill Brook or the wetlands, LURC may require Cherryfield Foods to reduce or even cease pumping. John Williams, executive director of LURC, observed that the permit "is much stricter than last year, and last year's was stricter than the year before."

Cherryfield Foods and the large producers are exploring other creative options for irrigation water. One proposal is to recycle fish hatchery wastewater and use it for irrigation. Another idea is to pump groundwater from an aquifer farther up the watershed, dump this cold, clean water into the Narragaugus River, where it would benefit that reach of river, and then divert it eight or ten miles downstream. The environmental community has been receptive to the growers' goodfaith efforts to find alternative supplies of water. The principal concern of Jeff Reardon of Trout Unlimited is that good science must provide the baseline. It will not do to remove the irrigation pipes from the rivers only to draw down the rivers through groundwater pumping that induces capture. Cherryfield Farms' hydrologist, Brad Caswell, is confident that groundwater pumping will provide the water needed for the blueberry growers without harming the salmon. Blueberry irrigation is seasonal and involves a relatively small quantity of water. "There is never any mining of water. You pump for three months, and within two months, you're right back to where you were," Caswell says.

Ironically, groundwater pumping may offer an intriguing solution for the salmon versus blueberry controversy. Carefully spaced wells, with restrictions on the quantity of water pumped and on the time of year of the pumping, may protect the rivers and their salmon and still allow blueberry irrigation. In Maine, an awareness of the relationship between groundwater and surface water has made possible a potentially viable solution.

Chapter 10

Size Does Count, at Least for French Fries

Minnesota's Straight River

"I wish to make it clear to you, there is not sufficient water to
irrigate all the lands which could be irrigated. . . ."
—John Wesley Powell (1893)

Ray Kroc, the founder of McDonald's, revolutionized the french fry in the
1950s. It was not mere marketing prowess that allowed him to do so. It
was science. He discovered that potatoes vary widely in their water content. A potato that contains too much water will become soggy when
fried. Kroc actually sent employees armed with hydrometers into the
potato fields of his suppliers to ensure that the potatoes contained the
optimum percentage of water. A freshly harvested potato typically consists
of 80 percent water. The french frying process essentially removes most of
that water and replaces it with fat. The high fat content makes french fries
unhealthy, but it also makes them delicious. The typical American consumes thirty pounds of french fries a year, a 700 percent increase since the
1950s, when Ray Kroc began to mass-produce french fries. According to
Eric Schlosser, author of *Fast Food Nation*, "French fries have become the
most widely sold foodservice item in the United States." Frozen french
fries have also nudged aside fresh potatoes, called "table stock" by the food
industry, in the at-home diets of many Americans. Potato manufacturers
have thoughtfully nurtured our enjoyment of convenience foods by pack-
aging french fries to suit our every whim for a fry of a certain size, shape,
or flavoring. The freezer section of a Safeway supermarket is likely to

143

carry some twelve different types of Ore-Ida french fries: shoestring, crinkles, twirls, crispers, fajita-seasoned, zesties, country style, tater tots, hash browns (country and southern style), potatoes O'Brien, and, of course, plain old french fries.

Any baking potato will suffice to make french fries, though the fast-food industry prefers Burbank russet potatoes, a variety that is mealy or starchy, not waxy. When ready for processing, the potatoes are washed, steam-peeled, sliced, and blanched, all of which ensures that the inside will have a fluffy texture. After quick drying, the potatoes are deep-fried for thirty seconds to produce a crisp shell. These steps usually occur at a processing plant located close to the potato fields to save on transportation costs. The fries are then frozen and shipped to a warehouse, which delivers them to retail outlets as needed. The fries remain frozen until the moment of service. At this point, they are deep-fried again for approximately three minutes.

Some potato species that we cultivate today were gathered and cultivated in the Peruvian and Bolivian Andes of South America for thousands of years before the first European explorations. Potatoes first reached North America from England in the early 1600s. The Irish potato blight in the 1840s taught the lesson that cross-fertilization and new cultivars ward off insects and fungi that attack potatoes. In the United States, the intense cultivation of Burbank russets has required growers to use large quantities of insecticides, pesticides, and herbicides to protect the single cultivar. One recent study found that babies in the Red River Valley in North Dakota, a major potato farming region, had low birth weights and a high incidence of birth defects, conditions blamed on the local use of herbicides and other agricultural chemicals.

The potato industry has recently fallen on hard times. To break even, a potato farmer must receive about $5 per hundred pounds. In 1996–97, potato prices fell to $1.50 per hundredweight. By 2001, the prices had declined to $1 per hundred pounds. Most small producers have left the business, and the process of consolidation has resulted in a small number of corporate farms, each growing thousands of acres of potatoes. As large as these farms are, the farmers are still beholden to the processors, who, in turn, must answer to the fast-food chains. In the business of potato farming, a very small number of buyers wield extraordinary power over a large number of sellers.

The advent of the fast-food industry and the converging technologies that made it possible have created American consumers who expect the same uniformity in their food products that they find in their vehicles, shoes, or notebook paper. In the past, fast-food french fries came in small waxed paper bags. The small bags would not stand up, so they often tipped over and spilled the fries, making a bit of a mess. For marketing reasons, in 1988, McDonald's began to offer consumers "super-sized" meals with larger portions of fries now served in rectangular boxes with flat bottoms. They were a huge hit.

French fries are a tremendously competitive component of the fast-food industry. The hook that keeps customers coming back to a particular franchise is not only the taste of the french fries but also their appearance. According to Dean John Gardner of the University of Missouri Agricultural Extension program, the fast-food industry decided that the french fry, to appeal aesthetically to consumers, had to be a certain length. It needed to jut out of the super-size box by just the right amount, so that the consumer can grasp the potato between index finger and thumb and dip it in ketchup.

— —

Ron Offutt grew up on his family's 240-acre farm in Moorhead, Minnesota. After graduation from college in 1964, he began to expand his family's potato growing operation. He recognized that the sandy soil of central Minnesota would provide an ideal medium for growing potatoes if the lands were irrigated. The R. D. Offutt Company now farms 200,000 acres of land in eleven states, with 66,000 acres in potatoes, making Ron the country's largest potato grower. His farms annually produce 2.9 billion pounds of potatoes.

As Ron's farming operation expanded, he needed a lot of tractors, so he acquired a John Deere franchise. Soon, RDO Equipment Co. became the nation's largest John Deere agricultural retailer *and* its largest construction equipment dealer, with forty-six stores in ten states. Ron also realized, in the 1970s, that it would be useful to own a french fry processing plant. So he bought one. In 1980, he completed construction of another processing plant in Park Rapids, Minnesota. He has since added two more processing facilities. Today, R. D. Offutt Company serves as the umbrella for a vast, vertically integrated agribusiness enterprise. Dean Gardner describes R. D. Offutt Company as "a classic, commercial success story for the production of an industrial potato for french fries." Industrial, he suggests, because the length and size of the potato is a critical part of the marketing. A uniform-length fry requires a uniform potato, which requires irrigation.

Until rather recently, many farms in the United States were "dryland farmed," meaning that the farmers had no system of irrigation. Their fortunes varied with the precipitation that Mother Nature provided, from flood to drought, in any given growing season. Many farmers, especially in the Midwest and the East, have come to realize that an occasional supplemental irrigation produces greater yields per acre and larger crops. Irrigation also enables farmers to apply fertilizers or pesticides to their fields through water-soluble solutions.

Americans' love affair with processed foods caused potato farmers to shift from dryland to irrigation farming. The problem with dryland potatoes is that their size, shape, and texture depend heavily on seasonal weather patterns. During the growing season, potatoes need constant moisture or they will have knobs and odd shapes. A misshapen or knobby potato is perfectly edible, but it is not an acceptable potato for the fast-food industry, at least in the United States. According to a potato processing executive, "American consumers were spoiled by the McDonald's of the world. They haven't made that mistake in Japan, where the specifications for potatoes are more reasonable. More of the potato gets used there than here." In Minnesota, potato farmers irrigate their fields because the two big suppliers for fast-food restaurants—Frito-Lay and Simplot—will contract only with potato growers who irrigate their fields in order to obtain potatoes with a uniform length, appearance, and color.

The R. D. Offutt Company farm near Park Rapids, Minnesota, in the Straight River basin, grows about 7,500 acres of Burbank russet potatoes, mostly for french fries, though also for tater tots, hash browns, and potato wedges. During the four-week harvesting season, potatoes are sent to the Lamb Weston/RDO Frozen processing plant in Park Rapids, which is a joint venture between Lamb-Weston Foods Corp. (a major supplier to McDonald's) and R. D. Offutt Company. The plant immediately processes some potatoes but stores the rest for up to eleven months. Storing potatoes creates two problems for processors. Most American consumers understand the first problem: they occasionally purchase a bag of potatoes, which they store under the sink and promptly forget. When finally discovered, the potatoes have become soft and flabby through dehydration and are suitable only for a child's science project. Once harvested, a potato begins to lose moisture to the air. To combat this problem, growers and processors store potatoes in a 95 percent humidity environment to prevent the loss of weight, which can be as much as 30 percent, or nearly one-third of the cash value.

Minnesota potato growers and processors face an additional problem. Most of us have enjoyed a summertime glass of iced tea with moisture on the outside of the glass. As we may remember from our own science classes, the cold glass chills the air immediately around it, and because the chilled air cannot hold the same amount of moisture as warmer air elsewhere in the room, water vapor condenses on the outside of the glass. The differential in temperature that produces condensation poses a problem for potato storage. The moisture in the high-humidity storage facility eventually condenses, which usually occurs on the facility's inside walls in a place with winters as cold as Minnesota. As moisture forms on the walls and ceiling of the plant, it begins to drip onto the potatoes, which, if wet, will eventually rot.

The humidity and temperature of stored potatoes are not important to the typical consumer who buys a large bag of potatoes, stores them in the garage or attic during the wintertime, and eats them over a six- or eight-month period. But humidity and temperature *are* critical for the fast-food industry. When a potato is stored at a cool temperature, its carbohydrates naturally turn to sugars. When baked, the potato will be somewhat sweeter from the sugars that caramelize during baking. If this potato is used for french fries, the caramelized sugar produces a brown color that is aesthetically unacceptable. As Larry Monico, director of operations for the R.D. Offutt farm in Park Rapids has explained, "We as Americans, or somebody, has decided that french fries should be white in color and not brown. If you made french fries out of potatoes that have been stored at a cold temperature, they would be brown in color like shoe leather. Not that they would taste bad, or anything else, but they are undesirable to us as consumers." Consequently, processors must use water to store potatoes at a precise temperature and humidity.

The Lamb Weston/RDO Frozen storage facility in Park Rapids, Minnesota, has a capacity of 26.5 million pounds of potatoes. They must store the entire crop so that there is not more than a one degree Fahrenheit difference between any two potatoes in the entire building. Otherwise, when fried, they might be slightly different colors. According to Larry Monico, "McDonald's won't accept french fries that aren't all white, and so, therefore, we have to keep the temperature constant so that they will all fry to

the same color." To achieve the required uniform humidity and temperature, the inside walls are entirely separated from the exterior walls by an air
space or cavity that creates an envelope separating the potato storage area
from the exterior walls. A separate furnace heats the cavity to a certain
temperature and prevents the outside air from affecting the temperature
and the humidity at which the potatoes are stored. A computer-controlled
system regulates the temperature and humidity in the storage area.

— —

The Straight River in north-central Minnesota, about 180 miles northwest
of the Twin Cities, is quite deep and meanders, contrary to its name, in a
series of S turns. Typical of rivers and streams in the upper Midwest, the
Straight River flows through glacial outwash. As a consequence of the
sandy soil, the surface and groundwater are very closely connected hydrologically. At the end of Minnesota's legendary winters, snowmelt rapidly
recharges substantial quantities of water to shallow aquifers that, in turn,
quickly transmit the water to the river.

In the past, local farmers eked out a living by dryland farming corn and
small grains such as wheat, barley, and oats. The sandy soil made farming a
marginal economic enterprise. The genius of Ron Offutt was to realize the
region's potential for growing potatoes, if the lands were irrigated. The uniform texture of the sandy soils, aided by the application of water, provided
an ideal medium for producing the uniform potatoes demanded by the
fast-food industry. The threat to the Straight River comes from this shift
from dryland to irrigated farming and from changes in the technology of
irrigation.

Airplane passengers regularly query flight attendants about conspicuous
green circles that dot the landscape of the Great Plains from North Dakota
to Texas and that contrast dramatically with the arid land surrounding
them. The circles are produced by center-pivot irrigation systems. In a center-pivot system, a well drilled in the center of a quarter-section (160 acres)
attaches by a swivel to aluminum pipes suspended six or eight feet off the
ground, which are supported by A-frame towers with tandem wheels on
the base. A hydraulic drive or a diesel or electric motor supplies power that
slowly pivots the pipes and towers in a circle around the well. The resulting irrigation-water pattern produces a perfect circle easily seen from
35,000 feet. Unlike older forms of row irrigation, center-pivot systems
allow farmers to tailor precisely the frequency and amount of water applied

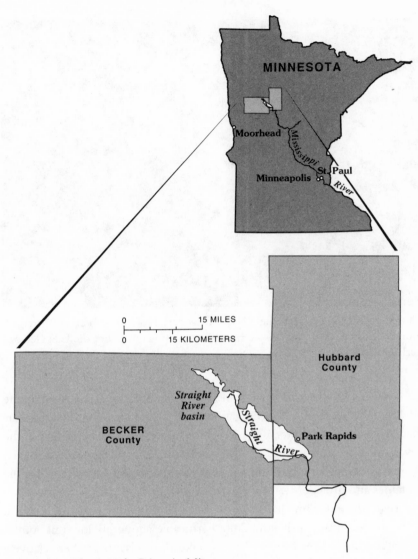

FIGURE 10.1. The Straight River in Minnesota.

in order to achieve better yields. Modern center-point systems reduce evaporation loss by using low pressure with specially designed nozzles that produce larger droplets aimed toward the ground and that can achieve an efficiency of 90 percent. Older systems relied on high pressure to spray fine mists of water into the air. Much of the water evaporated before it ever reached the ground.

FIGURE 10.2. Minnesota's Straight River meanders. Note the center-pivot irrigation systems on either side of the river. Photograph courtesy of the U.S. Geological Survey.

Center-pivot irrigation has transformed the Straight River basin; in the
1940s, there were only five irrigation wells in the area. By 1998, farmers
had drilled seventy center-pivot irrigation systems within two miles of the
river, and they now pump almost 3 billion gallons of groundwater each
growing season. Groundwater adjacent to the Straight River irrigates the
potatoes and provides water for processing.

Beneath and immediately adjacent to the Straight River, the glacial
outwash constitutes a shallow, quite permeable aquifer. Below this aquifer
lies a confining layer of glacial till, a mixture of clay and other relatively
impermeable sediments, and below that lies a deeper aquifer from deposits
during earlier glacial periods. The confining layer retards but does not
completely block water moving between the shallow and deep aquifers.
Pumping from the deep aquifer will increase recharge from the shallow
aquifer to the deep aquifer and, depending on the location of the well, may
also reduce discharge from the shallow aquifer to the Straight River. One
thing is certain: groundwater pumping from the *shallow* aquifer reduces
discharge from the aquifer to the Straight River.

Hydrologists are confident about this conclusion for a quite surprising reason. All water bodies contain radioactive isotopes, the product of either natural geologic processes or atomic fallout from nuclear bomb tests that stopped in the 1950s. Because isotopes have differing half-lives, the law of radioactive decay allows hydrologists to calculate the length of time that it takes for precipitation to infiltrate the ground and to discharge to a stream. It turns out that 95 percent of the water in the Straight River comes from discharge from the shallow aquifer. As of 1988, about half the irrigation wells pumped water from the shallow aquifer and the other half from the deeper aquifer.

One of Minnesota's most productive trout fishing streams, the Straight River contains brown trout that can weigh up to nine pounds. Although brown trout are not as sensitive to water temperatures as other trout species, they still require cold, clear water. Reduced flow in the Straight River produces higher ambient water temperatures that threaten the brown trout. A 1994 U.S. Geological Survey (USGS) report identified three factors that degrade the Straight River's trout habitat: (1) a decrease in stream flow from groundwater withdrawals for irrigation that reduces discharge from the aquifer to the stream; (2) higher-temperature irrigation water that percolates into the groundwater system and then discharges to the river; and (3) the introduction of agricultural chemicals to the river when irrigation water percolates into the ground and then discharges into the river. According to the USGS, the river's flow typically decreased during the summer, "possibly as a result of ground-water withdrawal for irrigation." Compared to farms in the West, Minnesota farmers use only a small amount of groundwater—approximately twelve inches per acre per year. Even this modest amount of pumping has the potential, according to the USGS, to reduce the Straight River's flow by as much as 34 percent during the irrigation season. This reduction in flow would increase the water temperature and might adversely affect the brown trout.

The USGS also found an increase in nitrate concentrations in the shallow aquifer along the Straight River. Farmers typically apply 235 pounds per acre of nitrogen fertilizer to grow Burbank russets. Biochemical processes convert organic nitrogen into inorganic nitrate that dissolves in water and leaches into the aquifer. Although the number of documented cases of human illness caused by nitrate-contaminated groundwater is small, the potential health hazards pose a significant environmental concern. A 1994 USGS study found that 6 percent of 600 groundwater samples from shallow wells in the Midwest had nitrate levels that exceeded the U.S. Environmental Protection Agency drinking water limit.

In the mid-1990s, Lamb Weston/RDO Frozen proposed a $60 million expansion of the potato processing plant at Park Rapids. The Minnesota chapter of Trout Unlimited, the Minnesota Center for Environmental Advocacy, and the Headwaters Chapter of the Audubon Society filed a lawsuit to prevent the state of Minnesota from issuing the necessary permits for the plant. The environmental groups feared that the plant's increased groundwater pumping would reduce Straight River flows and that the plant's effluent would adversely affect water quality. The lawsuit ultimately was settled when Lamb Weston/RDO Frozen agreed to change its operations in significant ways. First, it funded monitoring and other data collection efforts. Lamb Weston/RDO Frozen donated in excess of $300,000 to the Minnesota Department of Natural Resources (DNR) to help fund a comprehensive watershed study and a hydrologic model that could predict changes in river flow from groundwater pumping. Between 1996 and 1998, DNR placed a moratorium on issuing new water appropriation permits in order to conduct its study, but the resulting model was not precise enough to provide sufficiently accurate data to predict the impact of specific wells on the river. Lamb Weston/RDO Frozen also capped wells located at the processing plant and drilled two new ones, at a cost of $100,000, about a mile north of the plant in an area that hydrologists determined would not affect the Straight River. The company made these changes solely for the possible benefit of the Straight River. To get the water from the new wells to the processing plant, it built an $80,000 pipeline. Lamb Weston/RDO Frozen also upgraded the wastewater treatment facilities, at a cost of $14 million, and uses the effluent from the treatment plant to irrigate nearby crops.

After DNR lifted its moratorium, Lamb Weston/RDO Frozen ultimately obtained the necessary permits and expanded the plant, which is an enormous operation. Each day, seventy-five semitrailer truckloads of potatoes arrive for processing. Each year, the plant receives almost one billion pounds of potatoes and produces approximately 540 million pounds of french fries. It takes two pounds of potatoes to make one pound of french fries that are acceptable to the plant's largest customer—McDonald's. The plant uses 600 million gallons per year of groundwater in its washing, peeling, and storing operations. It's a lot of water, but R. D. Offutt Company's potato farming and processing businesses employ approximately 600 people and generate $11 million in annual payroll, which has a huge impact in rural Minnesota.

For the moment, the Straight River trout population is in no danger. However, a tall stack of groundwater permit applications waits to be processed by DNR. A large increase in irrigation for potatoes, with new wells being drilled in the deeper aquifer, would change the equilibrium. A 1999 Minnesota DNR study concluded: "Potential expansion in potato farming and irrigation could put the Straight River trout population at further risk of thermal impact and eventually raise water temperatures beyond their threshold of survival." Increased pumping from the deeper aquifer would increase recharge from the shallow aquifer, thus reducing discharge from the shallow aquifer to the river. Lower flows would mean higher ambient water temperatures and less dilution of nitrates that contaminate the river. One long-term answer, of course, is for us, as American consumers, to accept french fries that have slightly different colors, or minor discolorations, or even ones that are not long enough to stick out from a super-size carton.

Chapter 11

The Black Mesa Coal Slurry Pipeline

The Hopi Reservation in Arizona

"The frog does not drink up the pond in which he lives."
—American Indian proverb

Shortly after taking office in 1962, President John F. Kennedy proposed the development of coal slurry pipelines as an economical way to transport coal. Most observers considered his proposal a political "thank you" to the coal mining industry, particularly in West Virginia, which had heavily supported him in the election and was suffering depressed economic conditions. In a coal slurry pipeline, finely ground coal mixed with water forms a slurry that is pumped through a pipe to a generating plant. At the end of the pipeline, large centrifuges extract the water from the coal, which is then burned to heat water, producing steam to spin the turbine that generates electricity. The Kennedy administration advocated the construction of ten pipelines but ultimately built only two, and one quickly closed. The one remaining, the Black Mesa pipeline, transports coal slurry 273 miles from a mine in northern Arizona, in the middle of the Hopi and Navajo reservations, to the Mohave Generating Station near Laughlin, Nevada, where the coal is burned to generate electricity for Los Angeles, Las Vegas, and Phoenix.

Black Mesa, a high-altitude plateau rising abruptly 3,000 feet above the surrounding lowlands, lies eighty miles east of Tusayan, Arizona. The name Black Mesa itself implies its rich coal deposit. The coal is anthracite, not bituminous, and is quite valuable for its low sulfur content and its high

155

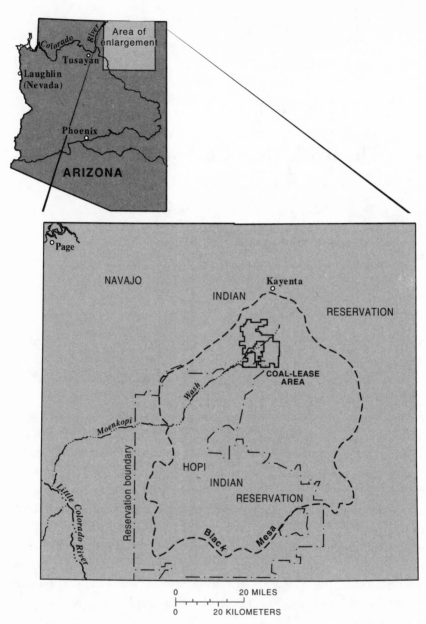

FIGURE 11.1. The Black Mesa area of northeastern Arizona.

heating value of approximately 10,700 British thermal units (Btu) per pound. When it burns, it produces less air pollution than coal mined in the eastern United States. Black Mesa is arid rangeland and sparsely populated. The population of the area, some 11,000 square miles, is less than 30,000; Tuba City is the largest city, with 7,300 people. Aside from jobs associated with coal mining, the area's economy is largely dependent on subsistence agriculture, sheep and cattle grazing, and a small amount of tourism.

The nation's only coal slurry pipeline depends entirely on pristine groundwater deposited thousands of years ago. In 1997, the United States Geological Survey (USGS), using naturally occurring radioactive isotopes, calculated that the water is between 10,000 and 35,000 years old. This extraordinary resource is some of the highest-quality water found anywhere in the United States. Peabody Energy Company extracts 1.3 billion gallons of groundwater a year—ten times as much water as that used by the entire Hopi tribe of 9,000 people—in a region that receives an average of eight inches of rain per year. The pumping threatens the drinking water supply of the Hopi tribe to provide electricity for curling irons, swimming pool pumps, and electric toothbrushes in Los Angeles, for opening garage doors and cans of tuna fish in Phoenix, and for the neon lights of the Las Vegas strip. The pumping is a classic example of the use of water in the American West. Peabody pumps this water because it has a need; but more importantly, it has the right to do so.

Peabody began as a retail coal business in Chicago, founded in 1883 by Francis S. Peabody. It has grown to become the world's largest private-sector coal business. It produces more than 9 percent of all the electricity in the United States and 2.5 percent of worldwide electricity. In fiscal year 2001, Peabody shipped a record 192 million tons of coal to customers in eighteen countries and five continents. Revenues totaled $2.67 billion.

In 1968, Peabody Energy Company (then Peabody Western Coal Company) began strip-mining Black Mesa. A lease from the U.S. Department of the Interior allows Peabody to mine almost 65,000 acres of Black Mesa and to pump groundwater for the slurry pipeline in exchange for payments made to the Navajo and Hopi tribes. Underlying Black Mesa are several different aquifer systems, the largest of which is the Navajo sandstone, or the N-Aquifer. Peabody pumps from the N-Aquifer, which contains an estimated 240 million acre-feet of water.

On the Hopi reservation, the largest source of surface water is Moenkopi Wash, which means "continuously flowing water place." Alvin

Honyumptewa, a seventy-year-old Hopi farmer, recently observed, "For the first time in my memory, I have not seen any water in Moenkopi Wash. We used to swim there all year long."

Vernon Masayesva, former tribal chair of the Hopi, remembers that when he was a boy, Moenkopi Wash contained sufficient water to irrigate fields, water livestock, and provide swimming holes during the hot summers. Today, Moenkopi Wash flows only intermittently. According to Masayesva, 90 percent of the springs on the Hopi reservation have dried up since he was young. He blames groundwater pumping by Peabody. The sale of water to Peabody, according to Masayesva, broke a Hopi religious law. A covenant between the Hopi and the deity, Maasaw, requires the Hopi to protect the earth's resources. It has become the central mission in Masayesva's life to halt the use of groundwater for the slurry pipeline. He has created a nonprofit organization, Black Mesa Trust, to help in the effort.

Masayesva described to me the powerful spiritual and cultural role that water plays in Hopi life. Hopi songs honor water, and easily 50 percent of Hopi surnames relate to water, including Yoyoki—"presently raining"; Yokawa—"it rained"; Yaeva—"the clouds build up"; Falaweapi—"lightening"; Omao—"cloud"; and Yaomon—"rain chief." Hopi religious ceremonies honor the rain, which connects them to the Creator. The first thing each morning, the Hopi look to the sky to see whether any clouds offer hope of rain. Throughout the year, elaborate religious rituals celebrate the balance and harmony in nature, especially the blessings of water. In Hopi mythology, Kokopelli—the familiar dancing flute player—plays his flute over springs to attract rain clouds. "Rain dances" evoke and celebrate the powerful role of water in sustaining life.

Springs, as a particular form of water, have enormous cultural significance for the Hopi, who are "farmers without water." As direct descendants of the Anasazi, the tribe has occupied the region for at least 1,500 years. Since 1150, Hopi have inhabited the village of Oraibi, making it the oldest continuously inhabited village in North America. Life on the Hopi reservation has changed little in centuries. Lacking major streams or rivers, the Hopi have nonetheless sustained themselves with subsistence agriculture. To water their crops, they rely on springs that flow from the sides of the sandstone mesas and down major washes between the fingers of each mesa. They capture this runoff in terraced landscaped gardens, where they plant maize, beans, melons, squash, corn, onions, radishes, chili peppers, and some fruit trees. Skillful terracing and the proper timing of planting, aided by the blessing of occasional rain, allow the Hopi to cultivate these fields without supplemental irrigation. Because few Hopi homes have running water, most people must haul five-gallon buckets of water to their homes from village pumps. Hopi water use is approximately forty gallons per capita per day, about one-fifth the U.S. average. The Hopi are extremely frugal with water.

The spring water that irrigates Hopi gardens provides a renewable supply of water that supports the modest needs of the villages. The Hopi celebrate springs in religious festivals, costumes, stories, and songs. In the Flute Ceremony, for instance, they pray to Paalölöqangw, the water serpent deity, to consecrate and regenerate the springs. During winter solstice ceremonies, the Hopi place feathered prayer sticks over each spring to protect the spring and to pray for help from the gods. They frequently make pilgrimages to remote springs to draw on the springs' regenerative power. Many Hopi believe that if the springs dry up, the Hopi people will return to the earth whence they came. Vernon Masayesva has ominously noted: "We have no other source of drinking water, and any significant depletion of our groundwater could spell doom for our tribe."

As Benjamin Franklin once noted, we learn the value of water when the well runs dry. Just as the value of real estate depends on location, location, and location, so, too, does the value of water. Farmers in California's Imperial Irrigation District pay $13.50 per acre-foot for Colorado River water, while Canyon Forest Village developers (discussed in chapter 14) anticipate spending $20,000 per acre-foot to transport water by railroad from the Colorado River to Williams. On the Hopi reservation, the springs have enormous cultural and religious value but no commercial value. The water pumped by Peabody has value only to facilitate the inexpensive transport of coal through the slurry pipeline. For Peabody, the well has not run dry, though the springs may soon.

Since the 1970s, coal mining has played a critical role in the lives of both the Hopi and the Navajo peoples. Mining has created 750 jobs that pay an average of $45,000 per year, a substantial wage in an area with 58 percent unemployment and a median income below $6,000 per year. Most Black Mesa mine workers are Navajo, perhaps because the mine is close to the Navajo town of Kayenta, but 130 miles from Hopi villages. This is a source of resentment among the Hopi, who expected more economic benefits than they have received. The lease generates royalty revenues of over $7 million a year for the Hopi, which accounts for more than 80 percent of the Hopi tribal government's annual budget. Given the meager resources of the tribe, the Hopi tribal council finds itself between a rock and a hard place. The current tribal leadership is understandably reluctant to do anything that might result in closing the mine.

What is the impact of groundwater pumping for the coal slurry pipeline on Moenkopi Wash and the springs? In 1978, the Office of Technology Assessment of the U.S. Congress prepared a report, *A Technology Assessment of Coal Slurry Pipelines*, that considered the environmental and social impacts of the Black Mesa pipeline. The report, quite remarkably, never mentioned that groundwater pumping for the pipeline might impact seeps, springs, and creeks on the Navajo and Hopi reservations. Initial USGS hydrologic studies concluded that the pumping did not affect surface flows because it came from the N-Aquifer—3,000 feet below the earth's surface—and because a confining layer above the N-Aquifer kept the shallower, unconfined aquifer separate from the N-Aquifer. Moreover, annual municipal use by the Hopi and the Navajo has increased slightly in recent years, reaching approximately 2,900 acre-feet in 1999, and leading Peabody to blame municipal pumping as the cause of declining spring flows. Yet doubts linger in the minds of many Hopi. The Hopi believe that there is a direct relationship between human behavior and natural forces. Vernon Masayesva *knows* that Moenkopi Wash and the springs have dried up since the onset of groundwater pumping by Peabody. He deeply believes that the cause is the company's groundwater pumping. Yet government reports and hydrologic models have not produced hard data to establish this link.

Masayesva finds this frightening. In his view, federal government and Peabody scientists regard Hopi beliefs as folklore and will consider only quantifiable, measurable data. They put cultural values and beliefs "into the category of Indian myth, a category considered inferior to western science." Masayesva's belief about the linkage between the pumping and the springs may turn out to be correct, even judged by the standards of federal scientists.

A 1997 USGS study found that water from the shallow aquifer may be leaking through the confining layer into the N-Aquifer. The supposedly impermeable layers that separate the deep, confined aquifer from the shallower, unconfined aquifer are not really *im*permeable but simply less permeable than other sediments. Over time, pumping from the N-Aquifer will probably accelerate leakage from the shallower aquifer into the deeper N-Aquifer. This increase in recharge to the N-Aquifer may decrease discharge to Moenkopi Wash and the springs. The USGS study also found that natural recharge rates to the N-Aquifer are only 2,500–3,500 acre-feet per year, substantially less than previously believed. This figure is significant because the pumping by Peabody *alone* exceeds recharge. Therefore, according to the rules of capture (recall chapter 3), the pumping must produce either a decrease in storage, a decrease in discharge, or a combination of the two.

Peabody denies that its pumping poses "any permanent or significant impacts to the aquifer or other water users." A company-commissioned hydrologic study, released in April 2001, concluded that Peabody's mining will consume less than 0.1 percent of the total volume of water in the aquifer, which is no doubt true. However, even a slight drawdown of the water table in the entire aquifer may have a profound localized impact by reducing discharge to nearby springs. Masayesva and others are not persuaded by the company's latest study. Every conclusion reached by Peabody's hydrologists that departed from earlier studies favored the company's position.

The Hopi are mistrustful of more than scientists. They have not been well served legally by the U.S. Justice Department, the U.S. Department of the Interior, or even their own privately retained counsel. A recent book by Charles Wilkinson, *Fire on the Plateau*, unearthed documents demonstrating that John Sterling Boyden, the lawyer who represented the Hopi tribe in the negotiations with Peabody in 1966, was simultaneously working for the coal company. Such a blatant conflict of interest violates the most basic rule of professional ethics. The lease was a sweetheart deal for the company. The Hopi tribe received only 3.3 percent of gross sales, about half what the federal government received for coal leases on federal land. Numerous taxes were waived. The lease did not even contain a reopener clause, a standard term in a contract that allows the parties to renegotiate provisions after a certain number of years. Finally, the company paid the Hopi only $1.67 per acre-foot of water, a tiny fraction of its market value.

If anything, the lease should have favored the tribe. In the mid-1960s, a massive water development bill, ultimately enacted in 1968 as the Colorado River Basin Project Act, made its way through Congress. A masterpiece of political logrolling, the bill secured the support of western senators and representatives by promising dams or other desired water projects.

Two dams in particular, the Marble Canyon and Bridge Canyon dams, were desired by Secretary of the Interior Stewart Udall and his brother, Representative Morris Udall, to provide hydroelectric power for the Central Arizona Project (CAP), a proposed 330-mile canal that would pump water uphill from the Colorado River to Phoenix and Tucson. Unfortunately, the two dams would also have flooded portions of Grand Canyon National Park. A bitter political fight, led by David Brower and the Sierra Club, caused Secretary Udall to abandon the dams. The problem then became where to find energy to move water through the CAP. The solution was Black Mesa coal. The lease with the Hopi provided coal not only for the Mohave Generating Plant but also for the Navajo Generating Plant near Page, Arizona, to power the CAP. Given this context, the terms of a fairly negotiated lease should have been extremely favorable to the Hopi.

In 1987, the Hopi Tribal Council and the Navajo Nation successfully renegotiated their leases to provide 12.5 percent royalties for the value of the coal and water revenues of $300 an acre-foot for the first 2,800 acre-feet and $600 an acre-foot thereafter. The new lease contained a reopener clause. Both the Hopi and Navajo considered the 1987 lease a significant improvement, which it was. However, neither the Hopi nor the Navajo knew that U.S. Interior Secretary Donald Hodel, who would have to approve the new lease, had met secretly to discuss its terms with a close personal friend who represented Peabody. In 1987, other coal leases carried a royalty rate of 20 percent, and the initial decision of the assistant secretary of the Department of the Interior was to increase the new lease's royalty rate to the same level. However, after meeting with his friend, Secretary Hodel intervened and instructed the assistant secretary not to increase the rate to 20 percent. Faced with an uncertain decision from Interior, the tribes settled for an increase to 12.5 percent.

Years later, the Navajo learned of Secretary Hodel's secret meeting and in 1996 filed two suits against the United States government, Peabody, and Southern California Edison (which owns a majority interest in the Mohave Generating Plant). In the suit against the government, the Navajo Nation claimed that Hodel's secret meeting violated his fiduciary duty, as secretary, to represent the best interests of the Nation. In 2000, a federal district court judge agreed and, in a blistering opinion, concluded that Hodel violated "the most fundamental fiduciary duties of care, loyalty and candor." The court observed: "There is no plausible defense for a fiduciary to meet secretly with parties having interests adverse to those of the trust beneficiary, and then mislead the beneficiary concerning these events." On appellate review, the U.S. Court of Appeals in August 2001 held that the United States government must pay damages to the Navajo (and perhaps the Hopi) for violating the trust relationship with the Navajo in connection with the coal leases.*

In the suit against Peabody, the Navajo (joined by the Hopi tribe) sought $600 million in damages for the loss of revenue between the 12.5 percent and the 20 percent royalty rates on the ground that Peabody, by lobbying Hodel, interfered with the fiduciary relationship between the Interior Department and the tribe. In March 2001, a federal judge rejected Peabody's effort to have the case dismissed.

These developments may soften the often harsh relationship between the Hopi and the Navajo Nation. Historic grievances, especially over land settlement issues, have divided the tribes. The Hopi protest over the impact of Peabody's pumping on Black Mesa's springs initially received no support from the Navajo. Yet, in April 2000, Navajos demonstrated at a Southern California Edison facility in Los Angeles to protest the impact of supplying groundwater to the Mohave Generating Station. In April 2001, Hopi *and* Navajo activists demonstrated outside the New York offices of the company that then controlled Peabody, to protest Peabody's mining of Black Mesa.

In October 2000, the Natural Resources Defense Council issued a report, *Drawdown: Groundwater Mining on Black Mesa*, arguing that the Secretary of the Interior has a duty to act to halt Peabody's groundwater pumping. The lease between the Hopi and Peabody contains an escape clause, inserted by Secretary of the Interior Stewart Udall because he was concerned about the environmental impacts of Peabody's pumping. The clause provides that if the secretary determines "at any time" that Peabody's pumping "is endangering the supply of underground water," he or she may require Peabody to "obtain water for its mining and pipeline operations from another source that will not significantly affect the supply of underground water in the vicinity." To date, no secretary has invoked this clause.

There is still no agreement on the basic hydrologic relationship between Peabody's pumping and the springs and creeks. Constructing hydrologic models is cumbersome and expensive, and the Hopi challenge

---

*In June 2002, the U.S. Supreme Court agreed to review the Court of Appeals decision.

many of the assumptions built into the existing models. But the cost in money and time of a prolonged fight over the accuracy and adequacy of hydrologic models is not the real problem. The *real* problem is that it may take years or even decades before the effects of current pumping become apparent. By then, it will be too late to save the springs and creeks.

The Hopi have an interest in economic development, including coal mining, and in the protection of their sacred springs and subsistence agriculture. Is there any answer? Sure. It doesn't take a Nobel Prize winner to figure it out. Remember, Black Mesa is the *only* coal slurry pipeline in the country. Oklahoma has made it illegal to use *any* water for a coal slurry pipeline. Coal from the Kayenta mine is shipped eighty-seven miles by electric train to the Navajo Generating Station. Every other coal mine in the country uses trucks or railroads to transport coal. Peabody could too, or it could shift from relying solely on groundwater to using municipal effluent for the coal slurry. The Tuba City and Kayenta municipal effluent plants produce almost 2,000 acre-feet per year; Peabody could eliminate over half its pumping by relying on effluent. Nearby shallow aquifers contain brackish water that Peabody could pump as a replacement for N-Aquifer water. But would these lower-quality sources be an adequate substitute? Yes, concluded a report of the Congressional Office of Technology Assessment. Indeed, given the scarcity of water in the region, the report advocated the use of low-quality water, such as municipal effluent or highly saline water.

In the wonderful world of western water, the most sensible solution is rarely adopted. Transporting the coal by rail or truck and substituting municipal effluent or brackish groundwater for N-Aquifer groundwater are options not currently on the table. Instead, there is substantial consideration being given to building a new pipeline that would draw 7,200 acre-feet of water from Lake Powell and transport it ninety miles and 2,900 feet in elevation to the Black Mesa mine and to Hopi and Navajo communities. The estimated construction cost for the pipeline is $165 million. Negotiations over the pipeline from Lake Powell are ongoing. The federal government would pick up most of the tab, with Peabody kicking in as well. Two advantages to this alternative are that the 7,200 acre-feet would settle Hopi and Navajo claims to water from the Little Colorado River and provide the tribes with additional water for their increasing domestic uses.

On the other hand, water in Lake Powell is Colorado River water, and claims of water rights from the Colorado River already exceed the reliable annual supply of water in the river. Some accommodation, therefore, would be necessary to free up rights to this 7,200-acre-foot block of water. As the Colorado River basin states continue their game of musical chairs, fighting over legal rights to Colorado River water, their congressional delegations may oppose federal funding for a pipeline that would divert water from Lake Powell. Arizona Senator Jon Kyl is a pivotal figure in these negotiations, and he has thus far withheld his approval of the pipeline. It may be impossible to persuade Congress to fund construction of a pipeline to move thousands of acre-feet of water to land located above an aquifer that contains hundreds of millions of acre-feet of water.

Neither the Hopi tribe nor the Navajo Nation nor Peabody Energy wants coal mining to stop. Coal lease revenues constitute such a significant portion of each tribe's governmental budget that it would create problems for the tribes if they lost these funds. Peabody faces a bright future from mining Black Mesa and currently profits substantially from its leases. When Hopi chairman Farrell Secakuku claimed that the company enjoyed a net profit of $60 million a year on Black Mesa coal, a spokesperson at Peabody called that estimate only "overstated." For the fiscal year ending March 31, 2001, Peabody had an operating profit of $341.8 million, up from $193 million in fiscal year 2000. Although Peabody has been careful not to divulge its profits from the mines at Kayenta and Black Mesa, its 2001 annual report notes that "the Southwest region," which apparently includes only the two Arizona mines, "realized an *increased* operating profit of $12.1 million" in fiscal year 2001.

As electricity blackouts rolled across California in 2000 and threatened other parts of the nation in 2001, attention focused on finding new sources of energy with which to produce electricity. The Bush administration's decision to seek to open the Arctic National Wildlife Refuge for oil exploration drew the most attention, but energy companies quietly began to enter leases to secure long-term supplies of coal. The investment community took notice, and the coal industry snapped out of a fifteen-year slump. Stock prices at the largest publicly traded companies doubled, and coal prices jumped from $20 to $40 per ton. Because energy demand has been rising 2 to 3 percent a year, while capacity has remained steady or even declined, this latest energy crisis presents a long-term problem for the country but a tremendous opportunity for the coal industry.

The Bush administration's energy plan, announced in May 2001, endorsed coal as a critical component in the solution to the country's energy needs. The coal industry received another boost when President Bush "clarified" his campaign pledge to regulate carbon dioxide emissions from power plants, which, scientists believe, are a major cause of global warming. The administration further enhanced coal as a viable energy source for the foreseeable future when it refused to endorse the Kyoto Accord on global warming. As with the Kennedy initiatives that led to the Black Mesa slurry line, critics considered these moves a payback to the coal industry, which contributed heavily to Mr. Bush's campaign, and to West Virginia, a traditionally democratic state, whose five electoral votes helped to provide Mr. Bush with his slim margin of victory. Whatever the motivation, Peabody Energy is nicely positioned to benefit, particularly from its resources of low-sulfur coal, such as those at Black Mesa. Enormous coal reserves lie beneath Black Mesa—one estimate places the reserves at 4 billion tons—enough to sustain coal mining at a significant level for decades to come. The problem is the need to find a win–win solution. A water pipeline from Lake Powell does not satisfy the win–win test because other Colorado River basin users are jealously eyeing the water that would be diverted to the pipeline.

The time to search for alternatives is at hand because the forty-five-year-old slurry pipeline has begun to leak. It must be refurbished or replaced in the short term at an estimated cost of $140 million, or an alternative method must be found to transport the coal. Transporting coal by railroad is an alternative that satisfies the win–win test, although it would involve certain capital expenses. It would require constructing a spur track from Black Mesa to the Burlington Northern Santa Fe Railroad (BNSF) main line, which traverses northern Arizona and skirts Laughlin, Nevada. At Laughlin, it would be necessary to construct another spur track to the Mohave Generating Station and to convert the boilers to handle solid coal rather than the pulverized coal delivered by the slurry system. Access to a rail system would dramatically enlarge the potential market for Black Mesa coal. At the moment, Peabody is captive to a single customer, Southern California Edison, which owns the Mohave power plant, because that is the only plant supplied by the slurry pipeline. If Peabody could get the coal to the BNSF main line, it would open up markets around the West. In response to the California energy crisis, American utilities announced plans to build more than 26,000 megawatts of coal-based generating plants. In July 2001, Peabody announced that it had entered into negotiations for new long-term coal supply agreements with several of these companies. These developments make clear that Black Mesa coal will find ready markets if it is available.

There is some question whether a rail transport system is economically feasible. A 1993 report, prepared for the U.S. Department of the Interior, considered alternatives to the slurry pipeline for transporting coal. However, the only alternatives given serious consideration involved the use of some other water source as a substitute for N-Aquifer water. The report dismissed a rail transport system because it would cost an additional $21 per ton to transport coal by rail rather than by slurry pipeline. The devil is always in the details, and reasonable changes in the economic assumptions built into the models of construction cost significantly affect resulting calculations of the economic feasibility of rail transport. The 1993 report estimated that it would cost several hundred million dollars for the railroad transportation system, but the report amortized this figure based upon an assumption that coal mining would end in the year 2020.

The win-win solution would be for the Hopi tribe, the Navajo Nation, Peabody Energy Company, and the federal government to negotiate a long-term lease—say fifty or seventy-five years in duration—that would eliminate the uncertainty now associated with pumping groundwater from the N-Aquifer. For such a long-term guarantee of access to Black Mesa coal, Peabody would surely put up considerable money toward the cost of the rail transport system. In 2000, Peabody and Southern California Edison pledged as much as $50 million toward the cost of the pipeline from Lake Powell. In September 2001, in an interview with Fred Palmer, Peabody Energy's vice president for legal and external affairs, I proposed this long-term lease, railroad spur line option. He said that Peabody had been discussing that themselves and that "we would be willing to sit down and look at that." Palmer's one concern is that the cost of coal must be kept competitive with the cost of natural gas, or the Mohave power plant might convert to natural gas.

The federal government would probably underwrite the majority of costs associated with solving this conflict over groundwater pumping, particularly given the federal government's woeful representation of the Navajo Nation and Hopi tribe. The federal government has repeatedly violated its fiduciary obligation to protect tribal interests. A financial settlement of tribal claims against the government could fund an alternative transportation system. The advantage to a rail transport system is that it costs only money. Water is not involved.

Perhaps even Senator Kyl would sign on. In 2000, when Secretary of the Interior Bruce Babbitt visited Arizona in an effort to push along the stalled negotiations over rights to water from the Little Colorado River, he likened the process to the peace negotiations in northern Ireland. The Clinton administration had recently brokered the Good Friday Accord. Babbitt commented: "If we can achieve peace in northern Ireland, we should be able to settle the Little Colorado River controversy." Senator Kyl responded: "The situation in northern Ireland only involved religion. This involves water."

Chapter 12

Is Gold or Water More Precious?

Mining in Nevada

"Water doesn't flow if it's level."
—Chinese proverb

The federal government owns 83 percent of the state of Nevada, a fact that irks many rural residents, who have a paranoid resentment about the presence of the federal government. The Sagebrush Rebellion, an organization that advocates local control over land owned by the federal government, has a strong presence in Nevada. Physical threats against U.S. Forest Service employees and bombings of Forest Service buildings have prompted some federal employees to relocate outside Nevada. In 1999, Humboldt-Toiyabe National Forest supervisor Gloria Flora resigned due to the "anti-federal fervor" in Nevada. She blamed county and state officials for encouraging "irresponsible fed-bashing." How did this state of affairs come to pass?

In 1995, a flood washed out a road on Forest Service land next to the Jarbidge River. Much to the annoyance of some locals, the Forest Service decided against rebuilding because erosion from the road threatened endangered bull trout in the Jarbidge. In 1998, county officials used a bulldozer in an unsuccessful attempt to reopen the road. The next year, a band of Elko, Nevada, residents who dubbed themselves the Jarbidge Shovel Brigade attempted to rebuild the road, until a federal judge stopped them. A tentative agreement between the Forest Service and Elko County to rebuild the road in a slightly different location unraveled in August 2000. As these events unfolded, it became apparent that the struggle was about much more than the road itself. As the environmental writer Ted Williams observed: "[T]he road was but 1½ miles long and led only to a dilapidated outhouse that wasn't even stocked with toilet paper." The road instead symbolized the federal government's control over Nevada. Notwithstanding this flare-up and the propensity of locals to refer to the Forest Service as "the Green Gestapo," Nevada's rural agricultural community has less to fear from the federal government than it does from its longtime ally, the mining industry.

The mining industry in the United States recently has fallen on hard times, as producers have increasingly explored and developed mines in Bolivia, Chile, Peru, Indonesia, and other third world countries with lenient environmental regulations. A stunning exception, however, is the gold mining industry, particularly in Nevada. Although Nevada is known as the Silver State, its gold production in 1998 reached 8,865,000 ounces, a state record, and a 16.8 percent increase over the former record in 1997. Nevada accounts for 74 percent of all gold mined in the United States and 11 percent of world production. If Nevada were a separate country, it would rank as the world's third-largest producer of gold, behind only South Africa and Australia. The increase of gold production in 1998 came largely from the Placer Dome Pipeline Mine and Homestake's Ruby Hill Mine, which began operations in 1997 and achieved full production in 1998.

Most people, when they think of Nevada, think of casinos. The booming population in Nevada has settled in the metropolitan areas of Las Vegas and Reno, which cater to the gaming industry. Approximately 90 percent of Nevada's 2.1 million people live in these two metropolitan areas. The remainder of the state looks much like it did a half century ago: 200,000 people spread thinly over 90,000 square miles. Although land and homes are cheap, jobs typically pay little more than the minimum wage. Things are quite different in the mining industry. In 1998, the average pay for a miner was $52,824, substantially above Nevada's average annual salary of $30,159. The mining industry employed 13,236 workers, and an estimated additional 43,000 jobs directly relate to the mining industry. Although the industry has a significant economic impact on the state as a whole, it is in the rural communities near the mines where the impact is greatest. Rural Nevada has considerable enthusiasm for the mining industry. In Eureka County, for example, 82 percent of employment is related to the gold mining industry.

In the United States, most mining occurs on land once owned by the federal government, thanks to the General Mining Law of 1872, which allows anyone who discovers and develops a valuable mineral deposit on federal land to obtain title to the land and to mine the resource free of charge and without competition. Although the law exempts federal lands reserved for particular purposes (for example, national parks), all other federal land is subject to the General Mining Law. Here is the kicker: the law allows miners to obtain title to the land for $5 an acre, a price that has remained unchanged since the nineteenth century. This arrangement recently prompted then Secretary of the Interior Bruce Babbitt to describe the General Mining Law as "an obscene example of corporate welfare." Defenders of the system, such as Richard Lawson, a retired four-star Air Force general who recently headed the National Mining Association, claim that reforming the law would threaten national security. "Destroying the mining law will risk the lives of our sons and daughters, for many will surely die in battle on some foreign shore because of it. Without the protection of the mining law, America cannot get the minerals it must have to remain free and secure, and we will go to war to get those precious metals." It's not clear how the general fits gold into this national security risk. In any event, although practically everyone agrees that the law needs a substantial overhaul, efforts to amend it have repeatedly failed.

In May 1994, Secretary Babbitt signed documents that transferred approximately 1,950 acres of federal land in Nevada to Barrick Gold Corporation, a Canadian company. Barrick paid the government $9,765 for the richest gold deposit in the United States, worth an estimated $10 billion. Disgusted that the General Mining Law mandated such a result, Babbitt called the transaction the "biggest gold heist since the days of Butch Cassidy." The attendant publicity from Babbitt's comments embarrassed Congress into placing a one-year moratorium on new claims to title to federal lands. Each year since, Congress has renewed the moratorium.

Barrick has done quite nicely with the land it received from Secretary Babbitt. It has developed two mines, the Betze-Post Mine and the Miekle Mine, in the area of the middle Humboldt River, located about a mile apart on the Carlin Trend and known collectively as the Goldstrike property. The company mines more than 435,000 tons of ore each day, which contain an average of 0.16 ounce of gold per ton. In 2001, Barrick's Betze-Post Mine, the largest open-pit gold mine in the United States, had a total production of 1.5 million ounces; the Miekle Mine produced 700,000 ounces, the highest production of any underground gold mine in the

United States. At a total cost of $193 per ounce but a realized price of $317 per ounce (between premium gold sales and the spot market), Barrick has seen a solid return on the $9,765 it paid the federal government for the Goldstrike property. Indeed, the heist is worse than anything Secretary Babbitt could ever have imagined. At the time Barrick acquired the Gold-strike property, the estimated reserves were 600,000 ounces of gold. But in a 2002 Analysts' Briefing (pitched to potential investors), Barrick proudly boasted: "At the end of 2001, reserves stood at 20.4 million ounces, after total production to date of 21 million ounces." The Goldstrike property is one of thirty-six operating gold mines in Nevada, most clustered in north-central Nevada along the Humboldt River and its tributaries. In June 2001, Barrick announced that it would acquire Homestake Mining Com-pany, thus creating the largest gold company in the world.*

Boom-and-bust cycles have historically plagued the gold mining industry, and recent years have been no exception. When inflation spun out of control in the early 1980s, investors flocked to the security of gold hold-ings. Prices soared, once hitting over $400 per ounce. Between 1989 and 1996, prices remained at an average of $375 an ounce. Gold companies responded to the high prices by ramping up exploration and production. In 1997, gold began to lose some of its luster as the stock market contin-ued its surge upward, the weakening Asian economies encouraged central banks to sell off large amounts of gold in exchange for stable foreign cur-rencies, and the creation of the new European Central Bank and its currency, the euro, produced further sales of gold. In June 2002, gold sold for around $320 an ounce on the spot markets. Although the industry has increased production, prices have decreased, requiring extensive cost-cutting and causing the consolidation of smaller players in the industry. The decreasing price has also resulted in significant economic dislocation in rural communities dependent on gold mining operations. Although some companies are extremely profitable, other marginal operations have shut down over the past three years.

There is something surely perplexing about the obvious unsustainabil-ity of gold mining. Not only is the value of gold entirely whimsical, depending on foreign policies of various countries, currency decisions of central banks, and the fashion industry, but the resource itself is finite. In

---

* In early 2002, Newmont Mining Corporation became the world's largest gold producer when it acquired Normandy Mining Limited of Australia.

1999, gold resources in Nevada totaled approximately 100 million ounces. These resources will sustain gold production at substantial levels for fifteen to twenty years. The legacy it will leave is questionable.

The practice of mining has undergone a profound transformation. Movies and novels celebrate the image of an independent prospector, pickax in hand, heading into the hills to unearth his claim. An alternative portrait has a miner panning for gold in a stream using a tin pan to separate the heavier gold nuggets from the lighter soil materials. In terms of modern mining practices, these images are curiosities of history. They succeeded only as long as gold was readily available in large nuggets and in shallow deposits near the earth's surface. When these methods no longer produced gold, miners turned to placer mining techniques. The placer miner first removed all surface vegetation and soil. He then dumped the gold-bearing soil, known as "pay dirt," into a sluice box, which is a wooden or metal trough with intermittent dams. The miner would run water through the sluice box and wash away the lighter materials—sands, silts, and clays—leaving the gold caught behind the internal dams. When the shallow claims played out, the miners dug drifts and vertical shafts to remove ore deposits from deeper in the earth.

The signature of today's gold mining industry is the open-pit mine, which allows the development of low-grade deposits. Open-pit mines can extract gold particles that are microscopic in size, literally too small to be seen by the naked eye. First, large construction vehicles remove hundreds of tons of ore, grind it down to smaller particles, then place it in enormous piles, perhaps 200 feet high. Next, a cyanide solution drips on the top of the pile, leaches through the pile, and amalgamates with gold as it moves downward. The solution is collected from beneath the pile and piped to a refinery for final processing. In the latest development in mining technology, Barrick processes gold at its Goldstrike property using an autoclave system or a roaster. The autoclave—essentially a giant pressure cooker—oxidizes the sulfide materials, which exposes the gold particles. The roasting process vaporizes carbon components of the ore; the gold-bearing solids are then put through an electrochemical process. In both processes, a carbon-in-leach system then extracts the gold from the slurry. The scale of these enterprises is stupendous. The Barrick Betze-Post Mine has a diameter of one and one-half miles, covers 8,000 acres of land, and reaches down 1,700 feet into the earth. It may take as much as fifty tons of ore to yield one ounce of gold, or three tons of ore to produce enough gold for a single wedding ring.

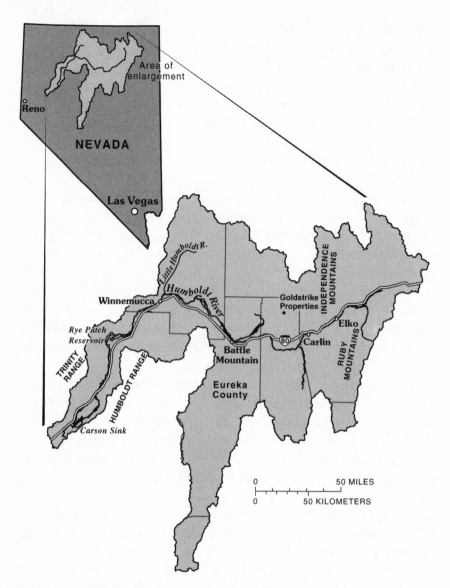

FIGURE 12.1. The Humboldt River basin in northern Nevada.

The Humboldt River, which begins and ends in Nevada, drains an area of 17,000 square miles in a sparsely populated section of north-central Nevada. In 2000, the population of the area's largest town—Elko—was 16,708. The Humboldt's headwaters are sixty miles from the Utah border, in the Independence and Ruby Mountains. Interstate 80 roughly parallels the Humboldt for its entire length, past the towns of Elko, Carlin, Battle Mountain, and Winnemucca, where the Little Humboldt River feeds into the Humboldt and the river turns southwest into a long, narrow basin between the Humboldt and Trinity Mountain ranges. Most of the river is diverted at Rye Patch Dam for irrigation by farmers. What little water escapes the dam finally evaporates in the desolate expanse of the Humboldt Sink approximately sixty miles from Reno. Under the prior appropriation doctrine, the river is fully allocated for agricultural purposes, primarily to irrigate alfalfa fields.

Until recently, groundwater withdrawals in the Humboldt River basin were for municipal use and irrigation. During the last decade and a half, groundwater withdrawals have increased significantly due to extensive pumping in "dewatering" operations at fourteen major gold mines centered on the Carlin Trend. In open-pit mining, heavy machinery digs the pit in concentric circles that get wider and deeper as the ore is removed from the pit. Eventually, the pit becomes so deep that it hits the water table. At that point, the bottom of the pit fills with water. This presents a problem for the mine operator, who cannot continue mining until the water is removed, a process known as "dewatering" the pit. To the mine operators, the water at the bottom of the pit is a waste product, a nuisance to be eliminated at the lowest possible cost, rather than a valuable resource to be conserved. Although the water has no value to the operators, the water is high-quality glacier water that can be traced back to the Holocene age, about 8,000 years ago. Bottled water companies would love to get their hands on this water, but it is apparently too far from a sizable population base to justify the transportation costs. So the mines must get rid of it, a lot of it.

To dewater the mine at Barrick's Goldstrike property, the company needed to lower the water table 1,650 feet. Barrick drilled seventy wells up to twenty-four inches in diameter to depths of 2,000 feet at a cost of $2 million per well. Dewatering the mine requires Barrick to remove from the Goldstrike property 30,000 gallons per minute; that's an acre-foot of water every eleven minutes. The company uses a small portion of this water in its gold processing operation, reinjects some of it into the aquifer, and has entered into an agreement with a neighboring ranch to irrigate 10,000 acres of alfalfa and to expand grazing areas for cattle. One might wonder about the wisdom, in the driest state in the country, of using groundwater for alfalfa, a high-water-use crop with a very low economic value, to feed cattle. But the water has no other value to Barrick. As it is, there is a lot left over. Barrick gets rid of the remaining water through a twenty-mile pipeline that empties into the Humboldt River.

Tom Myers was working on his Ph.D. in hydrology at the University of Nevada, Reno, when the Sierra Club hired him to investigate the issues associated with dewatering. He was flabbergasted by what he discovered. An idealistic young scientist, Myers cares deeply about issues of what has come to be called "environmental justice." When corporations and governments make decisions about, for example, where to site hazardous waste landfills, often the locations are smack in the middle of low-income racial-minority communities. Exposure to the dangerous chemicals discarded in the landfill disproportionately impacts local residents. Mine dewatering struck Myers as a dramatic example of environmental injustice.

In the course of his work for the Sierra Club, Myers met Glen Miller, a professor of environmental and resource sciences at the University of Nevada, Reno, who studies the mining industry. In 1995, they decided to found Great Basin Mine Watch, a nonprofit organization composed of traditional environmentalists, Native Americans, ranchers, and an independent prospector, to monitor the effects of mine development. Since then, Myers has become the organization's full-time director and has embarked on a fund-raising campaign to sustain its activities. Myers says that he "loves the Great Basin Desert" and thinks that dewatering is "destroying thousands of miles of the Great Basin" and, in particular, harming the Western Shoshone homelands.

Myers and Miller are particularly concerned about the quantity of groundwater pumped in the dewatering process. Each year, the mines pump groundwater at an amount that is twice the annual flow of the Humboldt River at Winnemucca. The groundwater being pumped today will create a deficit for future years. When the mines shut down the pumps, two things will happen. First, water will seek an equilibrium and flow back into the dewatered pits, eventually creating "pit lakes." The Betze-Post pit lake will hold 580,000 acre-feet of water, making it Nevada's second-largest human-made lake, exceeded only by Lake Mead. Due to the complicated chemical processes used in extracting the ore, the water in these new lakes is likely to be contaminated by arsenic, antimony, and other heavy metals.

Second, once the mines cease dewatering, the stress on the Humboldt River, tributary creeks, and adjacent springs will be profound. By the year 2010, the mines will have pumped 4 or 5 million acre-feet of groundwater, most of it from dewatering, and most of it dumped into the Humboldt

River, where it will flow out of the basin into the Humboldt Sink. To put it in perspective, the mines will have pumped one and a half trillion gallons, give or take a few billion, or twenty times the average annual flow of the Humboldt River. Today's overdrafting of the aquifer and dramatic lowering of the groundwater table will reduce surface flows in the Humboldt in the future. It is not a question of whether, but only of when and how much. You may ask: where is the water going to come from to create the pit lakes? Gravity causes water to seek the lowest level, and for twenty years, the mines have sucked water from adjoining uplands. Those lands consist of porous soils that have transmitted the water pumped by the mines. That process will continue. Dewatering has already caused the Humboldt River to recharge water that has reached the mine pits. But we haven't noticed because the water dumped into the Humboldt River from dewatering effectively hides the fact that pumping has reduced the Humboldt's baseflow. When the mines cease dewatering, today's temporary but artificial period of abundance will be replaced by a huge sucking sound as the water in the river percolates into the soil in a frantic but futile effort to reach the water table some 1,500 feet below the river bottom.

But for now, the Humboldt is enjoying historically high levels of water flow, even though, paradoxically, the surrounding water table has fallen as much as 1,000 feet. All will be well until the situation changes—when the mining companies finish mining the gold reserves in fifteen to twenty years, cease the dewatering operation, and then move on in search of other gold exploration opportunities. The Humboldt River faces a grim future.

Meanwhile, industry hydrologists insist that the impact on surface flows will be minimal. They argue that the dewatering comes from deep bedrock aquifers unconnected to the shallower alluvial aquifers. As with most complicated questions of hydrology, each side can rely on a range of data and produce results that cannot be dismissed easily as "true" or "false." It all depends on the assumptions built into the hydrologic model. Nevertheless, the U.S. Bureau of Land Management's (BLM) 1991 environmental impact statement (EIS) for Barrick's Betze project contained a stunning set of conclusions. "The cone of depression created in the water table by dewatering operations would continue to *expand* for approximately 25 to 30 years *after* dewatering ceases. . . . Throughout most of the recovery period, groundwater would flow radially into the Betze pit from the surrounding rock. Therefore, all wells, seeps, springs, and creeks would be hydrologically up-gradient of the Betze pit. . . . " (italics added). If the surface waters are up-gradient, then by the law of gravity, the water must move from the surface into the pit—over decades at least—until the cone of depression refills. In addition, it defies common sense to suggest that groundwater pumping of such magnitude will not impact surface flows. In law, many arguments are "reasonable," while others are simply ludicrous. What's the difference? Lawyers sometimes joke that a reasonable argument is one that you can make while keeping a straight face. The argument that pumping 4 to 5 million acre-feet of groundwater will not significantly affect the Humboldt River and its tributary springs and creeks fails the "straight face" test.

In June 2000, Tom Myers completed a hydrologic study that analyzed the economic and environmental impacts of gold mining. He concluded that "[t]he complex hydrology of the area renders estimates of impacts very uncertain. However, it is certain that river and stream flows will decrease." Myers has found it challenging to communicate these concepts. "Almost every newspaper reporter asks me: 'Can you see the effects of this dewatering now?' I really have to say—no, it's not drying up the river now because they're pumping it into the river. Reporters have a hard time grasping the long-term consequences and the ranchers are the same way. Plus, the industry claims it's all deep water. That's ridiculous! The deep well pumping and surface flows are connected."

Nevada law would normally prohibit groundwater pumping in excess of natural recharge from rainfall. But in 1989, the Nevada state engineer decided to allow overpumping of the basin. According to Hugh Ricci, the current state engineer, the decision was made on the ground that dewatering was "a temporary use of groundwater, the quantity was relatively small and the basin would come back into equilibrium in a relatively short time." In hindsight, the engineer was wrong on all three counts. Few people would describe thirty to forty years as temporary, 4 to 5 million acre-feet as relatively small, or sixty to one hundred years as a relatively short time.

The fact that the mines treat this water as a waste product has resulted in uncertainty as to whether the mines need to obtain a water-right permit under Nevada law. Nevada applies the prior appropriation doctrine both to the diversion of surface water and to the pumping of groundwater. This system usually protects existing farmers and ranchers from harm from a junior pumper, such as the mines. The prior appropriation system requires that permit holders use the water for a beneficial purpose. However, most western states treat mine dewatering as an activity that does *not* require a water-right permit because the dewatered water is not used for a beneficial purpose. Thus, quite perversely, the rules of prior appropriation do not apply to mines. One might have thought that logic would dictate the opposite. But that's where economics comes in.

In the late 1990s, the Newmont Gold Company filed a number of applications for prior appropriation permits, which Hugh Ricci granted in April 2001. Recognizing that the mining industry "has been a predominant economic force in Nevada since before statehood," Ricci concluded that dewatering was a beneficial use of water, even though the "use" most mines make of the water is to dump it into the Humboldt River. Unless he allowed Newmont to dewater the pit, the mining would cease. According to Mike Turnipseed, former state engineer and current director of the Nevada Department of Conservation and Natural Resources, the state is nevertheless concerned about the long-term impacts of dewatering. Turnipseed has mused: "Is the Humboldt River going to go dry for a century? We don't think so. We'd like to have a scientist tell us."

He's gotten his wish. An April 2002 final environmental impact statement, prepared by the BLM in connection with Newmont's proposal to deepen its Gold Quarry pit, concluded: "Flows in springs, seeps and streams would eventually return to premining conditions after pumping has ceased and the groundwater cone of depression has recovered sufficiently. Recovery of the water table to near original levels may take over 100 years." The good news is that "95 percent of groundwater recovery would occur within 60 years after dewatering ceases."

Nevada averages nine inches of rain per year, and even small variations in groundwater–surface water interactions may profoundly affect stream and spring flows and fish and wildlife habitat. A 1995 U.S. Geological Survey report concluded that expected groundwater pumping by mines would significantly impact surface flows. A recent report by Newmont suggests that significant impacts on springs and creeks have already occurred. Several springs have dried up, and dozens of others are threatened. In the future, the Humboldt River's flow in one location may fall by as much as 25 percent. The Newmont study also predicts that Suzy and Lower Maggie Creeks, tributaries of the Humboldt River, will completely dry up during the late summer and early fall. Rock Creek will also suffer a 25 percent reduction in flow. Maggie and Rock Creeks are home to the Lahontan cutthroat trout, a species listed as threatened under the Endangered Species Act.

Long-term losers from the diminished flows in the Humboldt River will be the region's long-term residents—the Western Shoshone people and the farmers and ranchers, all of whom rely on the river to grow alfalfa for their cattle. The Humboldt River is fully appropriated: in a typical year, farmers divert the entire flow of the Humboldt River so that no water is left to flow into the Humboldt Sink, the barren terminus of the river. For the moment, the farmers are happy because the unprecedentedly high flows attributable to an augmented supply from dewatering the mines provide farmers with literally more water than they can use. This era of excess will come to a crashing halt when dewatering ceases. Then, farmers will be faced with the daunting task of trying to prove that a specific mining company "caused" the loss of their surface water rights. Good luck. Failing to secure relief from the mines, farmers may begin to challenge each other's rights under the prior appropriation system, a fratricidal process of litigation that will splinter the community. One can confidently predict that some farmland will be taken out of production because the Humboldt River will not provide adequate water to sustain irrigation at current levels.

The Western Shoshone people describe their ancestral homelands, the Great Basin of Nevada, as *Newe Sogobia* or "the people's earth mother." The region's mountains, plants, animals, and waters all are associated with stories fundamental to Shoshone identity that recognize their kinship with the land. The Shoshone's history, like that of many other native peoples, contains sad chapters of unrelenting exploitation, as settlers, with the approval and support of the federal government, entered tribal lands, mined the resources, and then pleaded for further access to and ownership of tribal lands. A massacre of 375 Shoshone in 1862 and 1863, under the direction of Colonel Patrick Edward Connor, caused the Shoshone to accept the Treaty of Ruby Valley to stop the slaughter. The treaty opened Shoshone lands to mining by white settlers. Many contemporary open-pit gold mines are located in Newe Sogobia, but the tribe has received precious little for these lands or the gold within them. In 1979, the Shoshone received $26 million from the Indian Claims Commission for 24 million acres, or little more than $1 per acre, for ancestral land then inhabited by nontribal members. The value of gold extracted from these lands between 1980 and 1997, according to a tribal estimate, is $21 billion.

In the early 1990s, the Shoshone people began to notice diminished flows in their springs. Shoshone religion, like Hopi religion, attaches great spiritual significance to water. The Shoshone believe that *Bah-o-hah*, "water spirits," live in springs and creeks. The cultural place of water in Shoshone life is central. The Shoshone conduct medicinal ceremonies at water sources to promote healing and well-being. If the springs dry up, the Shoshone predict a future of perpetual poverty, loss of their lands, harm to their culture, and ultimately a decline in their population. The tribe's environmental coordinator, Bernice Lalo, described the drying up of springs as "cultural genocide." Mine dewatering has already dried up springs near the Betze Mine and the Lone Tree Mine. Environmental impact studies have documented that mine dewatering may dry up additional springs and creeks near the Twin Creeks, Mule Canyon, and Newmont's Gold Quarry mines. The Shoshone are also concerned about dewatering's impact on religious sites at Rock Creek and Tosawihi quarries. The Shoshone have good reason for concern: without water, their cultural and economic integrity will almost certainly be destroyed.

To the state of Nevada, gold mining's economic benefits apparently outweigh the industry's impact on the environment, including the state's springs and rivers. Humboldt basin farmers have not strongly opposed mine dewatering, perhaps because they believe that the mining companies will eventually purchase their lands and water rights. The Shoshone people, in contrast, do not accept these trade-offs but lack the political or economic leverage to halt dewatering.

Chapter 13

All's Fair in Love and Water

"Oysters, down in Oyster Bay, do it. Let's do it, let's fall in love."
—Cole Porter

Oysters enjoy a legendary reputation as aphrodisiacs. Lori McKean and Bill Whitbeck, authors of *The Joy of Oysters*, describe oysters as "nature's Viagra." Casanova, they suggest, considered oysters "a spur to the spirit and to love" and would down fifty oysters and *then* feed, be fed, and slurp oysters with his lover. On the other hand, macho James Bond, Agent 007, rebuffed a voluptuous companion's proffer of oysters by saying, "Well, I don't need these." Perhaps he feared for his reputation as a lady's man; on the other hand, it's just as well that the world was not forced to endure a film starring an oyster-stimulated James Bond.

When estuary water temperatures trigger the reproductive urge, female and male oysters release eggs and sperm into the water. Given that oysters do not move together to copulate or do anything else to enhance reproduction, it's a wonder that any little oysters develop. The eggs and sperm float off in search of each other. Should they join to become spat—young oysters—they need a place to call home. Tiny hairs protruding from the developing shell allow spat to feed on algae and plankton. After a couple of weeks of floating around munching algae, spat weigh enough to settle to the bottom and attach to whatever happens to be there. Unless it's something solid, spat will not survive. The usual medium—called cultch—is old oyster shells. Once nestled in, spat remain in place and, with luck, grow into adult oysters. For this to happen, however, the estuary must receive an adequate flow of freshwater.

The Apalachicola River empties into the Gulf of Mexico at Apalachicola Bay, off the southernmost point on Florida's panhandle. A wide, shallow estuary, Apalachicola Bay covers 210 square miles behind a chain of barrier islands. Robert J. "Skip" Livingston, a professor of biological science at Florida State University and author of *Resource Atlas of the Apalachicola Estuary*, describes the bay as "an anachronism, the last big

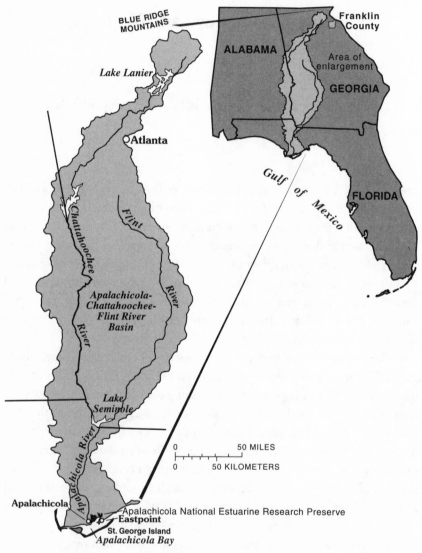

FIGURE 13.1. Apalachicola-Chattahoochee-Flint River basin.

coastal ecosystem that works." Apalachicola Bay supports an astonishingly diverse ecosystem that yields 90 percent of Florida's (and 10 percent of the country's) commercial oyster harvest. The most productive estuary in Florida, the bay provides important nursery habitat for shrimp, red snapper, speckled sea trout, and blue crabs. Commercial fishing in the region generates more than $100 million per year. Congress, in 1979, created the Apalachicola National Estuarine Research Reserve, almost 250,000 acres, to provide long-term protection of the estuary.

Archaeologists have discovered oyster shell dumps, called "middens," on the shores of Apalachicola Bay that confirm that Native Americans ate oysters for thousands of years before European colonists began to slurp this curious bivalve creature. Pierre de la Charlevoix, a late-seventeenth-century explorer, described the bay as "the kingdom of oysters, as the great Bank of Newfoundland, and the gulf and the river St. Lawrence are that of the cod-fish." Apalachicola Bay oysters, *Crassostrea virginica*, known as the American or eastern oyster, are distinguished by their rounded green shell and mild, slightly sweet flavor.

Oyster fishing in Apalachicola Bay is centered in the town of Apalachicola (population 2,334 in 2001) and the neighboring community of Eastpoint (population 2,158). To describe the area as rural is an understatement. The population of the entire county (Franklin) is only 11,057; an area of 544 square miles, it has a population density of only twenty persons per square mile. It takes an hour-and-a-half drive to reach a Wal-Mart or a movie theater. The entire county does not have a single stoplight, only a blinking red light in the town of Apalachicola.

Located eighty miles southwest of Tallahassee and sixty-five miles east of Panama City, the town of Apalachicola remains a quaint fishing village, unlike other areas on the Florida coast that have become resort towns. Oysters occupy such a central place in the economy of the town that the local radio station has the call letters WOYS and bills itself as "Oyster Radio, 100.5." Most oystering in Apalachicola Bay occurs on public reefs, oyster bars open to anyone. On approximately 600 acres, the government has granted leases to certain families, including Tommy Ward's. In the early 1900s, Tommy's great-grandfather developed oyster beds on barren bay bottom and began to cultivate oysters. The state eventually rewarded his efforts with a perpetual right to maintain these beds. Tommy and his family have pioneered an oystering technique that uses a scrape to harvest oysters. This device washes sediment off the oysters, which makes it easier for spat to grab hold. They also discovered a better cultch—scallop shells, which they plant on their beds to catch spat.

Although Tommy's family has made a living oystering in Apalachicola Bay for four generations, the fishing industry that supports the town is declining. Fewer than 500 fishermen remain. Many oystermen have begun working at a new jail nearby. The new prison jobs offer steady hours and decent pay, but the town of Apalachicola's way of life may change forever.

Apalachicola Bay oysters depend on water from the Apalachicola River. Estuaries are remarkably dynamic ecosystems that exist at the buffer zone between a river's freshwater and the ocean's saline water. Skip Livingston suggests that water flow in the Apalachicola estuary performs a function similar to blood in a human body. Freshwater flows move dissolved nutrients and particulate organic materials from upland drainage areas into the estuary. Simultaneously, these flows remove excretory products from sedentary organisms. The Nature Conservancy's biohydrologist Brian Richter and his colleagues have shown that variations in freshwater flow from day to day, and season to season, may be more important to the ecological health (or degradation) of a river than the presence of industrial pollutants. In particular, naturally occurring floods perform a critical function in maintaining the full spectrum of biological diversity. Oysters in Apalachicola Bay depend on nutrients washed downstream in the Apalachicola River by periodic flooding of the extensive swamps in the floodplain adjoining the river. Oysters also depend on a sufficient amount of freshwater arriving at the estuary to encourage oyster spawning and discourage shellfish predators from moving into the estuary.

When the Apalachicola estuary receives smaller volumes of freshwater, that creates two problems for oysters. First, lower flows mean fewer nutrients coming down the river and less food for oysters. For oyster nutrition, phytoplankton (microscopic plant life that drifts in the ocean) provide a critical link between inorganic compounds and organic matter. Phytoplankton productivity correlates directly with the input of freshwater from the Apalachicola River into the estuary: reduced freshwater flows therefore reduce phytoplankton productivity. Second, less freshwater means that the water in the estuary has a higher salinity. Higher salinity enables ocean-dwelling oyster predators, such as stone crabs, oyster drills (a type of snail that, as its name suggests, has a rasplike tongue that bores a hole through the oyster shell), and queen conchs, to move from the Gulf of Mexico into the estuary and onto the oyster beds. According to Graham Lewis, a scientist with the Northwest Florida Water Management District, commercial oyster harvests significantly correlate with river flows with about a two-year lag: low flows one year produce lower oyster harvests two years later. Skip Livingston and other scientists have found that high salinity in the estuary significantly contributes to oyster predation.

The Apalachicola-Chattahoochee-Flint (ACF) River basin embraces almost 20,000 square miles in Georgia, Alabama, and Florida (figure 13.1). The headwaters of the Chattahoochee River rise in the Blue Ridge Mountains of north Georgia. The river flows 434 miles down from the mountains, through Lake Lanier, a popular recreational spot that may draw 800,000 visitors on a summer holiday weekend, and past metropolitan Atlanta, where it serves as the area's drinking water supply. As it flows south to its confluence with the Flint River at Lake Seminole, it forms the border between Georgia and Alabama. More than a dozen dams and hydro-electric plants strictly regulate the Chattahoochee's flow.

The Flint River originates south of Atlanta and flows 350 miles, first south, then curving west to join the Chattahoochee at Lake Seminole. Below the lake, the river, now called the Apalachicola, enters Florida and flows 106 miles to its terminus at Apalachicola Bay in the Gulf of Mexico. Florida's largest river, with an average flow of almost 20,000 cubic feet per second (cfs), the Apalachicola has the most extensive forested floodplain of any river in Florida. The river, normally several hundred feet wide, expands to four and one-half miles during high flows. The lower reaches, part of the Gulf Atlantic Coastal Plain, consist of shoals, tupelo swamps, channels, sloughs, and natural levees. The Apalachicola River supports the largest variety of freshwater fish in Florida, the second-highest concentration of amphibians and reptiles in North America, and rare crayfish, freshwater mussels, torreya trees, and a species of tree found nowhere else in the world—the Florida yew.

Until recently, Apalachicola Bay has been healthy. However, three major factors have contributed to harming the bay: (1) upstream diversions of water from the Chattahoochee for Atlanta's booming population; (2) uncontrolled diversions from the Flint along with groundwater pumping adjacent to the Flint for agricultural irrigation by Georgia farmers; and (3) extensive dredging of the Apalachicola River by the U.S. Army Corps of Engineers (Corps). A critical pressure on water in the ACF basin is population growth. Since 1950, the population of the Atlanta metropolitan region has grown from less than 500,000 to over 4 million. Eighty-nine percent of the population in the ACF basin resides in Georgia, most in metropolitan Atlanta. Between 1990 and 2000, the state's population jumped 26 percent, the sixth-largest increase of any state. Water use for municipal and industrial purposes is projected to climb from 618 million gallons per day (mgd) in 1995 to 872 mgd by 2050. Metropolitan Atlanta's breakneck growth is devouring fifty acres of land a day. To put such dramatic population growth in perspective, consider that metropolitan Atlanta grows by the total population of the town of Apalachicola every month.

The irrigation practices of Georgia farmers also have undergone a profound transformation in recent years. Southern Georgia benefits from average annual precipitation of fifty inches of rain, more than enough water for southern Georgia farmers to raise corn, soybeans, and wheat by dryland farming. According to Dr. James E. Hook, director of an agricultural research center at the University of Georgia, improvements in the technology of center-pivot irrigation systems made them increasingly attractive for irrigating larger tracts of land. In the 1970s, Georgia farmers began clearing scrub oak and pine from lands too sandy for dryland farming but perfect, if irrigated, for row crops and vegetables. Center-pivot irrigation systems tapped into the abundant resources of the Floridan Aquifer. One of the largest aquifers in the United States, the Floridan has enormous annual recharge from precipitation. In the Flint River basin in southwest Georgia, shallow wells less than 100 feet deep easily yield 1,000–2,000 gallons per minute. Until recently, Georgia law required neither a permit to install a high-capacity groundwater well nor a report by the farmer of the amount pumped.

In the 1980s, Georgia farmers faced severe summer droughts and plummeting prices for various commodities, including soybeans and wheat. The only farmers who stayed in business were irrigators. Irrigation also enabled farmers to expand the number of acres dedicated to peanuts and cotton. Between the early 1970s and the early 1990s, the number of acres irrigated by Georgia farmers jumped fivefold to more than 1 million. In 1988, the state began to require irrigation permits but issued almost 12,000 within three years. Once issued, the permits required no further reports, conservation measures, or restrictions during drought. The early 1990s witnessed substantial changes in farm ownership as successful irrigation farmers bought out now-bankrupt dryland farmers. Once more, irrigation increased. Banks, not inclined to take risks with dryland farming, began to demand that farmers submit irrigation plans before lending money for seed and fertilizers. According to the Georgia Extension Service, irrigated acreage in Georgia jumped to approximately 1.5 million acres in 2000. In 1998, legislation purported to regulate agricultural wells that produced more than 100,000 gallons per day, but it had enormous loopholes. The law grandfathered all existing users, granted permits in perpetuity, and regulated only the pumping rate and the maximum number of acres, rather than a specific volume of water per year. Between 1970 and 1990, groundwater withdrawals in the ACF basin increased by 240 percent. In 1995, Georgia farmers used 350 mgd of ACF basin water, most of it groundwater. Agricultural water use in Georgia is expected to increase to 569 mgd by 2050.

The new millennium, according to Hook, "brought a whole new dimension to irrigation in Florida. Fear! What had seemed an inexhaustible supply of runoff was now challenged by Florida and Alabama." The neighboring states claimed that Georgia farmers who depended on the Floridan Aquifer were reducing flow in the Flint River. Severe droughts in 1998 and 1999 caused the Georgia Environmental Protection Division (EPD) to stop issuing new permits, but farmers ignored the law and installed hundreds of new wells and irrigation systems.

EPD and Flint River farmers eventually hammered out an agreement: EPD would grant permits for the illegally installed wells, the farmers would agree not to drill new wells, and proposed legislation would restrict pumping during severe droughts. In 2000, the Georgia legislature ratified this agreement, known as the Flint River Drought Protection Act (Flint River Act). La Niña weather patterns produced a third consecutive drought in 2000, but the Flint River Act was not yet in effect. Farmers continued to irrigate while Atlanta and neighboring cities mandated bans on outdoor water use, a dichotomy that brought forth charges that farmers were using excessive amounts of water. ACF basin rivers experienced record low water levels.

In March 2001, as the drought continued for a fourth year, Harold Reheis, director of EPD, declared a "severe drought," which triggered the Flint River Act. Under EPD regulations, an auction was held—using the Internet—in which farmers who diverted surface water from the Flint quoted per-acre prices that they would accept for refraining from irrigating during the 2001 season. After several rounds of bidding, the state accepted bids averaging $135 per acre to take 33,000 acres out of production. To fund the program, the state used a portion of its share of the national tobacco settlement money. Not all Georgians are happy with the Flint River Act. The *Atlanta Journal-Constitution* editorialized: "It's a stupid idea to reward farmers for not irrigating crops. . . . [The Flint River Act] is, in fact, nothing more than another farm subsidy."

Further harm has been done to Apalachicola Bay by extensive dredging of the Apalachicola River undertaken by the Corps to allow a tiny number of barges to carry fertilizer, fuel, coal ore, asphalt, and agricultural products to small ports in Georgia and Alabama. The number of barges on the river declined from 204 in 1993 to only forty-seven in 1999. The $3 million annual cost of dredging comes to $30,000 per barge. The dredging has created enormous sand piles along the river's bank and has cut off twenty-five miles of the river's floodplain. Dredging threatens oysters and other marine life in Apalachicola Bay by reducing the amount of nutrients that floodwaters remove from the floodplain and transport down the river to the estuary. In 2001, U.S. Senator Bob Graham of Florida attacked the dredging as the poster child for wasteful Corps projects. Congress in the same year appropriated $4.9 million to remove the dredged sand piles. The Corps' dredging led an environmental organization American Rivers to place the Apalachicola on its 2002 list of America's Most Endangered Rivers.

A double whammy occurs when droughts cause low flows. Farmers have the greatest need to irrigate during drought conditions, precisely when river flows and surface reservoirs are also low, which requires municipalities to increase pumping to cover the shortfall. The combination further reduces freshwater inflow to the estuary. A 1998 U.S. Army Corps of Engineers environmental impact statement (EIS) concluded that "reduced river inflow would result in reduced nutrient loading. Decreased nutrient loading has the potential to have far-reaching ramifications throughout the estuarine system." In the normally drab language of environmental impact statements, this conclusion was the equivalent of uppercase, bold-faced letters, followed by an exclamation point! The EIS concluded that the decline in oysters might "reach as high as 50 percent under certain conditions of critical low flows." The Floridan Aquifer contributes significant groundwater discharge to baseflow in the Flint River. Indeed, the EIS found that "the effect of pumping 1 gallon of groundwater from the Upper Floridan Aquifer would be about a 0.6-gallon reduction in the groundwater contribution to stream flow." In other words, 60 percent of the groundwater pumped by Georgia farmers would otherwise discharge into the Flint River.

The ACF basin is the centerpiece of a bitter struggle among Alabama, Georgia, and Florida over the right to use the water. The fight erupted in 1989 when the Corps, in response to a request by Georgia, recommended that water stored in Lake Lanier be reallocated to meet the future needs of Georgia cities. Alarmed that Georgia might be attempting to hoard the water, Florida and Alabama filed suit in 1990 to stop the Corps from reallocating the water. The struggle eventually led, in 1997, to an agreement among the states known as the Apalachicola-Chattahoochee-Flint River Basin Compact (ACF Compact), ratified by all three legislatures and approved by Congress.

Struggles over interstate rivers have beset the U.S. West for over 100 years. The great rivers in the American West, including the Columbia, Snake, Colorado, Missouri, Rio Grande, Platte, Republican, and Arkansas, run through or serve as boundaries between states. Squabbles among states have led to settlements in the form of interstate compacts, U.S. Supreme Court decisions and decrees, and congressional intervention. But the ACF Compact is unusual, as it allocates waters in an eastern river. Its necessity exposes as myth the idea that the East has an unlimited quantity of water.

The ACF Compact authorizes the ACF Basin Commission to "develop an allocation formula for equitably apportioning the *surface waters* of the ACF basin among the States. . . ." The states were supposed to agree on this formula by December 31, 1998, or the compact would terminate. Despite a series of time extensions, the states failed to reach a settlement until January 2002, when the negotiators announced that they had agreed "in principle" to a formula. But they released no details, and the agreement quickly unraveled. In March 2002, the states returned to the bargaining table. The apportionment only of surface water is curious indeed, for it exempts pumping by Flint River farmers from control by the commission. Curious, too, is the compact's voting-rights mechanism, which grants each state one vote, but requires that the decisions be unanimous. These provisions effectively give Georgia a veto over any allocation formula and take off the table pumping by Georgia farmers. As a practical matter, Georgia cities and farms can divert and pump with impunity.

Although I have not found anyone in Florida who wishes to take the credit (or blame) for these provisions, there is someone who represented Georgia who will do so. "I drafted the compact," boasts Professor Charles

T. DuMars of the University of New Mexico School of Law. A sage and wily veteran of western water wars, DuMars had firsthand experience representing New Mexico in a dispute with Texas over the Pecos River. New Mexico suffered a bitter loss because the Pecos River Compact included groundwater, and a unanimous vote provision allowed Texas to block changes. Now, DuMars represents Georgia. One consultant for the state of Florida, perhaps bitter because Florida is the downstream state with no leverage over Georgia, referred to DuMars and his associates with a sense of admiration as "the New Mexico water mafia."

The chief antagonists—Florida and Georgia—have very different notions about how to share the water resources of the ACF basin. Georgia is relying on the principle of state sovereignty to argue against any restriction on groundwater pumping. Georgia advocates keeping the reservoirs, most of which are located in Georgia, filled as though a drought were imminent; the continuing diversions necessary to accomplish this would effectively lower river flows and would provide Georgia with water for future growth. Florida's position, developed in consultation with The Nature Conservancy's biohydrologists, is that releases from the reservoirs should mimic historic (predam) flows. Occasional high flows are critical for the oysters. To protect the Apalachicola Bay estuary and the fishing industry, Florida is even willing to accept a smaller overall quantity of water. This may be the only instance in an interstate dispute over water in which a state's priority is to protect the environment rather than to obtain the maximum quantity of water.

Georgia will surely not agree to an allocation formula that favors Florida. To avoid this possibility, Georgia has manipulated the variables in the hydrologic model (for instance, the amount of water used by farmers) to support an allocation formula that will reduce the flow received by Florida. This observation doesn't apply only to Georgia. Florida has done the same thing; its modifications to the hydrologic model favor its preferred allocation. At this point in the struggle over the allocation formula, according to The Nature Conservancy's Brian Richter and his colleagues, the states "have slipped into a battle of the [hydrologic] models." The states, as one might have predicted, disagree about the relationship between groundwater pumping and river flows.

— —

There is no honor among thieves, nor among states as they struggle over the control of water—regardless of whether the states are western, eastern, or southern. In interstate water disputes, states argue for whatever position will secure for them the largest amount of water. Nor do states feel obliged to be consistent from one piece of litigation to another. Arguments of convenience and self-interest dictate each state's position. From the states, we hear howls of protest that other states have failed to protect the flows in interstate rivers from diminution through groundwater pumping, but less concern for how a state's own pumpers may be producing the same effect. Consider some examples.

Colorado, the state with the strongest protection for surface flows, is cavalier about groundwater pumping when the pumps are located just upstream of an interstate border. Lenient regulation of pumping helps Colorado irrigators, hurts the interests of downstream states, and reduces Colorado's obligation to produce water under interstate compacts. Still, Colorado rails against Nebraska for failing to curb groundwater pumping and cites this as a reason why Colorado should not be required to release flows for the protection of endangered species in Nebraska. Nebraska sanctimoniously attacks Wyoming for permissive groundwater rules and simultaneously deprives Kansas of water owed under interstate compacts. New Mexico demands that Colorado account for reduced flows under the Rio Grande Compact, but New Mexico allows groundwater pumping that violates its obligations to Texas under the Pecos River Compact. Texas complains about New Mexico's groundwater pumping but chooses not to curb pumping from the Edwards Aquifer under the doctrine of capture. Idealism has had no place in fights over water.

In the 1930s, Arizona even threatened armed conflict against California. The Great Colorado River War of 1934 arose when California began construction of Parker Dam on the Colorado River, which serves as the border between California and Arizona. Arizona feared, reasonably enough, that California was trying to hoard all the water and, just as important, the hydropower to be generated by a series of dams on the Colorado River. The governor of Arizona, Benjamin Moeur, milked this issue for all it was worth, prompting the comment, "Jesus may have walked on water, but Arizona has a governor who ran on the Colorado River." Governor Moeur sent the National Guard to "repel the threatened invasion of the sovereignty and territory of the state of Arizona. . . ." When the small truck convoy of troops arrived in Parker, Arizona, they still had to travel eighteen miles upriver to reach the dam site. Two of the governor's representatives did so—on the *Julia B*, a ferryboat. The *Los Angeles Times* rushed a "war correspondent" into the "theater of war," who wryly dubbed the ferryboat captain "Admiral" of the "Arizona Navy." Arizona became a laughingstock. The military war ended after Congress, in 1935, passed legislation specifically authorizing the construction of Parker Dam, but a war of words and politics continues to this day.

Like family relationships or feuds between neighbors, fights between states over water never quite get sorted out or resolved. Instead, new layers are added to rich mosaics. Disputes between states persist because the stakes are so high. The fight between Arizona and California over the Colorado River continues seven decades after the Great Colorado River War. As an old water proverb has it: Water flows uphill to wealth and power. Or downhill, in the case of Los Angeles. In the immortal words of L.A. Power & Water's William Mullholland, speaking about L.A.'s plundering of the Owens Valley, "If we don't take the water, we won't need it."

If the Great Colorado River War offers any lesson, the struggle over the waters of the ACF basin will not end anytime soon. As the fight continues, nothing will prevent Georgia farmers and cities from increasing the amount of water that they pump and divert. Although priority of use does not, in theory, create water rights in eastern riparian states, the more that Georgia comes to depend on this water, the harder it will be to free up the water for oysters in Apalachicola Bay.

Chapter 14

The Future of Water

Tourism and Grand Canyon National Park

"When the well's dry, we know the worth of water."
—Benjamin Franklin (1746)

One of life's great treats is to hike in Grand Canyon National Park across gorgeous rock formations barren of plants and greenery, and then stumble upon an oasis of a seep or spring that supports ferns and other vibrant green plants. It provides a chance to fill up one's canteen and to marvel at the life-giving power of water. Even a modest reduction in discharge would dry up many of these seeps and creeks.

The town of Tusayan, Arizona, lies just outside the South Rim section of Grand Canyon National Park, the most popular destination for tourists visiting the Grand Canyon. As the number of visitors to the Grand Canyon climbed from 2.2 million in 1970 to almost 5 million in 2000, the National Park Service struggled to accommodate them. In 2000, the over-whelming number of visitors led The Wilderness Society to declare the Grand Canyon one of the fifteen most endangered wild lands. The Grand Canyon National Park management plan proposes to limit the number of visitors and to ban automobiles altogether. A light-rail system or natural gas–powered buses would transport tourists around the South Rim section of the park. The park must also address a shortage of housing for park employees and concessionaires. The explosion in tourism at the park has also created problems just outside the park for the U.S. Forest Service, which manages Kaibab National Forest.

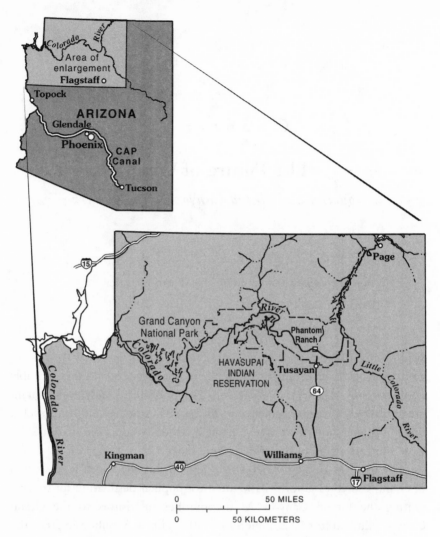

FIGURE 14.1. The Grand Canyon and vicinity in northern Arizona.

The Forest Service's traditional focus has been to regulate mining, logging, and grazing in national forests. As the West's population has increased and as tourism has sparked interest in the West's physical splendors, recreation has become the dominant use of Forest Service lands. Enthusiasts of camping, hiking, fishing, mountain biking, all-terrain vehicle riding, snowmobiling, downhill and cross-country skiing, climbing, whitewater rafting, kayaking, and trail running insist that the Forest Service manage federal forests to protect and encourage these recreational activities. All over the West, development is occurring immediately adjacent to federal lands as the private sector tries to accommodate the demand for recreational opportunities by building vacation homes, condominiums, hotels, motels, recreational vehicle campgrounds, restaurants, and retail shops. These developments next to national parks, forests, monuments, and wildlife refuges pose special challenges for federal land managers. Citizens want increased access to federal lands for recreation, but using groundwater to serve development on private lands threatens sensitive springs and creeks located on federal lands.

Canyon Forest Village Corporation (CFV), a development group that owns considerable acreage in and around Tusayan, has proposed land exchanges that would swap 272 acres of Forest Service land in Tusayan for 2,118 acres of their private land, called inholdings, located within Kaibab National Forest. The proposal would involve the construction of lodging, dining areas, retail shops, information and orientation facilities for the national park, housing for federal employees of the park, a transportation staging area, a parking lot for the banned automobiles, condominiums, recreational facilities, and a Native American marketplace constructed by CFV and managed by Native American groups. In total, the proposal would involve construction of 900 hotel rooms, 2,375 housing units, and 240,000 square feet of commercial space.

All this proposed development raises very serious questions about the availability of water, whether from underground or from the surface, because the Tusayan region receives on average only fifteen inches of rain per year and most of that is lost to evapotranspiration and surface runoff. Only about 0.3 inch per year recharges to the aquifer. Any groundwater pumping must therefore take water out of storage and/or decrease discharge to streams, seeps, and creeks. Because the South Rim is 4,500 feet above the bottom of the Grand Canyon at Phantom Ranch, the geology allows for myriad seeps, creeks, and even streams in the canyon to receive discharges from the aquifer. But it is feared that increased pumping to support new development will reduce flows to these surface watercourses. The small seeps and creeks serve as critical water sources for the birds, bats, small mammals, amphibians, and reptiles that inhabit the canyon. They also offer comfort to hikers, especially backpackers, who traverse the Tonto Plateau midway between the South Rim and the Colorado River.

West of the South Rim lies the Havasupai Indian Reservation. Tourism forms the basis of the tribe's economy, as upward of 12,000 people each year hike or travel on horseback into the canyon to enjoy Havasu Springs. The springs emerge from an arid part of the canyon in a most improbable form. The waters are turquoise and cascade over travertine cliffs into pools that better resemble a Caribbean coral reef pool than an Arizonan desert spring. Havasu Springs are fed by precipitation on the rim that filters into the aquifer and eventually discharges and creates the springs. The tribe fears that new, large-capacity groundwater wells will substantially diminish the flow of Havasu Springs. The springs have not only economic but also spiritual and cultural importance to the Havasupai people. Lincoln Manakaja, chair of the Havasupai tribe, put it this way:

> We as Havsu 'Baaja, the people of the blue-green water, will fight to stop the pumping of water from under the Coconino Plateau. Long before there were hydrologists, we knew the flow of the water. It starts as snow and rain on Wii Hagnbaja, the San Francisco Peaks. It then flows underground through the veins of our Mother, to our place of origin, under our resting place after the great flood, and then to our homes in Supai Canyon and what used to be our homes and gardens in the Grand Canyon. Our Mother's veins are the fractures and faults of the Coconino Plateau; these are the pathways for the water, the lifeblood, to flow for all creatures and plants to survive.

The geology of the Grand Canyon is astonishingly complicated, the product of almost 2 billion years of tectonic plates colliding, creating vast seas during some periods and gigantic deserts during others. The intricate layers with myriad faults and fractures pose a real challenge to hydrologists trying to predict how groundwater wells in Tusayan might impact Havasu Springs or the seeps, springs, and creeks in the Grand Canyon.

Because the proposed CFV development involved Forest Service land, it triggered preparation of an environmental impact statement (EIS) under the National Environmental Policy Act. An EIS must detail the environmental impacts of the proposed federal agency action (approval of the land swap), identify the adverse environmental effects if the proposal is implemented, and consider alternatives to the proposed action. The Forest Service's final EIS concluded that prior to construction of the first groundwater well in Tusayan in 1989, groundwater flow in the aquifer around Tusayan was in dynamic equilibrium. In other words, groundwater discharge to the springs approximately equaled recharge to the aquifer. In this situation, *any* new groundwater pumping will reduce spring flows. A 1996 groundwater model predicted that pumping in the Tusayan area would reduce flows in Havasu, Hermit, and Indian Garden Springs; the latter is well known to anyone who has hiked down Bright Angel Trail off the South Rim because it is the lush oasis one encounters halfway to the Colorado River.

The EIS considered a range of possible alternatives in connection with the proposed development, most of which involved bringing new wells on line. Under the alternative preferred by the Forest Service and CFV, groundwater would have provided the primary source of water for the Tusayan development. The developer favored using groundwater because it was cheap and convenient. Its consulting hydrologist concluded that the impact on Havasu, Hermit, and Indian Garden Springs would range between 1 and 5 percent of the flows over a fifty- to one-hundred-year time horizon. Any hydrologic study is subject to some uncertainty, particularly one attempting to predict water flows in a geological setting as complicated as the Grand Canyon. Consultants for the Havasupai tribe concluded that groundwater pumping would significantly reduce the flow in Havasu Springs.

The potentially adverse environmental consequences of new groundwater wells prompted environmental organizations, especially the Grand Canyon Trust, to mobilize its members to urge the Forest Service to consider new alternatives. The Havasupai tribe also opposed any increase in groundwater pumping. CFV faced an uncertain and potentially expensive fight if it pressed for the groundwater alternative. First, both the Forest Service and the National Park Service were insisting on a set of mitigation options and monitoring procedures. CFV was looking at the prospect of having to monitor indefinitely flows in the creeks and to manage a major problem should it turn out that groundwater pumping caused reduced flows in the springs and seeps. It was unclear what would happen in that event. Second, the Havasupai tribe has federal reserved rights to the surface flows in Havasu Creek as it passes through the reservation. A recent Arizona Supreme Court decision makes clear that these rights would trump CFV's groundwater rights. CFV wanted to avoid prolonged litigation with the tribe over whether it could use groundwater for the development. In short, CFV faced unknown costs and uncertain litigation. These were enormous deterrents. Hundreds of millions of dollars rested on the outcome.

CFV began to explore other options and to work closely with the Havasupai tribe and with prominent environmental organizations, especially the Grand Canyon Trust, the National Parks Conservation Association, and the Natural Resources Defense Council, in a search for an alternative supply of water. Together, CFV, the tribe, and environmentalists proposed a new alternative (Alternative H) that staff of the Kaibab National Forest endorsed in August 1999. Alternative H would bring water for the development from the Colorado River near Topock, Arizona. This involves several remarkable steps. First, CFV must acquire rights to Colorado River water from the Central Arizona Water Conservation District. Then they must arrange for the water to be hauled by tank cars owned by the Burlington Northern Santa Fe Railroad to Williams, Arizona, a distance of approximately 190 miles. Finally, developers must arrange for additional transport by railroad or construct an underground pipeline to move the water the final sixty miles to Tusayan.

Under Alternative H, CFV would divert the water at Topock, where the elevation is 500 feet above sea level, and move the water to Tusayan, where the elevation is 7,000 feet. Only in the world of western water could the idea of transporting water by train and/or pipeline 250 miles and 6,500 feet in elevation seem sensible. After all, the costs and challenges are quite staggering. Securing water rights to the already overappropriated Colorado River water alone would be challenge enough, but then CFV would need to spend approximately $15 million in capital costs for the sixty-mile pipeline, storage facilities, and loading facilities at Topock. Third, Burlington Northern Santa Fe would charge $1,200 to haul each 23,500-gallon tank car from Topock to Williams. At this rate, it would cost CFV $16,800 to move each acre-foot of water from Topock to Williams! Yet CFV's accountants crunched the numbers and decided that the project made economic sense, even though the costs are staggering compared with any other western water project. Alternative H also has the advantage of avoiding unknown costs and the uncertainty of litigation.

Alternative H anticipates water conservation and reuse programs that are truly state-of-the-art. The development, once built, would generate approximately 140,000 gallons per day (gpd) of wastewater that would be treated by a solar aquatic wastewater treatment plant, which uses no chemicals and less energy than conventional treatment systems. CFV might use this water for landscape irrigation, fire fighting, and possibly toilets and washing machines in dual-plumbed facilities, or it might be treated by reverse osmosis for reuse as a potable water supply. Alternative H would also (1) limit the amount of landscaping, thus reducing the amount of water for that purpose; (2) require low-water-use plants, to be irrigated with drip irrigation, which is highly efficient; and (3) require the lodging units to have low-flow toilets and no bathtubs as additional water conservation measures. The impetus for these conservation measures came from what appears at first blush to be an unlikely source—the developer, CFV. But the incentive for CFV is huge: every drop of water conserved or reused is one drop less that must be transported 250 miles by railroad and pipeline from Topock to the South Rim.

CFV anticipated having four separate water systems: a potable system, an effluent system, a water harvesting system, and a sewer system. Consider the harvesting system. When completed, the project would have 1.5 million square feet under roof (commercial, retail, lodging, and residential). If CFV could collect 50 percent of the snow and rain that falls on the roofs, it would harvest 20 million gallons per year. CFV estimated that the total development would require 60 million gallons per year, or approximately 180 acre-feet per year (af/yr); harvesting is therefore particularly attractive. Another harvesting possibility is the new Grand Canyon National Park transportation facility. If the light-rail system comes on line, people will leave their automobiles in a parking lot adjacent to the development in Tusayan. The planned 3,500-space parking lot would cover forty-five or fifty acres of land, and the runoff from the parking lot presents another opportunity for some serious water harvesting. Of course, this would entail state-of-the-art water treatment technologies to remove oil and other impurities to prepare the harvested water for reuse in irrigation or even as the potable supply. By using water-efficient systems, CFV hoped to keep water use for domestic purposes down to thirty to forty gallons per capita per day, an extraordinarily low figure for the United States.

The Southwest director of the National Parks Conservation Association, a nonprofit environmental organization that participated in developing Alternative H, observed that it "will raise the bar for development next to national parks and be a model for other situations." CFV's proposal received an American Society of Landscape Architects Planning Award for its water conservation features.

If the design and engineering of an adequate water supply for the development sounds complicated, so too is the legal apparatus necessary for CFV to obtain rights to Colorado River water. Lawyers for CFV, the

Havasupai tribe, and the environmental organizations developed quite ingenious solutions. First, CFV entered into a "fifth priority" contract with the Secretary of the Interior. Although the state of Arizona has rights to 2.8 million acre-feet per year (maf/yr) from the Colorado River, any state water user must obtain a water delivery contract from Interior. As the name suggests, fifth-priority water takes its place in line behind four other users. Only in years when other users fail to use Arizona's 2.8 maf allotment is fifth-priority water available. For CFV, the good news is that the water is astonishingly cheap, $0.25 per acre-foot; the bad news is that fifth-priority water does not provide a permanent supply. It would, however, provide a partial solution because Arizona is not currently using its entire 2.8 maf allotment. When fifth-priority water is available, CFV would divert it from the Colorado River at Topock and place it on the railroad cars for transport to Tusayan. To augment fifth-priority water, CFV contracted with the Central Arizona Water Conservation District (CAWCD), which manages the Central Arizona Project, to acquire excess water from the project, up to 40,000 af/yr over ten years. Through an aqueduct and pumping system, CAWCD transports water from the Colorado River at Lake Havasu to central and southern Arizona for use by cities and farms (figure 14.1). For a number of reasons, current water use is well below capacity, so excess water is available now.

But CFV does not need the water now; it needs it in the future. Here's where things get interesting. Under a separate contract, Phoenix's largest water provider, the Salt River Project, would recharge CFV's excess Central Arizona Project water in groundwater aquifers in central Arizona near Phoenix. Recharging water in this fashion would earn CFV credits for subsequent recovery of the water. The recovery—and this is the hook— would occur at Topock, *not* in central Arizona where the Central Arizona Project (CAP) recharge occurred! To provide water for users in the Phoenix area sometime in the future, the Salt River Project would withdraw the water that CFV recharged in central Arizona. Then CFV would divert water at Topock, and CAWCD would reduce its diversion from the Colorado River by an equal amount.

Whether any water actually will get recharged in central Arizona is not yet clear, for Arizona has a curious program called "in lieu" recharge. Under this program, farmers who currently pump groundwater would refrain from pumping and, "in lieu" of pumping groundwater, use Colorado River water delivered through the CAP instead. This creates credits for future pumping of the water that could have been pumped but was not. If it sounds like smoke and mirrors, then you understand perfectly. No water is actually recharged; less groundwater is pumped. It's a system that moves water from one user to another but avoids the cost of infrastructure—a pipe—to move the water. A paper transfer allows CFV to divert water at Topock and reduces by the same amount the water that CAWCD can divert at its Havasu pumping plant.

How would these restrictions on the developer be enforced? Here the lawyers for CFV, the government, the tribe, and the environmental organizations were equally creative. CFV entered into two covenants (restrictions on the land) that control water use. Alternative H would allow CFV to use limited quantities of groundwater only during initial construction and during emergencies, such as train derailment, a break in the pipeline, a flood, an earthquake, or other specific conditions identified in the water-use covenant. If CFV were to violate the terms of either covenant, one of six "benefited" parties could take action to halt the violation. The benefited parties are the Havasupai tribe, Grand Canyon National Park, Kaibab National Forest, and three environmental organizations—the Grand Canyon Trust, the Natural Resources Defense Council, and the National Parks Conservation Association. These covenants, once recorded in the appropriate county land office, are enforceable agreements that "run with the land" under Arizona law. In other words, they restrict not only CFV but also future property owners and occupants. By purchasing property from CFV and by obtaining the benefits from controlled development of this fragile resource, the property owners would waive their existing rights to use groundwater under Arizona law.

In September 1999, the cities of Flagstaff and Williams, which lie about an hour south and east of Tusayan, appealed the Kaibab National Forest's endorsement of Alternative H to the chief of the Forest Service, who upheld the decision in November 1999. In March 2000, the Coconino County board of supervisors approved the project unanimously, with one supervisor, Paul Babbitt, brother of Secretary of the Interior Bruce Babbitt, having recused himself. The ordinance enacted by the board placed further restrictions on groundwater use to eliminate perceived loopholes. CFV may not use groundwater during the construction phase, and drought is no longer classified as an emergency under the covenant.

Not everyone is happy with CFV, and significant hurdles remain before the first spade of dirt is turned over for the development. First, competing economic interests are trying to derail the project. The town of Tusayan is largely owned by the family or friends of Robert Thurston, who first arrived in the area in 1927. As things currently stand, the family controls the existing housing and retail markets. CFV, with 272 newly developed acres, would profoundly affect the control of the Thurston family. Given the limited availability of lodging in Tusayan, hoteliers in the cities of Flagstaff and Williams cater to tourists headed to the Grand Canyon. Local governments and businesses fear that CFV would siphon off millions of dollars and cripple the local economies. Flagstaff and Williams, as well as the Grand Canyon Improvement Association, a group of Tusayan merchants, and the Flagstaff Innkeepers Association, filed suit in federal court in Washington, D.C., in January 2000 challenging the Forest Service's decision. The suit claimed that the Forest Service land swap would be a horrible deal for the federal government because, in evaluating the swap, the Forest Service appraised its land in Tusayan at $20,000 an acre, but comparable private land in Tusayan allegedly sells for as much as $1 million per acre.

Second, the consensus among environmental groups unraveled when the Sierra Club vowed to fight the project. In March 2000, the Sierra Club filed a second federal court suit. The Sierra Club asserted that the covenants do not offer sufficient assurance that CFV will not rely on groundwater. They fear, once approval is granted, that CFV will figure out some way to rely on groundwater rather than undertake the expense of moving Colorado River water by rail and pipeline. But the Sierra Club also opposes the development itself. The Sierra Club's Arizona conservation chair, Sharon Galbreath, commented, "Building northern Arizona's largest shopping center at the entrance to the Grand Canyon is simply a bad idea." Some opponents have criticized the Forest Service because they claim that the land swap would promote development that would not otherwise occur. They believe that the owners of the private inholdings would never have developed those properties because they were too small or remote for viable commercial projects.

The National Park Service, the Forest Service, the Havasupai tribe, and the environmental organizations that endorse CFV have a completely different understanding. To them, it seems clear that the growth in tourism will continue. CFV would relieve some pressure on Grand Canyon National Park by moving some employees to decent housing outside the park and by facilitating the movement to rid the park of all automobiles.

Although the inholdings may not be developed imminently, development eventually will occur. Given these realities, CFV provides the most environmentally sensitive development, and it removes forever the possibility that the inholdings, once developed, would rely on groundwater.

Immediately after the March 2000 decision of the Coconino County Board of Supervisors to approve the proposal, the competing economic interests gathered signatures for a referendum petition that placed the ultimate decision before Coconino County voters in November 2000. The referendum battle turned out to be a particularly bruising one. According to Geoff Barnard, president of the Grand Canyon Trust, an environmental organization that supported CFV, "This election is about one single thing: It's about protecting one group of people from competition." The Flagstaff, Williams, and Tusayan hoteliers had a lot riding on the outcome. Between 1995 and 2000, they had built over 3,000 new motel rooms—rooms that would likely have lower occupancy rates if CFV were built. On the other side, CFV developer Thomas De Paulo of Scottsdale had spent $19 million in his nine-year effort to obtain approval for CFV. De Paulo contributed another $900,000 toward a media blitz to persuade Coconino County voters to approve CFV. But De Paulo's efforts were to no avail, as voters rejected the proposal by a 64 to 36 percent margin. Although explanations for the result vary, many residents in Coconino County's largest city, Flagstaff, have jobs in the motel industry or in tourism generally. There may also have been a visceral reaction to the idea of encouraging any development near the Grand Canyon. On the other hand, the American Society of Landscape Architects was incredulous. "Why isn't this exemplary, prize-winning project going to be built?," asked an article in the Society's publication, *Landscape Architecture*. It blamed Tusayan commercial interests for running a misleading campaign that portrayed CFV as an "outlet mall." It noted that within days of the vote "construction fencing went up on private land in Tusayan—for a strip mall."

In 2001, both of the federal lawsuits resulted in findings that halted the land exchange, at least for the moment, principally because the Forest Service's EIS failed to analyze the amount of groundwater that could be used during the construction phase of the project. One judge also found that the covenants should have been finalized and made available to the public for comment *before* the Forest Service approved the land exchange. The judges remanded the case to the Forest Service to correct these deficiencies in the EIS.

For his part, De Paulo has vowed not to abandon the project. CFV has appealed the most damaging of the two federal suits. On the political front, Arizona law requires De Paulo to wait a year before submitting another proposal for a vote by the board of supervisors. In January 2002, De Paulo told me that the new proposal will resemble the earlier one, with one significant change: it will omit the transient lodging component. Perhaps that will eliminate the opposition from local motel owners. In the next round, CFV would slightly modify its method of transporting Colorado River water to the development. Rather than divert water from the river near Topock, CFV has contracted with CAWCD to acquire sufficient water to supply CFV for 100 years. Over the next five to ten years, CFV will store that water in recharge facilities near Glendale, west of Phoenix, then extract it as needed. The proposal still requires using the Burlington Northern Santa Fe Railroad to transport the water to Williams, and additional rail transportation or a pipeline to get the water to Tusayan.

The CFV story demonstrates the critical role of the National Environmental Policy Act, with its requirement that federal agencies prepare an environmental impact statement before they embark on any significant federal action. The EIS brought public scrutiny to bear on the Forest Service's preferred alternative, which would have relied on groundwater and would have posed a terrible threat to springs and seeps along the South Rim of the Grand Canyon. Public reaction caused the developer to work closely with the principal environmental organizations to forge the CFV proposal, a creative, environmentally sensitive plan. Unlike so many other groundwater–surface water interaction plans around the country, this one came to terms with the hydrologic reality. Even then, the Forest Service must undertake additional studies, concluded the federal courts, before the exchange may go forward.

If the land exchange eventually takes place, a significant advantage for Kaibab National Forest and the springs and seeps in Grand Canyon National Park would be the elimination of CFV's private inholdings. If CFV develops its private inholdings, Arizona law would allow new groundwater wells to service the development. Between 1994 and 1998, the Arizona Department of Water Resources granted permits for three new groundwater wells in Tusayan. Only one well existed before 1994. To save Havasu Springs and the Grand Canyon's seeps and springs, it is imperative to halt further reliance on groundwater as a source for new development.

That the preferred environmental option seems so surreal speaks volumes about the economic and political context of the whole project. Alternative H involves taking large quantities of water out of the Colorado River Basin, where the water flows naturally, and moving it hundreds of miles by railroad and pipeline. The success of CFV depends on the developer acquiring water rights to the Colorado River, the most hotly contested and heavily litigated river in American history. Under the Law of the River, as the set of rules governing the Colorado is known, various states and Mexico have annual rights to over 16.5 million acre-feet. However, scientific studies have proven that the average annual flow in the Colorado over the last 500 years is only about 13.5 maf. There are more paper rights than wet water. The developers nevertheless remain confident that they can secure rights to the relatively modest quantities of water they need. But, while CFV has dodged one hydrologic problem, it is exacerbating another. There is simply not enough water in the river to satisfy expected demand.

Alternative H is remarkable in another regard. In the West, we regularly move water hundreds of miles from its source to agricultural fields or a growing city. Transboundary water diversions supply Los Angeles, San Diego, Denver, Albuquerque, Phoenix, and Tucson. But these and other large-scale water projects have been made possible only by the infusion of enormous amounts of federal dollars. No one in the private sector would ever have built the multibillion-dollar Central Arizona Project. Alternative H would cost CFV over $20,000 per acre-foot of water, an investment of entirely private money. At a time when the Imperial Irrigation District in California charges its members $13.50 per acre-foot for Colorado River water, CFV is prepared to pay 1,500 times that amount for the same water! Prognostications of the future are hazardous, or maybe only foolish, yet this development offers a clear vision of what lies ahead. Water is worth a lot more money than people have realized. No farmer in his or her right mind would ever pay $20,000 for an acre-foot of water. Not even growing marijuana would justify such an expense. But the value of water is relative, and if we shift the perspective from cost per acre-foot to cost per gallon, the picture looks quite different. Now the cost to CFV works out to $0.06 per gallon. Compared to bottled water, which sells for up to $12 per gallon, it looks like a great deal. And so it is for the developers and for those who will purchase commercial or residential property at CFV. As the old adage about real estate goes, everything depends on "location, location, location." For property at the gateway to one of the most magnificent splendors on earth, a somewhat higher water bill is no big deal.

Chapter 15

The Tragedy of Law and the Commons

"All the water there will be, is."

—Anonymous

In medieval England, the common law developed a "right of commons" that allowed the king's subjects to use the crown's uncultivated land for pasture and firewood. In the early American colonies, a similar system permitted citizens to pasture their animals on the town square or green. Along the eastern seaboard, these open areas in the middle of cities and towns remain, though not many cattle now graze the Boston Common. But from the seventeenth to the nineteenth centuries, Bostonians considered the common a mutual heritage for their livestock. Those who visit Boston and find its narrow streets and meandering byways frustrating to navigate in the twenty-first century should remember that the roads follow paths trodden down by livestock on their way to and from the common.

Allowing citizens' limitless use of a common area inevitably produces what biologist Garrett Hardin called "the tragedy of the commons." For common-pool resources, those not owned by individuals, such as air, water, oceans, and wildlife, individuals will act to maximize their individual welfare, which simultaneously reduces total social welfare. To return to Hardin's commons, citizens with cattle have an incentive to increase the size of their herds to take advantage of the free grazing opportunity. At some point, however, the aggregate effect of such individual decisions will be that grazing exceeds the capacity of the common and begins to degrade it. At that point, how will rational individuals respond? By continuing to increase the number of animals that they graze on the common. The benefit from the grass eaten by each additional animal goes entirely to the animal's owner, but the burden from the degradation is shared among all citizens who use the common.

We have witnessed the same phenomenon in our environment. Fouled air, polluted water, overgrazed public lands, clear-cut public forests, overharvested fisheries, and overhunted buffalo reflect the cumulative impact of the choices of individual citizens, acting as rational economic beings. Economists describe these activities as creating externalized costs, costs that are not absorbed by individuals but are imposed on their neighbors or on society generally. Notable recent examples of the tragedy of the commons include overfishing in Chesapeake Bay, exploitation of blue fin tuna and swordfish, and overharvesting of Maine lobsters. As long as the resource is public and no barriers limit entry to the business, the potential exists to decimate the common resource.

So it is with groundwater. The doctrines of capture and reasonable use encourage exploitation of a common-pool resource. The legal rules governing groundwater use reward rational economic individuals by assuring them that the biggest pump wins. Rivers, springs, lakes, wetlands, and estuaries around the country face an uncertain future because most states have separate legal rules for regulating surface water and groundwater. For surface water, riparian law or the prior appropriation doctrine governs; but for groundwater, either a different system of prior appropriation or the doctrines of capture or reasonable use prevail.

A complete misunderstanding of hydrology has been memorialized in many states, where groundwater and surface water are legally two unrelated things. Surface and groundwater law in most states developed along tracks that appeared to be parallel but that would eventually collide. The collision eventually occurred when groundwater pumping, through the capture process, began to reduce the flow in lakes, rivers, and streams.

Most states have failed to eliminate the gap between law and science. In lieu of legal reform, Americans have shown limitless ingenuity in devising technological fixes for water supply problems by altering the hydrologic cycle to sustain existing usage. This book's stories have revealed quite curious proposals: moving water by railroad and pipeline from Topock Gorge to the Grand Canyon's South Rim; refilling depleted lakes in Florida with additional pumped groundwater; running a pipeline from Lake Powell to the Hopi reservation in northern Arizona; pumping groundwater from the Edwards Aquifer and dumping it into San Antonio's River Walk; recharging effluent in Sierra Vista to reduce pumping's impact on the San Pedro River by creating a "mound" between the city's wells and the river; dewatering gold mines in Nevada and dumping that water into the Humboldt River; using a canal to move water from the American River to the Cosumnes River. Each "solution" reflects our belief that we can control nature, even as we ignore reality. Each proposal offers an immediate yet temporary fix to a larger problem. These alternatives are band-aids that may prevent an infection from getting worse, but they are not cures for the disease. They instead allow us to ignore the inescapable reality that our uses of water are not sustainable over the long term.

As a society, we must address the problems of population growth, wasteful water consumption practices, and inappropriate agricultural water use. Growth poses the ultimate threat to our springs, streams, rivers, wetlands, and estuaries. Tucson's growth dried up the Santa Cruz River. Municipal population growth in San Antonio and Sacramento has placed endangered species in jeopardy. Metropolitan Atlanta's water consumption threatens a way of life in the tiny town of Apalachicola, Florida. Suburban development outside Boston supports a lifestyle of sprawling homes and lawns that sometimes dries up the Ipswich River. In Florida, pumping by Tampa Bay Water has damaged houses and turned lakes into dry weed beds. Population increases in a relatively small city like Sierra Vista imperil a premier bird watching site. Even areas remote from population pressures suffer consequences associated with population growth. Although farming blueberries in Maine, mining gold in Nevada, bottling spring water in Wisconsin, farming potatoes in Minnesota, and mining coal in Arizona all occur in sparsely populated areas, each activity is driven by a burgeoning population's demand for more and more of everything.

We waste an appalling amount of water. Peabody Energy's coal slurry pipeline, Barrick Gold Corporation's mine dewatering operation, and, of course, the Texas catfish farm come to mind as examples. So do golf courses in California's deserts that each pump millions of gallons per day to keep fairways green and artificial lakes in Phoenix's suburbs, filled entirely with groundwater.

In the West, farmers annually use about 80 percent of each state's water, in part to grow alfalfa, cotton, wheat, corn, and rice—crops that grow perfectly well in other parts of the country without the need for irrigation. The federal government encourages this water use by providing below-market-rate electric power to run farmers' groundwater pumps and by subsidizing various crops. As a consequence, farmers grow a water-guzzling crop like cotton in Arizona's Sonoran Desert. As we have seen, agricultural water use is increasing in the Midwest, the East, and the South; farmers have shifted from dryland farming to irrigation farming to grow potatoes in Minnesota, blueberries in Maine, and corn, soybeans, and wheat in Georgia.

As our water use spirals upward, we must begin to rethink the economic structure by which we value (and usually undervalue) our water resources. At the same time, we must act to protect our rivers, springs, wetlands, lakes, and estuaries from groundwater pumping. We humans have the capacity, if we choose to exercise it, to rise above our basest self-interest and to act for the long-term best interests of generations to come. The predicate for noble sacrifice is knowledge of the consequences of our actions. For groundwater pumping, we have lacked that awareness, for the problem has been, literally, out of sight and out of mind. Now that we understand how water moves and how groundwater pumping affects the environment, it is time to act.

There is considerable urgency. My stories, unfortunately, illustrate what the future holds. Because groundwater moves so slowly, it may take years or decades of groundwater pumping to affect rivers, streams, creeks, springs, wetlands, lakes, and estuaries. The hidden tragedy and irremediable fact is that groundwater pumping that has *already* occurred will cause environmental damage in the future. Over the next generation, other stories like the ones I recount will come to light. What we *can* control is future pumping. Let's consider how to reform the system.

— —

We did not get into this pickle overnight, nor will the cure come quickly or easily. To change direction will be like trying to redirect an ocean liner; it will take time. But there is reason to be optimistic. If we stop interrupting the hydrologic cycle, springs will rise and rivers flow again. Nature has enormous regenerative capacity. The solution involves charting a new course for the future based on wise policies, then making a commitment to stay the course. It can be done. In the process, there is a role for every individual and for local, state, and federal governments.

Elwood Mead, for whom Lake Mead on the Colorado River is named, served first as Wyoming's state engineer and then as head of the U.S.

Bureau of Reclamation. He feared that creating a market in water rights would enable people to profit from a free public resource and would lead to monopoly:

> In monarchies streams belong to the crown . . . [b]ut in a republic they belong to the people, and ought forever to be kept as public property for the benefit of all who use them, and for them alone, such use to be under public supervision and control.

I suppose, a century later, that the poster children for Mead's fears are Perrier and T. Boone Pickens. We should indeed resist efforts by entrepreneurs to hoard a public resource. Yet some economists, under what is dubbed free-market environmentalism, believe that privatizing all interests in water will yield transferable rights that, according to the laws of supply and demand, will inevitably move water toward the highest-value uses. These economists think that the only way to avoid the tragedy of the commons is to end free access to the common-pool resource (groundwater) and to create, as a substitute, a system of private property rights in water. There are both economists and environmentalists who yearn for an ideal world: water as private property in the vision of economists; water as a public resource for environmentalists. That ideal world is not the one we inhabit. Nor is it a world that we can achieve anytime soon. Politics simply will not permit it. Nor is it, I believe, a world that we want. Proposals that conceive of water either as exclusively a public resource or as entirely private property are merely simplistic appeals from opposite ends of the rhetorical spectrum. Their proponents fail to appreciate the historic development of our laws and institutions, the localized context of water conflicts, and the inescapable reality that our *current* system recognizes that water is both a public resource *and* a private property right. Not only is recognizing and accepting this duality critical to saving our rivers and streams, it also yields the most desirable outcome.

The notion of water as a public resource has an appealing ring in the abstract; but in the concrete, water allocation decisions would be made by public officials (elected or appointed). Not many economists believe that legislative decisions are made strictly in the public interest. As for leaving the choices to government bureaucrats, they may make decisions for self-interested reasons, such as to maximize the budgets of their agencies. For many elected officials, the horizon is only as far away as the next election. Water allocation choices in many states simply reflect the legislatures' responses to political pressure from important economic constituencies. In Texas, for example, the legislature passed a rather feeble effort at reform that is long on planning but, because of the enormous clout of groundwater pumpers that include the city of San Antonio, is short on sanctions. Oklahoma permits limitless groundwater pumping, a result that favors the state's oil industry. In Nebraska, where farmers heavily depend on groundwater, the legislature's reform effort left control in the hands of local natural resources districts that are unlikely to impose serious restrictions on groundwater pumping. In Colorado, the state legislature has classified groundwater as "tributary," "non-tributary," and "not non-tributary," the last being an infelicitously titled category that favors the fast-growing, politically powerful suburbs of Denver. In short, when elected officials allocate water, they cater to the interests of powerful constituents. Any effort at reform must come to terms with this unblinking reality.

On the other hand, those who worship at the shrine of the market must put their faith in egregious fictions, such as the assumption that consumers have perfect knowledge of all available choices. For water rights, in particular, the market is less than efficient because of what economists call transactions costs, those costs necessary to make the market work. It takes time and money to identify willing sellers of water, to evaluate the value of their water rights, to determine whether the water rights of third parties may encumber the sale, to negotiate the terms, and to assess whether the proposed contract is enforceable.

Any market system has difficulty internalizing environmental values. Economists expect, in a private property system, that the rational owner will protect the environment on his property. But the holder of a groundwater right has no incentive to protect streams or rivers on someone else's (or the government's) land. Therefore, simply creating private property rights in groundwater may not eliminate the degradation of rivers and riparian habitat or other environmental harm from pumping. A property right in groundwater creates an incentive for landowners to protect the resource only to the extent necessary to assure them access to the full quantity of their rights. This incentive is modest because pumpers will almost always be able to pump the full measure of their rights, regardless of how many other wells draw from the same aquifer. Over time, their collective action may draw down the water table, which will increase the costs of energy to lift water from a lower level, but probably will not prevent pumpers from obtaining all the water they need.

To control the impact of groundwater pumping on the environment, we must combine a command-and-control model of government rules and regulations with the market forces of transferable rights and price incentives. The 1980 Arizona Groundwater Management Act could serve as a template for other states. Though hideously complex in particulars, this act is elegantly simple in structure. First, it quantified existing water uses and extended grandfathered right protection to them. Second, it prohibited new groundwater wells, except for those drilled under carefully controlled circumstances. Third, it established a state administrative agency, the Department of Water Resources, to administer and supervise all groundwater uses. Finally, it imposed water conservation standards on all users. Operating like a ratchet, the act progressively tightens the standards for water use by the cities, mines, and farms in five separate stages through the year 2025. In each interval, users must comply with increasingly stringent water conservation standards. In short, the act took the status quo as the baseline, carefully regulated new users, and required existing users to engage in conservation. Although the act has not operated exactly as intended, it has achieved two goals that any meaningful groundwater reform must embrace: first, it has protected the rights of existing users by creating quantified water rights that are transferable and therefore valuable; second, it has allowed the state of Arizona to break free of the relentless cycle of increasing use by placing restrictions on individual freedom to pump groundwater.

The creation of a system of private property rights may help to avoid the tragedy of the commons. Consider the Maine lobster fishing industry. John Tierney, writing in *The New York Times Magazine*, contrasted unregulated lobster fishing in Maine with a regulated system in Australia. In Maine, overharvesting has decimated lobster stocks, forcing Maine lobster fishers to work longer hours tending many more traps that now must be located tens of miles farther offshore, all to harvest a smaller number of lobsters of greatly reduced size that fetch lower prices. The tragedy of the commons is alive and well off the Maine coast. Australian lobster fishers faced the same ruinous competition for a finite supply until, in the 1960s, the Australian government limited the total number of traps the lobster fleet could use. It assigned licenses for these traps to the existing fishers. Newcomers must buy a license from someone already in business; over time, these licenses have become valuable commodities. More importantly, the lobster population has rebounded and Australian lobster fishers work fewer days, with shorter hours and fewer traps, and earn a great deal more money than their Maine counterparts. The Australian lobster fishers have a vested interest in the health of the fishery. The licensing system has averted the tragedy of the commons. The state of Maine has taken steps toward the Australian system by closing some areas of the coast to new lobster fishers, limiting each fisher to 800 traps, and banning fishing on Sundays. Maine lobster landings jumped from approximately 20 million pounds in 1985 to almost 60 million in 2000. Although the causes for this dramatic rise are complicated, most experts believe that the state restrictions have contributed significantly. Maine lobster fishers, who have a substantial stake in the health of the fishery, have endorsed these restrictions.

Some may object that creating grandfathered water rights for existing users transforms a right of use into a valuable property right, thus generating a windfall for current users. In many states, this windfall will go mostly to farmers because they consume so much groundwater. When Arizona created such a system, one opponent protested that "we do not want the farmers retiring to La Jolla and raising martinis." He was right, of course. But there is no politically viable alternative. Existing groundwater pumpers represent a powerful political force in every state, one with sufficient leverage to block any reform effort that tramples on their interests. Most political scientists agree that if you pit a small group of fiercely committed voters against a large number of indifferent or mildly involved voters, legislators will vote in favor of the small group's position. (I would argue that this is why legislatures routinely defeat proposed handgun legislation.) For reasons of equity, vested legal rights, and political feasibility, we must protect the rights of existing users, even if we think they are using water in a wasteful fashion.

States need to foster a market in water rights by allowing the easy transferability of rights from existing users to newcomers. Much groundwater pumping currently sustains low-value economic activity, such as growing alfalfa for cattle feed. To correct this wastage, state law must facilitate the movement of water from low-value uses to higher-value ones by establishing a water-rights market as the mechanism for accomplishing the shift. Water markets rely on voluntary free-market decisions made by willing buyers and sellers and take many forms, including purchases, transfers, lease options, exchanges, and forbearance agreements. The arrangements may be temporary or permanent; the only limitations are the creativity of the parties and their lawyers. For an example of creativity, environmental organizations concerned with maintaining minimum in-stream flows have purchased options from farmers that allow them to lease water during years when the river or stream suffers low flows. Under another arrangement, cities have paid farmers to conserve water by lining their ditches with concrete, while in return the cities acquired rights to some portion of the water conserved.

One brake on the creation of water markets comes from federal and state programs that provide farmers with low-cost water and from federal programs that pay farmers to grow water-guzzling but low-value crops, such as cotton. An Arizona farmer, when asked how he determined which crops to grow, thought for a moment and, with a twinkle in his eye, replied: "First, I look up at the snowpack in the mountains. Next, I consider the flow level in the river. Finally, I find out what crops the federal government is subsidizing." The elimination of such subsidies would price water more realistically, remove the incentive to grow crops of marginal value, and encourage the development of a water-rights market.

We need significant reform if we are to prevent further degradation of our rivers, streams, wetlands, and estuaries. Government rules and regulations deserve a prominent place in our reform efforts to facilitate water marketing and to protect the environment. The states have available at least eight different avenues for reform.

1) States should carefully craft water conservation standards. A water conservation program seems, intuitively, like a good idea: "Let's save water." However, the Arizona Groundwater Management Act's twenty years of experimentation with conservation standards send a mixed message. The act's elaborate and detailed conservation standards have prompted the user groups (cities, farms, and mines) to fight tooth and nail over every regulation proposed by the Department of Water Resources. Quarrels over agricultural efficiency ratios, municipal per capita per day water consumption, and "mining conservation technology consistent with reasonable economic return" have delayed implementation and consumed enormous amounts of time, energy, and money. Each legislative session has found users pushing bills to create loopholes in the conservation standards. The lesson from this experience is that simple conservation standards, ones that are easy to administer and implement, have the greatest likelihood of success. Complicated ones, fraught with complexity and elaborate monitoring and

enforcement programs, may be counterproductive. They will result in countless drafts, innumerable public meetings, and detailed administrative rules and regulations. Whether the users actually conserve water as a result of the standards is another matter entirely; they may be too complex to yield effective enforcement.

2) State legislatures should establish minimum stream flows and protect those flows from pumping of hydrologically connected groundwater. Through a combination of statutes, judicial decisions, and administrative rules, the state of Washington has developed a system that other states should emulate. The legislature authorized the state Department of Ecology to establish minimum water levels for streams and lakes to protect fish, game, other wildlife resources, and recreational and aesthetic values. The minimum levels become appropriations within the prior appropriation system and will be protected against subsequent groundwater pumping of hydrologically connected water. As a result, the Washington Department of Ecology has denied a number of permits for new wells.

3) States must pull the plug on unregulated groundwater pumping. Individuals should have no right to drill new wells that contribute to the tragedy of the commons and that shunt externalities off to their neighbors or society. States should ban absolutely the drilling of new wells within prescribed distances from any watercourse or wetland. Oregon law, for example, allows the state's Water Resources Department to designate "critical groundwater" areas and to impose restrictions on new pumping from wells within a mile of the river. The Oregon system, because it is relatively easy to administer, reduces transaction costs. All parties understand the rules for these wells.

Some may protest that restricting new pumping would violate the takings clause of the U.S. Constitution, which prohibits the government from taking private property for a public purpose without compensating the owner. However, courts have concluded that the property right is merely a right of use. Until the water is used, there is no water right. Therefore, a change in state law that operates prospectively to regulate existing wells and to prevent the drilling of new wells does not violate the takings clause. Those courts that have addressed the issue have upheld restrictions on pumping as reasonable exercises of the states' regulatory power.

Indeed, it is unclear whether a change in state law that halted *exist-*

ing pumping would trigger an obligation on the state to pay compensation. Most states consider groundwater a public resource that is subject to state management. In 2000, the Hawaii Supreme Court held that the water resources of the state, including groundwater, are subject to the public trust. That is, the state holds title to the water in trust for the people of the state, both present and future generations. In Arizona, Michigan, and Wisconsin, recent lawsuits claim that groundwater pumping that harms the states' watercourses violates the public trust.

4) States should impose an extraction tax on water pumped from any well within a certain distance of any river, spring, or lake. The target is any well whose cone of depression directly intersects the river and any well that intercepts water on its way toward the river. Such a tax would encourage existing pumpers to conserve water and new pumpers to locate wells farther away from watercourses.

5) State governments should also undertake the mundane, though critical, task of data collection. Most states have no idea how many wells have been drilled within the state or how much water they pump. States should require all existing well owners to register with the state and to install water meters that measure the water pumped. States should also prohibit drilling any new well without obtaining a permit from the state. This permitting and data collection should include domestic wells, which are currently exempt from regulation in most states. Some states have hundreds of thousands of domestic wells, a huge loophole in those states' regulatory systems. Gross abuses of this exemption have occurred in some states, such as Washington, where developers have drilled clusters of wells to serve entire subdivisions and have claimed each well as exempt, even though the cumulative pumping vastly exceeds the maximum for an exempt well. The Washington Supreme Court finally ended this abuse in March 2002. Other states must pass legislation or strictly enforce existing laws to prevent such crude efforts to circumvent state regulation.

6) States should also require that any new pumper offset or mitigate the impact on the environment. It makes no sense to allow developers to drill new wells in an aquifer already under stress. Arizona has a mitigation program that requires developers to demonstrate an "assured water supply"; one way to do so is by purchasing and retiring agricultural rights. Oregon has given the designation "Scenic Waterway" to

certain rivers, which are then protected by the requirement of mitigation whenever a new well would reduce the flow in the river by a
specified amount. Oregon also allows a surface water diverter to
undertake conservation measures, such as lining the ditch that carries
water from the river to the field, and to obtain rights to the conserved
water. However, the program also allocates 25 percent of the conserved
water for in-stream flow. Thus, the program creates an incentive for
conservation and reserves a portion for the environment. To be effective, any mitigation measure must avoid complicated and expensive litigation over subtle issues of hydrology and must, therefore, be simple
and easy to administer.

7) States (especially local governments) must also use financial incentives
as a significant part of water policy. Quite simply, we are not paying the
true cost of water. When homeowners or businesses receive a monthly
water bill from a city's water department or a private water company,
that bill includes only the extraction costs of drilling the wells, the
energy costs of pumping the water, the infrastructure costs of a distribution and storage system, and the administrative costs of the water
department or company. Water rates, with rare exceptions, do *not*
include a commodity charge for the water itself. The water is free. As
a consequence, this pricing structure shunts off on other customers (or
on society generally) many other costs: groundwater users do not pay,
for example, the cost of harm to rivers and riparian habitat, of dried-
up lakes, of water-quality degradation, or of subsidence caused by
groundwater pumping.

Even though water is a scarce commodity, most Americans have not
yet faced the condition that economists call *scarcity*, which occurs
when people alter their consumption patterns in response to price
increases. Our habits of water use will not change until the cost of
water rises sufficiently to force an alteration. Therefore, we must
increase water rates so that all users pay the *replacement* value of the
water, which is not just the cost of drilling a new well, but also the cost
of retiring an existing user's well.

Economists agree that significant price increases would create
incentives for all users to conserve. All farmers, homeowners, businesses, or industrial users could then decide for themselves which uses
of water to continue and which to curtail. Rate increases would
encourage the elimination of marginal economic activities and the

movement of water toward more productive uses. An increase in rates might stimulate new technologies and water harvesting efforts. It would certainly encourage greater use of effluent.

Existing groundwater pumpers must pay more, perhaps considerably more, for the water they pump. If the states extend grandfathered protection to existing users, states should encourage water conservation through pumping taxes on groundwater. Such taxes must be scheduled in a way that is sensitive to the economies of rural regions and that gives groundwater pumpers adequate notice that they will have to pay more for the privilege of pumping. Pumping taxes that increase water rates on farmers raise other issues as well—of equity and history. It is unreasonable to expect farmers suddenly to pay much higher water rates. Increases need to be phased in over time so that farmers can adjust acreage, cropping selection, and other variables necessary to transition from low-value crops to ones with higher economic value. Such changes are already occurring in California, where recent legislation has created water marketing mechanisms that encourage farmers to conserve and to sell or lease water rights to municipalities. Pumping taxes should begin at a modest level and increase over time to encourage water conservation and simultaneously to facilitate water marketing. Taxes ought to target pumping that most damages the environment—in other words, pumping near rivers, streams, springs, wetlands, and lakes.

Clearly, we should shelter persons of fixed or moderate income from any significant increase in water rates for basic domestic needs. On the other hand, residential use that exceeds a certain threshold often reflects water use associated with discretionary uses, such as swimming pools or lush outdoor landscaping, as in the Ipswich River Basin. Water rates ought to target such discretionary uses and discourage them by imposing graduated (nonlinear) rates for consumption above the threshold amount.

A major impediment to using financial incentives is the existence of state public utility commission rules that permit private water companies to charge customers only for the "cost of service," which may not include costs associated with obtaining long-term, renewable water supplies. State public utility law must allow private water companies to pass on to their consumers all costs associated with obtaining access to renewable supplies and with building the infrastructure to reuse effluent. Although one can debate the specific characteristics of a particular pricing structure, the principal point remains that we are not paying the true value of the water we are using.

8) Whenever a water rights transfer occurs, the state should require that a small percentage of the water be dedicated for environmental purposes. States should not get too greedy with this environmental dedication, however, or it will be self-defeating. The prospective parties to a transfer will, of course, consider the economic consequence of the dedication on their proposed transfer. If the dedication is too onerous, the sale or lease will not take place. But a modest dedication, phased in over time and applied to all transfers of water rights, has great potential for environmental restoration.

Several states have developed "conjunctive management" programs that coordinate the use of ground and surface water to maximize economic benefit. Although conjunctive management receives high praise from most commentators, it often does not solve the problem of reduced surface water flows caused by groundwater pumping. Indeed, it may exacerbate the problem. New Mexico, for example, allows a surface water diverter who suffers harm from groundwater pumping to make good the deficiency by pumping groundwater herself. However, the new well will almost assuredly capture water from the source of the surface water right. Although New Mexico protects the individual appropriator, the cumulative impact is to reduce further the flow in the river.

The U.S. Congress has historically deferred to the states with respect to water laws. Proposals for federal regulation of groundwater traditionally gave rise to a chorus of howls from states' rights advocates, especially those in the West, who, as author Wallace Stegner once observed, perceive the role of the federal government as "Get out! And give us more money!" But in the last generation, federal law has quietly but profoundly displaced state water law. Federal reserved water rights, the Clean Water Act, the Wild and Scenic Rivers Act, the Safe Drinking Water Act, the National Environmental Policy Act, and the Endangered Species Act impose federal standards, rules, and regulations that may profoundly impact state water law allocations. Although it might be preferable philosophically to leave this matter to the states, they have done an abysmal job of protecting the environment from groundwater pumping.

Congress has constitutional authority under its commerce power to impose federal regulations on groundwater pumpers, yet there are two good reasons why it should not do so. First, it would provoke a bruising political battle. The political capital expended to win that fight could be better spent elsewhere. Second, as my stories have revealed, the impact on the environment from groundwater pumping takes many forms. Imposing a uniform federal template on the nation is likely to exclude some pumping that should be regulated and to include some pumping that poses no serious risk of harm.

In my judgment, offering the carrot of federal funds is a far better approach than wielding the stick of federal regulation. Under its taxing and spending power, Congress should create a program funded by federal tax dollars to reward states that protect their environments from groundwater pumping (a form of gentle coercion). A host of federal programs (e.g., federal highway funds) give the states money but attach conditions. Under a similar program, if a state wished to protect rivers and streams, it could accept the federal money in return for meeting federal standards. If, on the other hand, a state preferred to maintain its independence, it could decline the federal funds and be free to establish its own standards paid for with its own internal revenues.

Mere reliance on market factors and command-and-control rules may not adequately protect important environmental values. Therefore, states should commit their resources to purchasing and retiring groundwater rights to protect critical watersheds and habitat. Where will funding for such programs come from? The states' general funds are a good place to start. Partnership with the federal government may provide a second funding source. The 1965 Land and Water Conservation Fund established a matching grant program to assist the states in acquiring water and land for outdoor recreation. In February 2002, the Bush administration proposed a Cooperative Conservation Initiative that would increase funding for the Land and Water Conservation Fund from $56 million to $200 million. The fund encourages the states to establish innovative conservation projects and to receive up to 50 percent of the cost from the federal government. The initiative may fund state plans for the acquisition and retirement of groundwater pumping rights in sensitive watersheds.

What is the role for individuals? Each of us can respond as a consumer and as a citizen. As consumers, we might examine how we use water. Despite the criticisms of Perrier, it is not a crime or a violation of any ethical or philosophical norm to drink spring water. Indeed, it's a healthy substitute for Pepsi, coffee, or beer—all made with water. It is true that any "spring" water sold in the United States that comes from a well will reduce flow in the nearby spring. But humans need water for survival, and various companies have bottled spring water since the nineteenth century. The environment has withstood this assault. Our democratic system still functions. In economic terms, human consumption is the highest-value use of water, and every physician will confirm that we don't drink enough. Our total consumption of drinking water—as a nation of 285 million people—is but a literal drop in the bucket compared to the groundwater pumped to grow alfalfa to feed cattle.

Yet some proposals for new bottled water plants, like Perrier's adjacent to the Mecan River in Wisconsin, are appalling. Perrier could have moved its proposed well a couple of miles away from the spring and still have obtained water with virtually the same chemical composition, but it couldn't have sold it as "spring" water. So my advice, the next time you turn your shopping cart up the "water aisle" in your favorite supermarket, is to pick up a twelve-pack of "artesian" water. Maybe Perrier will hear you.

Our consumer preferences for "spring" water, gold jewelry, and blemish-free french fries involve innocent choices made by individuals, but their cumulative impact has the potential to devastate springs and rivers. As consumers, we might cut back on french-fry consumption; it would be good for our hearts as well as for our rivers. Because most domestic water use goes for exterior purposes (lawns, swimming pools, gardens), homeowners might rethink their choice to water a sprawling lawn with groundwater. They might also install low-flow faucets, showerheads, and toilets. These involve relatively pain-free changes.

The contribution that each of us can make as a citizen will depend on how much time, energy, or commitment we have. A happy theme of this book is the recognition of local heroes—individuals fighting to make a difference. Tom Maddock, Steve and Cathy Monsees, Vernon Maseyesva, Ed Baum, Kerry Mackin, Brian Richter, Jeff Mount, Mike Eaton, Terri Wolfe, and Tom Myers, among others, deserve our gratitude. (Their grass-roots organizations, and others like them, need support. They are listed in the appendix.) The involvement of concerned citizens is critical, because countless other stories like the ones in this book are unfolding. It is not yet clear whether the rivers in these other stories will dry up like the Santa Cruz River in Arizona or be saved like the Mecan River in Wisconsin. Their fate depends on how we respond.

Appendix

Organizations Committed to Protecting the Environment from Groundwater Pumping

The following environmental organizations and community groups are concerned about the impact of groundwater pumping on the environment. This appendix may aid readers who wish to become involved or to learn more about a particular controversy. I am sure that this list is not exhaustive, as there must be dozens of other wonderful, community-based organizations doing extremely important work.

Organizations Involved in the Case Studies in this Book

Introduction. Perrier's Search for New Sources of Spring Water

In Wisconsin:
Waterkeepers of Wisconsin
P.O. Box 66
Briggsville, WI 53920
E-mail: wow@friendsofthemecan.com
(608) 981-2534 or (920) 787-4808

Concerned Citizens of Newport (CCN)
N9947 Thompson Drive
Wisconsin Dells, WI 53965
E-mail: ccn@saveamericaswater.com

Save America's Water
P.O. Box 573
Shawano, WI 54166
Phone: (715) 524-5998
Fax: (call first) (715) 524-9958
E-mail: WeCan@saveamericaswater.com

In Michigan:
Ms. Terry Swier
Michigan Citizens for Water Conservation
P.O. Box 1
Mecosta, MI 49332
(231) 972-8856
E-mail: mcwc@saveMIwater.org

In Florida:
Ms. Terri Wolfe, President
Save Our Springs Inc.
P.O. Box 174
Crystal Springs, FL 33524
E-mail: sos@3oaks.com
Web site: Saveourspringsinc.org

Chapter 4. The San Pedro River
Professor Thomas Maddock III
Codirector, Research Laboratory for Riparian Studies
Department of Hydrology and Water Resources, Bldg. 11
The University of Arizona
Tucson, AZ 85721
Phone: (520) 621-5082
Fax: (520) 621-1422
E-mail: maddock@hwr.arizona.edu

Mr. Andy Laurenzi
Ms. Holly Richter
The Nature Conservancy
1510 E. Ft. Lowell Road
Tucson, AZ 85719
Phone: (520) 622-3861
Fax: (520) 620-1799
E-mail: laurenzi@tnc.org, hollyrichter@theriver.com

Tricia Gerrodette, President
Huachuca Audubon Society
P.O. Box 63
Sierra Vista, AZ 85636

Robin D. Silver, M.D.
Conservation Chair
Center for Biological Diversity
P.O. Box 39382
Phoenix, AZ 85069-9382
Phone: (602) 246-4170
Fax: (602) 249-2576
E-mail: rsilver@biologicaldiversity.org
Web site: www.biologicaldiversity.org

Sonoran Institute
7650 E. Broadway Blvd., Suite 203
Tucson, AZ 85710
Phone: (520) 290-0828
Fax: (520) 290-0969
Web site: www.sonoran.org/si/index.html

Chapter 5. *Tampa Bay's Avarice*
Ms. Terri Wolfe, President
Save Our Springs, Inc.
P.O. Box 174
Crystal Springs, FL 33524
E-mail: sos@3oaks.com
Web site: Saveourspringsinc.org

Chapter 6. *The Edwards Aquifer*
Mr. Ken Kramer, Director
Lone Star Chapter
Texas Sierra Club
P.O. Box 1931
Austin, TX 78767
Phone: (512) 477-1729
Fax: (512) 477-8526
E-mail: lonestar.chapter@sierraclub.org
Web site: www.texas.sierraclub.org

Ms. Melinda E. Taylor
Program Manager for Ecosystem Restoration
Environmental Defense
44 East Avenue, Suite 304
Austin, TX 78701
Phone: (512) 478-5161
Fax: (512) 478-8140
E-mail: melindataylor@environmentaldefense.org
Web site: www.environmentaldefense.org

San Marcos River Foundation
P.O. Box 1393
San Marcos, TX 78667
Phone: (512) 393-3787
E-mail: wassenich@sanmarcos.net
Web site: www.sanmarcosriver.org

Chapter 7. Ipswich River in Massachusetts
Ms. Kerry Mackin
Executive Director
Ipswich River Watershed Association
240 County Road, P.O. Box 576
Ipswich, MA 01938
Phone: (978) 356-0418
Fax: (978) 356-1993
E-mail: irwainfo@ipswichriver.org
Web site: www.ipswichriver.org

Mr. Lou Wagner
Massachusetts Audubon Society
Advocacy Department
South Great Road
Lincoln, MA 01733
Phone: (781) 259-9500
Fax: (781) 259-1089

Mr. Robert L. Zimmerman, Jr.
Executive Director
Charles River Watershed Association

2391 Commonwealth Avenue
Newton, MA 02166
Phone: (617) 965-5975
E-mail: crwa@crwa.org
Web site: www.crwa.org

Chapter 8. The Cosumnes River

Michael R. Eaton, Esq.
Director, Cosumnes River Project
The Nature Conservancy
13501 Franklin Blvd.
Galt, CA 95632
Phone: (916) 683-1699
Fax: (916) 683-1702
E-mail: meaton@cosumnes.org

Ms. Ellen Mantalica
Coordinator, The Cosumnes Research Group
Center for Integrated Watershed Science & Management
Kerr Hall 183
University of California
Davis, CA 95616
Phone: (530) 754-9133
Fax: (530) 754-9141
Web site: watersheds.des.ucdavis.edu/crg/

Chapter 9. Wild Atlantic Salmon

Mr. Ed Baum, Fisheries Consultant
Atlantic Salmon Unlimited
P.O. Box 6185
Hermon, ME 04402-6185
Phone/Fax: (207) 848-5590
E-mail: ASUnlimited@aol.com

Atlantic Salmon Federation
Maine Council
14 Maine St., Suite 308
Brunswick, ME 04011
    or

RR3 Box 86
Bangor, ME 04401
Phone: (207) 725-2833
Fax: (207) 725-2967
E-mail: asfme@blazenetme.net

Mr. Jeff Reardon
New England Conservation Director
Trout Unlimited
14 Maine St., Suite 304
Brunswick, ME 04011
Phone: (207) 373-0700
E-mail: jreardon@tu.org

Mr. Matthew Scott
Executive Secretary
Project Share
RFD 1, Box 428
Belgrade, ME 04917
Phone: (207) 495-3409
E-mail: mscott@clinic.net

Chapter 10. Minnesota's Straight River
Minnesota Trout Unlimited
P.O. Box 11465
St. Paul, MN 55111-0465
Web site: www.mntu.org

Minnesota Center for Environmental Advocacy
26 E. Exchange Street, Suite 206
St. Paul, MN 55101-1667
Phone: (651) 223-5969
Fax: (651) 223-5967
Email: mcea@mncenter.org
Web site: www.mncenter.org

Carolyn Raffensperger, Esq.
Executive Director
Science and Environmental Health Network

3704 W. Lincoln Way #282
Ames, IA 50014
E-mail: raffensperger@cs.com
Web site: www.sehn.org

Chapter 11. The Black Mesa Coal Slurry Pipeline

Mr. Vernon Masayesva
Black Mesa Trust
P.O. Box 33
Kykotsmovi, AZ 86039
Phone: (480) 675-0870
Web site: www.blackmesatrust.org

Natural Resources Defense Council
Regional Office
71 Stevenson Street, #1825
San Francisco, CA 94105
Phone: (415) 777-0220
E-mail: nrdcinfo@nrdc.org

Black Mesa Recovery Campaign
c/o Glen Canyon Institute
P.O. Box 1925
Flagstaff, AZ 86002
Phone: (928) 556-9311
Fax: (928) 779-3567
Web site: www.glencanyon.org

Chapter 12. Gold Mining in Nevada

Tom Myers, Ph.D.
Director
Great Basin Mine Watch
P.O. Box 10262
Reno, NV 89510
Phone: (775) 348-1986
Fax: (775) 324-7667
E-mail: tom@black-rock.reno.nv.us
Web site: www.greatbasinminewatch.org

Western Shoshone Defense Project
P.O. Box 211308
Crescent Valley, NV 89821
Phone: (775) 468-0230
Fax: (775) 468-0237
E-mail: wsdp@igc.org

Chapter 13. Apalachicola Bay

James E. Hook, Ph.D.
Lead Research Scientist
National Environmentally Sound Production Agriculture Laboratory
The University of Georgia
Coastal Plain Experiment Station
P.O. Box 748
Tifton, GA 31793-0748
Phone: (229) 386-7274
Fax: (229) 386-7371
E-mail: nespal@tifton.cpes.peachnet.edu
Web site: nespal.cpes.peachnet.edu

Ms. Layne Bolen
The Nature Conservancy
Apalachicola River & Bay Project Manager
P.O. Box 876
Apalachicola, FL 32329-0876
Phone: (850) 653-3111
Fax: (850) 653-3526
E-mail: lbolen@tnc.org
Web site: www.nature.org/florida

Mr. Brian D. Richter
Director, Freshwater Initiative
The Nature Conservancy
490 Westfield Road
Charlottesville, VA 22901
Phone: (804) 295-6106
Fax: (804) 979-0370
E-mail: brichter@tnc.org
Web site: www.freshwaters.org

Professor Robert J. Livingston
Center Director
Center for Aquatic Research and Resource Management
Florida State University
Tallahassee, FL 32306-2043
Phone: (850) 644-1466
Fax: (850) 644-9829
E-mail: livingst@bio.fsu.edu

Chapter 14. Grand Canyon National Park

Grand Canyon Trust
2601 N. Fort Valley Road
Flagstaff, AZ 86001
Phone: (928) 774-7488
Fax: (928) 774-7570
Toll free: (888) GCT-5550 (1-888-428-5550)
E-mail: info@grandcanyontrust.org
Web site: www.grandcanyontrust.org

National Parks Conservation Association
1300 19th Street, Suite 300
Washington, DC 20036
Phone: (800) 628-7275
Fax: (202) 659-0650
Web site: www.npca.org

Natural Resources Defense Council
Regional Office
71 Stevenson Street, #1825
San Francisco, CA 94105
Phone: (415) 777-0220
E-mail: nrdcinfo@nrdc.org

National Organizations

The Nature Conservancy
Attn: Treasury (Web/Support)
4245 N. Fairfax Drive, Suite 100
Arlington, VA 22203

Phone: (800) 628-6860
Web site: nature.org
E-mail: comment@tnc.org
(For information on The Nature Conservancy's Freshwater Initiative,
go to their Web site: www.freshwaters.org)

National Parks Conservation Association
1300 19th Street, Suite 300
Washington, DC 20036
Phone: (800) 628-7275
Fax: (202) 659-0650
Web site: www.npca.org

Natural Resources Defense Council
40 W. 20th Street
New York, NY 10011
Phone: (212) 727-2700
Fax: (212) 727-1773
E-mail: nrdcinfo@nrdc.org

Trout Unlimited
1500 Wilson Blvd., #310
Arlington, VA 22209-2404
Phone: (703) 522-0200
Fax: (703) 284-9400
E-mail: trout@tu.org
Web site: www.tu.org/index.html

American Rivers
1025 Vermont Avenue, N.W., Suite 720
Washington, DC 20005
Phone: (202) 347-7550
Toll-free: (877) 347-7550
Fax: (202) 347-9240
Web site: www.americanrivers.org

National Audubon Society
700 Broadway
New York, NY 10003

Phone: (212) 979-3000
Fax: (212) 979-3188
E-mail: audubonaction@audubon.org
Web site: www.audubon.org

Sierra Club
85 Second Street, 2nd Floor
San Francisco, CA 94105-3441
Phone: (415) 977-5500
Fax: (415) 977-5799
E-mail: information@sierraclub.org
Web site: www.sierraclub.org

Glossary

Acequia: A community organization in the Hispanic Southwest that controls the distribution of water on the basis of need rather than prior appropriation.

Acre-foot of water: The volume of water required to cover one acre of land to a depth of one foot, or 325,851 gallons.

Algae: Aquatic one- or multicelled plants without true stems, roots, and leaves but containing chlorophyll. Algae may produce taste and odor problems in water.

Alluvial: As an adjective: of, pertaining to, or composed of alluvium. As a noun: an alluvial deposit.

Alluvial valley: The deposits of erosion from surrounding mountains.

Alluvium: Debris from erosion, consisting of some mixture of clay particles, sand, pebbles, and larger rocks. Usually a good porous storage medium for groundwater.

Aquifer: A geologic formation containing enough saturated porous and permeable material to transmit water at a rate sufficient to feed a spring or for economic extraction by a well. Combination of two Latin words, *aqua* or water, and *ferre* to bring; literally, something that brings water.

Artesian well: A well in which water rises to the surface without pumping from a permeable geologic formation that is overlain by an impermeable formation.

Baseflow: Water that flows regularly (i.e., not floodwater temporarily stored in riverbanks) from an aquifer into a river or stream. Baseflow is particularly important to river ecosystems during periods of little or no precipitation.

Bedrock: Consolidated rocks that form the bottom and sides of a valley. Bedrock is nearly impermeable and is a barrier to groundwater flow.

Bosque: A Spanish word meaning a grove of trees (pronounced BOS-kay).

Brackish: Water with a salt concentration greater than freshwater and less than seawater.

Capture: The amount of increased groundwater recharge, decreased groundwater discharge, or both, due to the stress of pumping from a well. Capture usually refers to water that is removed from an aquifer via groundwater pumping when this water would (without pumping) flow to support a river ecosystem.

Computer model: A computer program used by hydrologists to simulate a hydrologic system. A computer model can estimate various aspects of a hydrologic system, including the impact of groundwater pumping on a nearby surface water body and on the water table.

Cone of depression: A drop in the water table around a well or wells that have been pumping groundwater. Depending on the rate of pumping and aquifer characteristics, a cone of depression can be shallow and extend only a few feet, or it can extend for several miles. Because water flows downgradient underground, a cone of depression pulls water from the surrounding area into it, thus affecting the nearby water table.

Confined aquifer: An aquifer bounded above and below by confining units (i.e., low-permeability layers of sediment or rock).

Confining layer: Body of material with low vertical permeability.

Confluence: Point of juncture of two or more streams.

Conservation easement: A restriction placed on land to preserve it from development.

Consumptive use: An activity that withdraws water from the basin and returns only some or none back to the basin.

Cubic feet per second (cfs): A unit expressing volume of flow in a river. One cubic foot equals 7.5 gallons.

Desalinization: A process of removing salts and other dissolved minerals from water.

Dewatering: The act of emptying pores filled with water from a sedimentary or rock layer.

Discharge: The outflow of water from the ground to a surface water body.

Dissolved oxygen: Gaseous oxygen dissolved in water.

Draft environmental impact statement (EIS): Publication that documents the environmental conditions, issues, and effects associated with an action affecting the environment and on which the public is invited to comment. Comments received from regulatory agencies, organizations, and individuals are addressed in the final EIS (see **final EIS**).

Drawdown: The lowering of the water table caused by the withdrawal of water from an aquifer by pumping.

Effluent: Sewage water that will go through or has undergone treatment.

Estuary: The lower portion or wide mouth of a river, where the salty tide meets the freshwater current.

Evapotranspiration: The compound word that refers to the net effect of both evaporation and plants' transpiration (see **transpiration**).

Federal reserved rights: Water rights that attach to federal land set aside by Congress or the president for a particular purpose.

Filtration: The process of passing water through materials with very small holes (pores) to strain out particles. Filtration can remove microorganisms, including algae, bacteria, and protozoa, but not viruses.

Final EIS: The final product of the environmental impact statement process, which responds to comments received on the draft EIS (see **draft EIS**).

Floodplain: Land adjacent to a river channel that is covered with water when the river overflows its banks.

Gaining stream/river: A stream or river that gains water from the adjacent groundwater system. This water is called baseflow.

Gallons per capita per day (gpcd): The amount of water used on average by an individual each day. Total gpcd is calculated by dividing total water use in the area, including industrial, commercial, and agricultural uses, by the number of users. Residential gpcd is the number resulting from considering only domestic water use.

Geologic formation: A persistent body of igneous, sedimentary, or metamorphic rock having easily recognizable boundaries that can be presented on a map as a practical or convenient unit for mapping and description.

Glacial till: Sediment left behind by glaciers (see **till**).

Grandfathered rights: When a state restricts water use but exempts existing users from the new limit, those existing users have grandfathered rights.

Groundwater: Water located beneath the surface of the earth.

Groundwater system: A geologic collection of adjacent aquifers.

Hydraulic connection: A saturated connection between a river or stream and the water table in the aquifer.

Hydraulic gradient: The change of pressure per unit distance from one point to another in an aquifer. When an area is "downgradient," it is at a lower level and water will flow in that direction.

Hydrologic model: A statement of simplified relationships abstracted from a natural hydrologic system. Model parameters are developed from selected observations of the properties of interest to suit the model purpose.

Infiltration: The process of water entering the soil or streambed surface.

Karst: A region made up of porous limestone containing deep fissures and sinkholes and characterized by underground caves and water that moves quickly through the fissures and caves.

Losing stream/river: A stream or river in which water flows from the river to the adjacent groundwater system.

Mountain front recharge: Natural recharge that occurs at the base of the mountains because of rainfall or snow melt at higher elevations.

Outwash: Washed, sorted, and stratified drift deposited by water from melting glacial ice.

Overdraft: Water withdrawn from an aquifer in an amount that exceeds recharge.

Overstory: The canopy of foliage of mature trees.

Perennial: A reach of river that flows year-round.

Permeable: The relative ease with which a geologic formation can transmit water.

Potable water: Water that is suitable for drinking; from a Latin word meaning "drink."

Prior appropriation: The system of surface water rights that rewards the earliest diverters with the greatest security ("first-in-time" is "first-in-right").

Pumping test: A hydrologic test in which an aquifer is pumped at a given location and its response to the pumping is observed (i.e., amount of water drawdown at the well and/or in surrounding monitor wells).

Reasonable use doctrine: The system of groundwater rights that allows a property owner to pump a limitless quantity of water so long as it is used on his or her land and used for a beneficial purpose.

Recharge: (verb) To add water to a groundwater system; (noun), the net amount of water added.

Return flow: Water diverted for use, either from a river or groundwater, that is not consumptively used and that flows back into the source. These flows may occur as surface or subsurface flows directly into a river.

Riparian: Of or pertaining to a river or river system.

Riparianism: The system of surface water rights in the eastern United States that allows those who own property on a river or lake to use that water.

Riparian vegetation: Vegetation located on the banks or in the vicinity of a river, stream, or other body of surface water.

River reach: An arbitrarily defined length/stretch of a river.

Rule of capture: The system of groundwater rights that places absolutely no restriction on the quantity of water that may be pumped or the location of its use.

Runoff: Water that runs off the ground surface and into a river or wash. It runs off the ground surface because the ground is saturated or impermeable and cannot absorb moisture.

Salinity: A measure of the salt concentration in water.

Saturated zone: The zone underground in which all voids in soil and rock are filled with water. The water table is the upper limit of this zone.

Sediment: Fragmented material that originates from weathering of rocks and is transported or deposited by air, water, or ice.

Sedimentary rocks: Rocks resulting from consolidation of sediments. The rocks can be formed in marine, estuarine, and continental environments.

Sinkhole: A portion of land that has collapsed because of either dewatering or dissolution of limestone in limestone aquifer systems.

Streamflow gauge: Device located on a river that measures water levels and stream flows.

Subsidence: Downward movement of the land surface associated with groundwater pumping, especially where pumping has caused the water table to drop. Subsidence is an essentially irreversible process not greatly ameliorated by later raising the water table.

Till: Unsorted, unstratified clay, silt, sand, gravel, or boulders of glacial origin.

Total dissolved solids (TDS): A measure of the minerals dissolved in water.

Transmissibility: The flow capacity of an aquifer measured in volume per unit time per unit width.

Transmissivity: The rate at which water flows through an aquifer.

Transpiration: The process of giving off moisture through the surface of leaves and other parts of plants.

Treatment plant: A facility using various physical and chemical processes to treat water or wastewater.

Turbidity: The reduction of transparency in water due to the presence of suspended particles; a cloudy appearance in the water.

Unconfined aquifer: Saturated zone between the water table and an underlying confining unit.

Water right: The entitlement to withdraw and beneficially use a specified amount of the water of a hydrologic system.

Watershed: The geographic area drained by a river or river system.

Water table: The surface in an unconfined aquifer at which pressure is atmospheric and below which the permeable material is saturated with water.

Well field: A group of wells in a particular geographic area, usually operated by one entity.

Wetland: An area that always has water at or near the surface. A natural wetland receives its water from a groundwater source and, in the American Southwest, is also called a *cienega*.

List of Acronyms

ACF	Apalachicola-Chattahoochee-Flint
af	acre-foot of water, or approximately 325,851 gallons
ALCOA	Aluminum Company of America
AMA	active management area, area of regulation under Arizona Groundwater Management Act
BLM	U.S. Bureau of Land Management
CAWCD	Central Arizona Water Conservation District
CEC	Commission for Environmental Cooperation, set up under the North American Free Trade Agreement
cfs	cubic feet of water per second
CFV	Canyon Forest Village Corporation
CPS	City Public Service
DER	Maine Department of Environmental Regulation
DHS	California Department of Health Services
DNR	Department of Natural Resources (of Minnesota and Wisconsin)
EIS	environmental impact statement
EPD	Georgia Environmental Protection Division
ESA	Endangered Species Act
FDA	U.S. Food and Drug Administration
FWS	U.S. Fish and Wildlife Service

gpd	gallons of water per day
gpm	gallons of water per minute
IRWA	Ipswich River Watershed Association
LURC	Maine Land Use Regulation Commission
maf	million acre-feet
mgd	millions of gallons per day
MWRA	Massachusetts Water Resources Authority
NMFS	National Marine Fisheries Service
NPDES	National Pollution Discharge Elimination System permit, under the Clean Water Act
SAWS	San Antonio Water System
SLAPP	strategic litigation against public participation
TNC	The Nature Conservancy
USGS	U.S. Geological Survey

Bibliography

General Background

Books

Ball, Philip. *A Biography of Water: Life's Matrix*. New York: Farrar, Straus and Giroux, 1999.

Childs, Craig. *The Secret Knowledge of Water: Discovering the Essence of the American Desert*. Seattle: Sasquatch Books, 2000.

De Villiers, Marq. *Water: The Fate of Our Most Precious Resource*. New York: Houghton Mifflin Company, 1999.

Hundley, Norris, Jr. *The Great Thirst: Californians and Water, 1770s–1990s*. Berkeley: University of California Press, 1992.

Koeppel, Gerard T. *Water for Gotham: A History*. Princeton: Princeton University Press, 2000.

Pielou, E. C. *Fresh Water*. Chicago: The University of Chicago Press, 1998.

Reisner, Marc. *Cadillac Desert: The American West and Its Disappearing Water*. New York: Viking Penguin Inc., 1986.

Reisner, Marc and Sarah Bates. *Overtapped Oasis: Reform or Revolution for Western Water*. Washington, D.C.: Island Press, 1990.

Worster, Donald. *Rivers of Empire: Water, Aridity, and the Growth of the American West*. New York: Pantheon Books, 1985.

Articles and Reports

Glennon, Robert Jerome and Thomas Maddock III. "In Search of Subflow: Arizona's Futile Effort to Separate Groundwater from Surface Water." *Arizona Law Review*, vol. 36, p. 567, 1994.

Glennon, Robert Jerome and Thomas Maddock III. "The Concept of Capture: The Hydrology and Law of Stream/Aquifer Interactions." *Proceedings of the Rocky Mountain Mineral Law Institute*, vol. 43, p. 22-1–22-89, 1997.

Western Water Policy Review Advisory Commission Report. *Water in the West: Challenge for the Next Century*. Denver, Colorado. June 1998.

Winter, Thomas C. et al. *Ground Water and Surface Water: A Single Resource*. U.S. Geological Survey Circular 1139, 1998.

Introduction

Books

Born, Steve et al. *Exploring Wisconsin Trout Streams: The Angler's Guide*. Madison: The University of Wisconsin Press, 1997.

Raffensperger, Carolyn and Joel Tickner, eds. *Protecting Public Health and the Environment: Implementing the Precautionary Principle*. Washington, D.C.: Island Press, 1999.

Articles and Reports

"Anti-Bottlers Form Coalition." *Chicago Tribune*, 30 May 2000.

Anthony, Ted. "Ancient Water Quenches Town's Thirst Environment: Parched Oakley, Utah, Finds a Massive Aquifer and a Taste of Yesterday." *Los Angeles Times*, 12 December 1999.

Bartolai, Elizabeth. "Most Lynn TWP Water Off-Limits." *Allentown Morning Call*, 29 October 1997.

Bartolai, Elizabeth. "Ontelaunee Creek Trout Counts Differ with 7 Months in Between; Perrier Has to Study Increased Water Withdrawal's Effects on Aquatic Life." *Allentown Morning Call*, 29 March 1998.

Bartolai, Elizabeth. "Perrier Wants to Triple Water Intake; Lynn TWP Residents Tour Facilities, Hear Details, But Some Still Gulp at Plan." *Allentown Morning Call*, 29 March 1998.

Bartolai, Elizabeth. "Perrier Says Withdrawals Below Limit; It Reports It May Be in Line with State's Request for 10 Percent Water Cutback." *Allentown Morning Call*, 30 June 1999.

Bartolai, Elizabeth. "Perrier Says It's Withdrawing 15 Percent Less Water from Springs; Deer Park Brand Water Is Taken from Lynn Township's Hoffman Springs, Bottled in Upper Macungie." *Allentown Morning Call*, 6 August 1999.

Bartolai, Elizabeth. "Citizens Group Monitors Ontelaunee Creek Quality: Lynn TWP Members Are Worried About Perrier Buying Land to Take More Water from Other Sources." *The Morning Call*, 20 February 2001.

"Bill's Author Sees Possible Passage of New Controls this Spring." Associated Press Newswires, 2 March 2000.

"Bottled Water Company Decides to Shift Springs Search." Associated Press Newswires, 26 February 2000.

Bottled Water Web. "The Worth of Water," 1999, <www.bottledwaterweb.com>.

"Bottling Up SW Wisconsin." *The Capital Times*, 23 June 2000.

"Bottling Water Raises Conservation Concerns, Perrier Wants to Drill for Water in the State-owned Mecan Springs Area, but with What Environmental Impact?" *Wisconsin State Journal*, 20 December 1999.

Burnett, Lee. "Pumping for Dollars." *Maine Times*, 27 January 2000.

Carter and Burgess. "High Capacity Well Application for The Perrier Group of America's Proposed Bottled Water Project." 19 June 2000.

Carter and Burgess. "Preliminary Design Report and Environmental Analysis for The Perrier Group of America's Proposed Bottled Water Project." 19 June 2000.

Concerned Citizens of Newport and Waterkeepers of Wisconsin. "Gov. Thompson Says—'Move On.'" Briggsville, Wisconsin. Press Release, 1 November 2000.

Concerned Citizens of Newport and Waterkeepers of Wisconsin. "Perrier Tests Raised Red Flags." Briggsville, Wisconsin. Press Release, 7 January 2001.

Dames & Moore. "Work Plan Groundwater Study Perrier Group of America." Big Spring Area, Adams County, Madison, Wisconsin, February 2000.

Dames & Moore. "Draft Interim Report: Wetland Resources Study." Big Spring Creek, Adams County, Madison, Wisconsin, 23 May 2000.

DeArmond, Michelle. "Morongo Tribe Unveils Plans for Bottling Plant." *The Press-Enterprise*, 12 January 2002.

Department of Urban and Regional Planning, University of Wisconsin–Madison/Extension. *Modernizing Wisconsin Groundwater Management: Reforming the High Capacity Well Laws*. August 2000.

"DNR to Hold Hearing on Perrier Well Request." *The Capital Times*, 21 June 2000.

Donnelly, Francis X. "Bottled Water Fight Grows, Mecosta County Residents, Officials at Odds over Proposed $100 Million Perrier Plant." *The Detroit News*, 20 May 2001.

"DRBC Amends Ground Water Regulations in Southeast Pennsylvania to Include 62 Additional Watersheds." *PR Newswire*, 25 June 1999.

Durantine, Peter. "Bottling Companies Tap into State's Groundwater." *Pittsburgh Post-Gazette*, 3 August 1997.

Food and Drug Administration, U.S. Department of Health and Human Services. *Code of Federal Regulations Title 21 - Food and Drugs Chapter I; Subchapter B - Food for Human Consumption; Part 165 - Beverages; Subpart B - Requirements for Specific Standardized Beverages*; 21 C.F.R. § 165.110, Bottled Water, 2000.

Gallagher, David F. "'Just Say No to H$_2$O' (Unless It's Coke's Own Brew)." *The New York Times*, 2 September 2001.

Gelt, Joe. "Consumers Increasingly Use Bottled Water, Home Water Treatment Systems to Avoid Direct Tap Water." *Arroyo*, 9, No. 1, March 1996.

Johnson, Malcolm. "Water Fight: Lines Drawn in Battle over Regulation, Protection of 'Liquid Gold.'" *The Grand Rapids Press*, 16 November 2001.

Jones, Meg. "Perrier Plan Meets Geyser of Opposition." *The Milwaukee Journal Sentinel*, 15 February 2000.

Jones, Meg. "Leave Water Alone, Voters Tell Perrier." *The Milwaukee Journal Sentinel*, 14 June 2000.

Kraft, George J. "Comments on the 'Great Spring Waters of America' Environmental Assessment." University of Wisconsin, 2 August 2000.

"Lafayette County Lays Out Welcome Mat for Perrier." Associated Press Newswires, 17 June 2000.

Lezin, Sophia. "Lynn Zoners Deny Plan to Draw Water from 3 Township Springs; Farm

Owner Wanted to Pump 700,000 Gallons a Week but Would Not Say Why; 140 Residents Attend Meeting to Protest." *Allentown Morning Call,* 27 March 1996.

Lezin, Sophia. "Don't Bottle Our Water, Say Local Activists; Hundreds of Thousands of Gallons Could Be Extracted Each Week from Eastern PA Springs." *Allentown Morning Call,* 24 November 1996.

Maier, Craig. "Neerah Springs vs. Perrier." *Portage Daily Register,* 24 June 2000.

Maller, Peter. "Latest Perrier Plan Gets a Dousing." *The Milwaukee Journal Sentinel,* 2 March 2000.

Maller, Peter. "Protesters Denounce Perrier Bottling Plans." *The Milwaukee Journal Sentinel,* 18 April 2000.

Maller, Peter. "Perrier Isn't Deterred by Bottling Plant Votes." *The Milwaukee Journal Sentinel,* 15 June 2000.

McCarthy, Guy. "Morongos Build Water-Bottling Plant." *The Press-Enterprise,* 3 January 2002.

Minnesota Department of Natural Resources. "Environmental Analysis and Decision on the Need for an Environmental Impact Statement (EIS)." Rev. 3-87, 2000.

"More Perrier Lawsuits Filed: New Complaints Aim to Stop the Company's Drilling of Wells." *Wisconsin State Journal,* 20 October 2000.

"Morongo Indians Plan Largest Bottling Plant in Nation." Associated Press Newswires, 11 January 2002.

Murphy, Grace. "Neighbors Question Bottling Plant Impact, Poland Spring Assures Hollis Residents It Will Protect Their Wells." *Portland Press Herald,* 18 August 1999.

Natural Resources Defense Council. *Clean Water & Oceans: Drinking Water: In Depth Report, Bottled Water, Pure Drink or Pure Hype?,* March 1999. (Available at www.nrdc.org/water/drinking/bw/bwinx.asp)

"Nature Preserve Usage Questioned." Associated Press Newswires, 12 January 2000.

Ness, Erik. "Spin the Bottle: Perrier Didn't Reckon on an Angry Citizenry When It Looked to Expand into the Midwest." *Grist Magazine,* 21 May 2001.

"New Laws for Great Lakes: Perrier Proposal Shows Holes in State's Water Management." *The Grand Rapids Press,* 3 December 2001.

"Newport Citizens Group Sues DNR." *Milwaukee Journal Sentinel,* 12 October 2000.

"Perrier on Ice: Plans Raise Serious Questions about Protecting State Groundwater." *The Grand Rapids Press,* 25 June 2001.

"Perrier Plan to Drill Near Stream Draws Dissenters: Senator, Conservationists 'Skeptical' about the Proposed Bottling Operation that May Affect a Prized Water Source." *Wisconsin State Journal,* 24 December 1999.

"Perrier Plans to Meet Residents of Adams County." Associated Press Newswires, 28 February 2000.

"Perrier Says Water, Well Tests 'Very Encouraging' but Foes Don't Want Plant." *The Capital Times,* 18 April 2000.

"Perrier Talking with DNR about Bottling Wisconsin Water." Associated Press Newswires, 23 December 1999.

Possley, Maurice. "Wisconsin Trout Lovers Fight Lure of Perrier." *Chicago Tribune,* 17 January 2000.

Possley, Maurice. "Perrier Drops Wisconsin Plan, Mecan Springs Furor Forces Bottled-Water Giant to Abandon Its Request for a Well on State-Owned Land." *Chicago Tribune*, 3 February 2000.

Price, Jenny. "DNR Says Perrier Wells Won't Hurt Area's Water." *The Milwaukee Journal Sentinel*, 26 July 2000.

"Protest Signs Greet Company Officials at Meeting." Associated Press Newswires, 18 April 2000.

"Public Objections to Water-Bottling Plan Heard." Associated Press Newswires, 16 March 2000.

"Residents Oppose Perrier Bottling Plans." Associated Press Newswires, 8 January 2000.

Saemann, Karyn. "Group Pledges to Fight DNR's Perrier OK." *The Capital Times*, 22 September 2000.

Sandin, Jo. "DNR Says Perrier Proposal Won't Deplete Water Supply." *The Milwaukee Journal Sentinel*, 25 July 2000.

Seely, Ron. "Questions Abound on Perrier Proposal, Company Is Said to Be Very Interested in Pumping Water from Mecan Springs." *Wisconsin State Journal*, 2 January 2000.

Seely, Ron. "Perrier Wants to Drill Multiple Wells in Springs, Bottler Tells State Officials More Testing Needs to Be Carried Out on the Site Before a Final Decision Is Made." *Wisconsin State Journal*, 12 January 2000.

Seely, Ron. "Disputes Follow Perrier, Despite Legal Challenges in Other States, Bottler Says Initial Uneasiness Often Abates." *Wisconsin State Journal*, 13 February 2000.

Seely, Ron. "Perrier Talks May Improve Options, Opponents Are Willing to Help the Bottler Find a Site that Better Suits the Needs of State Residents." *Wisconsin State Journal*, 25 February 2000.

Seely, Ron. "Perrier Meets Opposition, Again Big Spring Crowd Wary of Proposal." *Wisconsin State Journal*, 2 March 2000.

Spencer, Theo. "Something to Gush About." *Gourmet*, February 2000.

Swiatek, Jeff. "Local Water Bottler Canon Springs Sold to Perrier Group." *Indianapolis Star*, 6 June 2000.

"Tribe Signs Arrowhead Water Deal." *Los Angeles Times*, 13 January 2002.

Vanden Brook, Tom. "Perrier Wants to Draw Water on State Land; Bottler's Proposal Sparks Concern for Trout Stream." *The Milwaukee Journal Sentinel*, 19 December 1999.

Vanden Brook, Tom. "Perrier Considering Other Midwest Springs for Plant." *The Milwaukee Journal Sentinel*, 23 December 1999.

Vanden Brook, Tom. "A Source for Worry." *The Milwaukee Journal Sentinel*, 13 February 2000.

Vanden Brook, Tom. "State DNR's Approval of Wells Seems Unlikely." *The Milwaukee Journal Sentinel*, 13 February 2000.

Vanden Brook, Tom. "State Quietly Tried to Woo Perrier." *Milwaukee Journal Sentinel*, 28 March 2000.

Vanden Brook, Tom. "Nation's Thirst Raises Fears for Springs." *USA Today*, 18 April 2001.

Waterkeepers of Wisconsin. "Adams County Passes Water Resolution." Briggsville, Wisconsin. Press release, 21 November 2000.

"Water-Tapping Forum Draws Protest; DNR Secretary Wants Tougher Laws." Associated Press Newswires, 15 February 2000.

White, Ed. "Osceola Bottled-Water Plant Approved." *The Grand Rapids Press*, 20 February 2001.

White, Ed. "Engler Aide Warned Perrier Could Undermine Effort to Save Water." *The Grand Rapids Press*, 15 May 2001.

Wisconsin Department of Natural Resources. "Mecan River System Fishery Area, Wausharar and Marquette Counties (Master Plan) Concept Element." 23 January 1985.

Letters, Memoranda, Miscellaneous

Culp, Peter W. "The Message on the Bottle: Commodity Fetishism vs. Market Power in the Bottled Water Industry" (unpublished student paper, The University of Arizona, James E. Rogers College of Law, 2000).

House, Samantha, Ho-Chunk Nation Cultural Resources Division. Legislative resolution presented to the Senate Oversight Hearing Committee, 22 August 2000.

House, Samantha, Ho-Chunk Nation Cultural Resources Division. Letter to David Weitz, Perrier Group of America, public affairs manager, Eau Claire, Wisconsin. 28 August 2000.

Lonetree, Willard, Ho-Chunk Nation, Recording Secretary of the Tradition Court. Memorandum to Samantha House and Larry Garvin, Ho-Chunk Nation Historic Preservation Department, Black River Falls, Wisconsin. 11 August 2000.

WIS. STAT. § 35.18(2) (1999).

WIS. STAT. § 281.17 (1999).

WIS. STAT. § 281.35 (1999).

Wisconsin Department of Natural Resources. "Wisconsin State Natural Areas Program" (visited May 3, 1999) <www.dnr.state.wi.us>.

Chapter 1. The Worth of Water in the United States

Books

Barlow, Maude, and Tony Clarke. *Blue Gold: The Fight to Stop the Corporate Theft of the World's Water.* New York: The New Press, 2002.

Bates, Sarah F. et al. *Searching Out the Headwaters: Change and Rediscovery in Western Water Policy.* Washington, D.C.: Island Press, 1993.

Horwitz, Morton J. *The Transformation of American Law, 1780–1860.* Cambridge: Harvard University Press, 1977.

Hundley, Norris, Jr. *Water and the West: The Colorado River Compact and the Politics of Water in the American West*. Berkeley: University of California Press, 1975.

Meyer, Michael C. *Water in the Hispanic Southwest: A Social and Legal History, 1550–1850*. Tucson: The University of Arizona Press, 1984.

Pisani, Donald J. *To Reclaim a Divided West: Water, Law, and Public Policy 1848–1902*. Albuquerque: University of New Mexico Press, 1992.

Pisani, Donald. *Water, Land, and Law in the West*. Lawrence: University Press of Kansas, 1996.

Rothfeder, Jeffrey. *Every Drop for Sale: Our Desperate Battle over Water in a World about to Run Out*. New York: Jeremy P. Tarcher/Putnam, 2001.

Shiva, Vandana. *Water Wars: Privatization, Pollution and Profit*. Cambridge: South End Press, 2002.

Stegner, Wallace Beyone. *The Hundredth Meridian: John Wesley Powell and the Second Opening of the West*, 2nd ed. New York: Penguin Books, 1992.

Webb, Walter Prescott. *The Great Plains*. Boston: Houghton Mifflin, 1936.

Wiel, Samuel. *Water Rights in the Western States*, 3rd ed. 2 vols. San Francisco: Ayer Publishing Company, 1979.

Worster, Donald. *Rivers of Empire: Water, Aridity, and the Growth of the American West*. New York: Pantheon Books, 1985.

Worster, Donald. *A River Running West: The Life of John Wesley Powell*. New York: Oxford University Press, 2001.

Chapter 2. Human Reliance on Groundwater

Books

Bear, Jacob et al. *Seawater Intrusion in Coastal Aquifers—Concepts, Methods, and Practices*. Dordrecht, The Netherlands: Kluwer Academic Publishers, 1999.

Bittenger, Morton and Elizabeth Green. *You Never Miss the Water Till . . . The Ogallala Story*. Littleton, Colorado: Water Resources Publications, 1980.

Bowden, Charles. *Killing the Hidden Waters*. Austin: University of Texas Press, 1977.

Chappelle, Francis. *The Hidden Sea: Ground Water, Springs, and Wells*. Tucson: Geoscience Press, Inc., 1997.

Clapp, Nicholas. *The Road to Ubar, Finding the Atlantis of the Sands*. New York: First Mariner Books, 1999.

Green, Donald. *Land of the Underground Rain*. Austin: University of Texas Press, 1973.

Kromm, David and Stephen White. *Groundwater Exploitations in the High Plains*. Lawrence: University of Kansas Press, 1992.

MacDonnell, Lawrence J. *From Reclamation to Sustainability: Water, Agriculture, and the Environment in the American West*. Niwot: University Press of Colorado, 1999.

Miller, Taylor et al. *The Salty Colorado*. Washington, D.C.: The Conservation Foundation and the John Muir Institute, 1986.

Opie, John. *Ogallala Water for a Dry Land*. Lincoln: University of Nebraska Press, 1993.

Pisani, Donald J. *To Reclaim a Divided West: Water Law, and Public Policy, 1848–1902.* Albuquerque: University of New Mexico Press, 1992.

Sax, Joseph L. et al. *Legal Control of Water Resources*, 3rd ed. St. Paul: The West Group, 2000.

Shurts, John. *Indian Reserved Water Rights: The Winters Doctrine in Its Social and Legal Context, 1880s–1930s.* Norman: University of Oklahoma Press, 2000.

Todd, David Keith. *Ground-Water Resources of the United States.* Berkeley: Premier Press, 1983.

Worster, Donald. *Rivers of Empire: Water, Aridity, and the Growth of the American West.* New York: Pantheon Books, 1985.

Articles and Reports

Alley, William M. et al. *Sustainability of Ground-Water Resources*, U.S. Geological Survey Circular 1186, 1999.

Galloway, Devin et al. *Land Subsidence in the United States*, U.S. Geological Survey Circular 1182, 1999.

Getches, David H. "The Unsettling of the West: How Indians Got the Best Water Rights," *Michigan Law Review*, vol. 99, p. 1473, 2001.

Solley, Wayne B. *Estimates of Water Use in the Western United States in 1990, and Water-Use Trends, 1960–1990.* Report to the Western Water Policy Review Advisory Commission, U.S. Geological Survey, Reston, Virginia. August 1997.

Tellman, Barbara et al. *AZ's Changing Rivers: How People Have Affected the Rivers.* Water Resources Research Center, College of Agriculture, The University of Arizona, Issue Paper #19, March 1997.

U.S. Geological Survey. *Land Subsidence in the United States* (eds. Devin Galloway, David R. Jones, and S. C. Ingebristen). Circular 1182, 1999.

Chapter 3. How Does a River Go Dry?: The Santa Cruz in Tucson

Books

Betancourt, Julio and Raymond Turner. *Tucson's Santa Cruz River and the Arroyo Legacy* (Book manuscript). Tucson: The University of Arizona Press, September 1990.

Leopold, Luna B. *Water, Rivers and Creeks.* Sausalito, CA: University Science Books, 1997.

Leopold, Luna B. and Thomas Maddock. *The Flood Control Controversy: Big Dams, Little Dams, and Land Management.* New York: Ronald Press Co., 1954.

Logan, Michael F. *The Lessening Stream: An Environmental History of the Santa Cruz River.* Tucson: The University of Arizona Press, 2002.

Sheridan, Thomas E. *Arizona: A History.* Tucson: The University of Arizona Press, 1995.

Articles and Reports

Alley, William M. et al. *Sustainability of Ground-Water Resources.* U.S. Geological Survey Circular 1186, 1999.

Arizona Department of Water Resources. *Third Management Plan for Tucson Active Management Area 2000–2010.* December 1999.

Gelt, Joe et al. *Water in the Tucson Area: Seeking Sustainability.* Issue Paper #20, 2d printing, Water Resources Research Center, College of Agriculture, The University of Arizona, Summer 1999.

Ground Water. Prepared for the City of Tucson, Arizona, September 1962.

Halpenny, Leonard C., Water Development Corporation. *Ground-Water Resources within the San Xavier Indian Reservation and Proposals Relating to Leases for Development of Ground Water.* Prepared for the City of Tucson, Arizona, September 1962.

Logan, Michael F. "Head-Cuts and Check-Dams, Changing Patterns of Environmental Manipulation by the Hohokam and Spanish in the Santa Cruz River Valley 200–1820." *Environmental History,* vol. 4, p. 405, 1999.

Park, Lt. John, Corps Topographical Engineers. "Report of Explorations for that Portion of a Railroad Route, Near the Thirty-Second Parallel of North Latitude, Lying Between Dona Ana, on the Rio Grande, and Pimas Villages, on the Gila." *Reports of Explorations and Surveys, to Ascertain the Most Practicable and Economical Route for a Railroad from the Mississippi River to the Pacific Ocean,* made under the direction of the Secretary of War, in 1853–4, According to Acts of Congress of March 3, 1853, May 31, 1854, and August 5, 1854, vol. II.

SFC Engineering Company et al. *Arizona Stream Navigability Study for the Santa Cruz River—Gila River Confluence to the Headwaters (Final Report).* November 1996.

Sheridan, David. *Desertification of the United States.* Council on Environmental Quality, 8 November 1999.

Tellman, Barbara et al. *AZ's Changing Rivers: How People Have Affected the Rivers.* Water Resources Research Center, College of Agriculture, The University of Arizona, Issue Paper #19, March 1997.

Tucson AMA Safe-Yield Task Force. "Issue: Central Arizona Groundwater Replenishment District." (Draft) 10 November 1999.

Tucson AMA Safe-Yield Task Force. "Issue: Conservation Related Incentives to Use Renewable Supplies." (Draft) 10 November 1999.

Tucson AMA Safe-Yield Task Force. "Issue: Opportunities to Increase Utilization of CAP in the Tucson AMA." (Draft) 10 November 1999.

Tucson AMA Safe-Yield Task Force. "Issue: Recharge Siting." (Draft) 10 November 1999.

Tucson AMA Safe-Yield Task Force. "Issue: Recovery of Recharge Credits." (Draft) 10 November 1999.

Tucson AMA Safe-Yield Task Force. "Issue: Renewable Supply Infrastructure." (Draft) 17 November 1999.

Tucson AMA Safe-Yield Task Force. "Issue: Exempt Wells." (Draft) 1 February 2000.

Tucson AMA Safe-Yield Task Force. "Issue: Agricultural Groundwater Rights." (Draft) 18 February 2000.

Tucson AMA Safe-Yield Task Force. "Issue: Cost-Effectiveness of Conservation Efforts." (Draft) 6 March 2000.

Tucson AMA Safe-Yield Task Force. "Issue: Industry Standards." (Draft) 6 March 2000.

Tucson AMA Safe-Yield Task Force. "Issue: Industrial Groundwater Rights." (Draft) 24 March 2000.

Tucson AMA Safe-Yield Task Force. "Issue: Residual Municipal Pumping." (Draft) 24 March 2000.

Tucson AMA Safe-Yield Task Force. "Issue: Sub-Area Management." (Draft) 30 March 2000.

Tucson AMA Safe-Yield Task Force. "Issue: ADWR's Compliance and Enforcement Approach." (Draft) 19 April 2000.

Tucson AMA Safe-Yield Task Force. "Issue: Regional and Community Efforts." (Draft) 19 April 2000.

Tucson AMA Safe-Yield Task Force. "Issue: Shift in Conservation Focus to End Users," (Draft) 20 April 2000.

U.S. Geological Survey. *Estimated Use of Water in the U.S. in 1965.* Circular 556, 2d printing, 1969.

U.S. Geological Survey. *Estimated Use of Water in the U.S. in 1970.* Circular 676, 2d printing, 1975.

U.S. Geological Survey. *Estimated Use of Water in the U.S. in 1975.* Circular 765, 2d printing, 1979.

U.S. Geological Survey. *Estimated Use of Water in the U.S. in 1980.* Circular 1001, 3d printing, 1985.

U.S. Geological Survey. *Estimated Use of Water in the U.S. in 1985.* Circular 1004, 2d printing, 1990.

U.S. Geological Survey. *Estimated Use of Water in the U.S. in 1990.* Circular 1081, 1993.

U.S. Geological Survey. *Channel Change on the Santa Cruz River, Pima County, Arizona 1936–86.* Open-File Report 93-41, Tucson, December 1993.

U.S. Geological Survey. *Estimated Use of Water in the U.S. in 1995.* Circular 1200, 1998.

U.S. Geological Survey. *Water-Quality Assessment of the Central Arizona Basins, Arizona and Northern Mexico—Environmental Setting and Overview of Water Quality.* Water-Resources Investigations Report 98-4097, Tucson, 1998.

Wagner, Raina. "A Wash in Tucson: Our 'Rivers' Lack Water but Brim with Activity." *The Arizona Daily Star,* 22 February 1998.

Chapter 4. A River at Risk: The Upper San Pedro River in Arizona

Books

Freeze, R. Allan and John A. Cherry. *Groundwater.* Englewood Cliffs: Prentice-Hall, Inc., 1979.

Leopold, Luna. *A View of the River.* Cambridge: Harvard University Press, 1994.

Leopold, Luna. *Water, Rivers, and Creeks.* Sausalito: University Science Books, 1997.

Savory, Allan with Jody Butterfield. *Holistic Management: A New Framework for Decision Making.* Washington, D.C.: Island Press, 1999.

Shelton, Richard. *Going Back to Bisbee.* Tucson: The University of Arizona Press, 1992.

Sheridan,Thomas E. *Arizona:A History*.Tucson:The University of Arizona Press, 1995.

Todd, David Keith. *Ground Water Hydrology*. New York: John Wiley & Sons, Inc., 1967.

Articles and Reports

16 U.S.C. 460xx-(a).

16 U.S.C. 460xx-1(d).

33 C.F.R. § 328.3 (2000).

Additions to the Big Cypress National Preserve; Establishing the San Pedro Riparian National Conservation Area; Designating the Horsepasture River as a Component of the National Wild and Scenic Rivers Systems; and Amending FLPMA: Hearings on S. 2029/H.R. 4090, S. 2442/H.R. 4811, S. 2707/H.R. 2826, and H.R. 2921 Before the Subcomm. on Public Lands, Reserved Water and Resource Conservation of the Committee on Energy and Natural Resources, United States Senate, 99th Cong., 2d Sess., S. Hrg. 99-1055, 23 September 1986.

American Rivers. America's 10 Most Endangered Rivers of 1999 (last modified 14 April 1999) <www.amrivers.org/99endangered.html>.

Arizona Department of Water Resources. *Preliminary Hydrographic Survey Report for the San Pedro River Watershed: In re the General Adjudication of the Gila River System and Source*, Volume 1: General Assessment. August 1990.

Arizona Department of Water Resources. *1984–1996 Annual Water Withdrawal and Use Summary*, Tucson AMA. 31 March 1998.

Arizona Department of Water Resources. *1997 Tucson AMA Water Use Summary*. 1 December 1998.

Arizona Department of Water Resources. *Report Concerning Revisions to the Hydrographic Survey Report for the San Pedro Watershed*, Superior Court of the state of Arizona in and for the County of Maricopa, 15 September 1999.

Arizona Department of Water Resources. *Notice of Errata in Report Concerning Revisions to the Hydrographic Survey Report for the San Pedro Watershed*, Superior Court of the state of Arizona in and for the County of Maricopa, 16 September 1999.

Arizona Department of Water Resources. *1998 Tucson AMA Water Use Summary*. 16 August 2000.

Arizona General Stream Adjudication Bulletin. November 1998–January 1999.

Arizona-Idaho Conservation Act of 1988, 134 *Cong. Rec.* H 10542, no. 150. 20 October 1988.

ASL Hydrologic & Environmental Services in conjunction with R. Allan Freeze Engineering, Inc. *Sierra Vista Subwatershed Hydrology Primer*. Produced for the City of Sierra Vista, Bella Vista Water Company, Inc. and Pueblo Del Sol Water Company, December 1994.

Bagwell, Keith. "15 Beavers to Get New Homes, Jobs on San Pedro River." *The Arizona Daily Star*, 3 August 1998.

Bodfield, Rhonda. "Panel Predicts a Dry San Pedro." *The Arizona Daily Star*, 15 September 1998.

Bureau of Land Management and the Sonoran Institute. *San Pedro and Santa Cruz Rivers Resource Directory*. August 1999.

Center for Biological Diversity v Donald H. Rumsfeld et al., 198 F. Supp.2d 1139 (D. Ariz. 2002).

Chandler, Colleen. "City Officials Declare War on Enviro 'Enemy.'" *Sierra Vista Herald*, 23 September 1995.

Christensen, Jon. "In Arizona Desert, a Bird Oasis in Peril." *The New York Times*, 4 May 1999.

Christensen, Jon. "Conserving a Fragile River Ecosystem: U.S., Mexican Authorities Try to Save the San Pedro River Basin from Overexploitation." *The New York Times*, 8 May 1999.

Commission for Environmental Cooperation. *Upper San Pedro River Initiative: Sustaining and Enhancing Riparian Bird Habitat on the Upper San Pedro River.* July 1998.

Commission for Environmental Cooperation. *Ribbon of Life: An Agenda for Preserving Transboundary Migratory Bird Habitat on the Upper San Pedro River.* 1999.

Davis, Tony. "Court Ruling May Limit Growth along San Pedro, Gila Rivers." *The Arizona Daily Star*, 29 September 1999.

Environment and Natural Resources Division, Directorate of Installation Support. *Ongoing and Programmed Future Military Operations and Activities at Fort Huachuca, Arizona Programmatic Biological Assessment.* U.S. Army Garrison, Fort Huachuca, Arizona, March 1998.

Environment and Natural Resources Division, Directorate of Installation Support. *Approval of Land Use and Real Estate Investment Strategies in Support of Real Property Master Planning (Draft Environmental Impact Statement).* U.S. Army Garrison, Fort Huachuca, Arizona. April 1998.

Environment and Natural Resources Division, U.S. Department of Justice. *Response to Arizona Department of Water Resources' Report Concerning Revisions to the Hydrographic Survey Report for the San Pedro Watershed.* Superior Court of the state of Arizona in and for the County of Maricopa, 16 September 1999.

Erickson, Jim. "Salsa Spans Border, Affiliations." *The Arizona Daily Star*, 8 March 1998.

Erickson, Jim. "San Pedro Back on River Group's Endangered List." *The Arizona Daily Star*, 12 April 1999.

Erickson, Jim. "Endangered Minnows May Make Waves." *The Arizona Daily Star*, 11 December 1999.

Erickson, Jim. "Leave It to Beavers: San Pedro's Transplants Are Staying Busy Building Dams and Changing the Ecology." *The Arizona Daily Star*, 2 April 2000.

Establishing the San Pedro Riparian National Conservation Area, Arizona, 132 *Cong. Rec.* H 5816, no. 110. 11 August 1986.

Establishing the San Pedro Riparian National Conservation Area in Cochise County, Arizona, in Order to Assure Paleontological, Scientific, Cultural, Educational, and Recreational Resources of the Conservation Area, and for Other Purposes. 100th Cong., 1st Sess., H.R. Rep. No. 100-2412, March 1987.

Fichtl, Ted. "Think About It: A New Perspective on Issues of Interest, Listen Up All You Ostriches." *Mountain View News*, 12 May 1999.

Fluid Solutions, ENTRANCO, ASL Hydrologic and Environmental Services, and U.S. Department of the Interior, Bureau of Reclamation. *Environmental Assessment for the Sierra Vista Water Reclamation Facility Effluent Recharge Project, Cochise County, Arizona (Draft)*. December 1998.

Fluid Solutions and U.S. Department of the Interior, Bureau of Reclamation. *Environmental Assessment for the Sierra Vista Water Reclamation Facility Effluent Recharge Project, Cochise County, Arizona (Final)*. November 1999.

Geophysics Study Committee, Geophysics Research Board, Assembly of Mathematical and Physical Sciences, National Research Council. *Studies in Geophysics: Scientific Basis of Water-Resource Management*. Washington, D.C.: National Academy Press, 1982.

Glennon, Robert Jerome and Thomas Maddock III. "In Search of Subflow: Arizona's Futile Effort to Separate Groundwater from Surface Water." *Arizona Law Review*, vol. 36, p. 567, 1994.

Glennon, Robert Jerome and Thomas Maddock III. "The Concept of Capture: The Hydrology and Law of Stream/Aquifer Interactions." *Proceedings of the Rocky Mountain Mineral Law Institute*, vol. 43, p. 22-1, 1997.

Graber, John. "Vangilder Wants to Fast Track Bridges." *Sierra Vista Herald*, 2 June 2000.

Hess, Bill. "Monsoon Arrives a Bit Early." *Sierra Vista Herald*, 7 July 1998.

Hess, Bill. "Residents Speak Out on River Report." *Sierra Vista Herald*, 9 July 1998.

Hess, Bill. "River Study Won't Use University Reports." *Sierra Vista Herald*, 18 March 1999.

Hess, Bill. "Article Brings Communications Issue to Forefront." *Sierra Vista Herald*, 10 May 1999.

Hess, Bill. "Panel: Stop Growth Frenzy." *Sierra Vista Herald*, 10 May 1999.

Hess, Bill. "'We're Not Ostriches,' Politicians Defend Performance." *Sierra Vista Herald*, 11 May 1999.

Hess, Bill. "River Task Force Told: Golf Courses Need to Use Treated Water." *Sierra Vista Herald*, 30 July 1999.

Hess, Bill. "BLM: We Need to Protect the River and the Economy." *Sierra Vista Herald*, 19 August 1999.

Hess, Bill. "People Boom Threatens Border—Environment Efforts May Be Derailed by Doubling of Population." *Sierra Vista Herald*, 20 August 1999.

Hess, Bill. "New Coalition Formed to Protect River." *Sierra Vista Herald*, 22 August 1999.

Hess, Bill. "Federal Agency Letter Stirs Council Members' Ire." *Sierra Vista Herald*, 18 May 2000.

Hess, Bill. "Audubon Society Requests a Place in Partnership." *Sierra Vista Herald*, 29 June 2000.

Hess, Bill. "Recharge Project Becomes Reality." *Sierra Vista Herald*, 13 July 2000.

Hess, Bill. "Keeping Tabs on Growth Key to Protecting Fort, Fed Official Says." *Sierra Vista Herald*, 17 August 2000.

Hess, Bill. "Army Aims Funds to Lower Water Use: The Nature Conservancy to Buy Easements Along San Pedro." *Sierra Vista Herald*, 25 August 2001.

Hess, Bill. "Easement Plan Won't Stop Post's Efforts for Less Water Use." *Sierra Vista Herald*, 27 August 2001.

Hogue, Ruth Ann. "Fuse Lit for Sierra Vista Boom." *The Arizona Daily Star*, 28 March 1999.

Ibarra, Ignacio. "Strong Opposition Voiced to San Pedro Water Plan." *The Arizona Daily Star*, 15 January 1995.

Ibarra, Ignacio. "Ft. Huachuca Commits to San Pedro." *The Arizona Daily Star*, 30 October 1999.

Ibarra, Ignacio. "San Pedro Management in Danger, Babbitt Says." *The Arizona Daily Star*, 10 November 1999.

Ibarra, Ignacio. "Eye on the Troubled San Pedro: Ecosystem in Transition, International Team Finds." *The Arizona Daily Star*, 28 November 1999.

Ibarra, Ignacio. "Eye on the Troubled San Pedro: U.S. Water Users Long for a Part of Mexican Supply." *The Arizona Daily Star*, 28 November 1999.

Kingsolver, Barbara. "San Pedro River." *National Geographic*, April 2000.

Koester, Pat. "County, Cities Join Forces to Fight Lawsuit Threatened by Radical Environmentalists." *Tombstone Tumbleweed*, 22 July 1999.

Lee, Bryan. "Outdoors Brush with History: Overgrown Town of Charleston Nestles beside the San Pedro River." *The Tucson Citizen*, 5 December 1997.

Nature Conservancy, The (Arizona Chapter). *1999 Annual Report*.

Nijhuis, Michelle. "Charting the Course of the San Pedro." *High Country News*, 12 April 1999.

Okimoto, Jolyn. "Doing What They Do Best: Beavers Improve San Pedro Habitat." *The Arizona Daily Star*, 29 May 2000.

Parnell, Michael. "Supervisors OK Plan for Bachmann Springs." *Sierra Vista Herald*, 2 May 2000.

Pearson, Rita, Director, Arizona Department of Water Resources. "Arizonans Can— and Will—Deal with the San Pedro River." *The Tucson Citizen*, 26 November 1999.

Pearson, Rita, Director, Arizona Department of Water Resources. "ADWR, Administering the GMA to Ensure Arizona's Water Future." *Arizona Water Resource*, March–April 2000.

"Public Vote Sought on Sierra Vista Homes." *The Arizona Daily Star*, 27 July 1999.

"River More than Local Issue" (Editorial). *The Arizona Daily Star*, 27 July 1999.

Rupkalvis, David. "Counties' Coalition Hears Report on Fort's Efforts to Save Water." *Sierra Vista Herald*, 16 February 2002.

San Pedro Expert Team. "Sustaining and Enhancing Riparian Migratory Bird Habitat on the Upper San Pedro River" (Public Review Draft). 15 June 1998.

San Pedro Expert Team. "Sustaining and Enhancing Riparian Migratory Bird Habitat on the Upper San Pedro River" (Final Review Draft). March 1999.

San Pedro Riparian National Conservation Area. *Hearings on H.R. 4811. Before the Subcomm. on Public Lands of the Committee on Interior and Insular Affairs, House of Representatives*, 99th Cong., 2d Sess., Serial No. 99-41, 15 July 1986.

San Pedro Riparian National Conservation Area, 132 *Cong. Rec.* E 2854, vol. 132, no. 112. 13 August 1986.

San Pedro Riparian National Conservation Area and the Reno/Las Vegas Catholic Diocese Land Conveyance. *Hearings on S. 252 to Establish the San Pedro Riparian National Conservation Area; H.R. 568 to Establish the San Pedro Riparian National Con-*

servation Area in Cochise County, AZ, in Order to Assure the Protection of the Riparian, Wildlife, Archeological, Paleontological, Scientific, Cultural, Educational, and Recreational Resources of the Conservation Area, and for Other Purposes; S. 575 to Convey Public Land to the Catholic Diocese of Reno/Las Vegas, NV (Before the Subcomm. on Public Lands, National Parks and Forests of the Committee on Energy and Natural Resources, United States Senate), 100th Cong., 1st Sess., S. Hrg. 100-103, 30 April 1987.

Saunders, Diane. "Citizens Group Turns in Petitions." *Sierra Vista Herald*, 24 August 1999.

Saunders, Diane. "Supervisors Give Thumbs Down to Management Area." *Sierra Vista Herald*, 21 November 2000.

Senate Concurrent Memorial 1006: *Environmental Standards—International Treaty or Federal Designation*. 1998 Ariz. Legis. Serv. Sen. Conc. Mem. 10006 (West).

Sharma, Vandana et al., Arizona Research Laboratory for Riparian Studies, Department of Hydrology and Water Resources, The University of Arizona. *An Analysis of the Effects of Retiring Irrigation Pumpage in the San Pedro Riparian National Conservation Area, Cochise County, Arizona*. 2000.

Southwest Center et al. v. William Perry. U.S. D.AZ. CIV 94-814 TUC ACM ORDER, 8 July 1996.

Southwest Center for Biological Diversity. "Ft. Huachuca Sued to Stop Harm to San Pedro River" (Press Release). 21 April 1999.

Southwest Center for Biological Diversity et al. v. Jamie Rappaport Clark et al., U.S. 90 F.Supp.2d 1300 (D.N.M. 1999).

Southwest Center for Biological Diversity v. William S. Cohen et al., U.S. D.AZ. Complaint for Declaratory and Injunctive Relief, 20 April 1999.

Tobin, Mitch. "Army Aims to Aid San Pedro." *The Arizona Daily Star*, 28 August 2001.

"Tough Words on San Pedro" (Editorial). *The Arizona Daily Star*, 15 November 1999.

Udall Center for Studies in Public Policy, The University of Arizona. "Public Input Digest for the Upper San Pedro River Initiative." September 1998.

The University of Arizona Department of Agricultural and Resource Economics. *Nature-Based Tourism and the Economy of Southeastern Arizona: Economic Impacts of Visitation to Ramsey Canyon Preserve and the San Pedro Riparian National Conservation Area*, undated.

Upper San Pedro Advisory Panel. "Advisory Panel Report on the Upper San Pedro River Initiative." November 1998.

U.S. Department of the Interior, Bureau of Reclamation. *Ground Water Manual: A Water Resources Technical Publication, A Guide for the Investigation, Development and Management of Groundwater Resources*, 1977.

U.S. Geological Survey. *Ground Water and Surface Water: A Single Resource*. Circular 1139. 1998.

U.S. Geological Survey. *Hydrogeologic Investigations of the Sierra Vista Subwatershed of the Upper San Pedro Basin, Cochise County, Southeast Arizona*. Water-Resources Investigations Report 99-4197. 1999.

U.S. Geological Survey. *Sustainability of Ground-Water Resources*. Circular 1186. 1999.

"U.S. House Approves $4 Million to Help Schools, Protect San Pedro, Buy Conservation Easements." *Sierra Vista Herald*, 19 October 2001.

Vionnet, Leticia B. and Thomas Maddock III. *Modeling of Ground-Water Flow and Surface/Ground-Water Interactions for the San Pedro Basin—Part 1—Mexican Border to Fairbank, Arizona.* Department of Hydrology and Water Resources. HWR No. 92-010, 1992.

Yozwiak, Steve. "Report: Growth Is Killing River, Overuse Imperils the San Pedro." *The Arizona Republic,* 16 June 1998.

Letters, Memoranda, Miscellaneous

Cochise County Supervisors. Letter to Ms. Ann Moote, Udall Center for Studies in Public Policy, Upper San Pedro Initiative. 16 July 1998.

Ellis, Bruce, Chief, Environmental Resource Management Division, Bureau of Reclamation. Memorandum to "Meeting Attendees," *Re: Underlying Geology at the Sierra Vista Wastewater Treatment Plant.* 30 April 1998.

Goreham, Fritz. Letter to Larry Linser, deputy director, Arizona Department of Water Resources, *Re: Water Supply Adequacy Decisions in the San Pedro Watershed.* 17 November 1993.

Goreham, Fritz, Field Solicitor, U.S. Department of the Interior. Memorandum to Gary Randall, General Litigation Section, U.S. Department of Jusice, *Re: Comments on the Ft. Huachuca–Bella Vista Water Co. Draft Settlement Concepts,* 2 February 1994.

Harlow, David, Field Supervisor, U.S. Fish and Wildlife Service. Letter to Cindy Lester, chief, Regulatory Branch, U.S. Army Corps of Engineers. 27 April 2000.

Harlow, David, Field Supervisor, U.S. Fish and Wildlife Service. Letter to Alexis Strauss, director, Water Division, U.S. Environmental Protection Agency. 27 April 2000.

Linser, C. Laurence, Deputy Director, Engineering and Adjudications, Arizona Dept. of Water Resources. Letter to William Sullivan, Martinez & Curtis, P.C. 29 September 1993.

Linser, C. Laurence, Deputy Director, Engineering and Adjudications, Arizona Dept. of Water Resources. Letter to William Swan, Office of the Solicitor. 31 March 1994.

MacNish, Robert, Adjunct Professor, Department of Hydrology and Water Resources, The University of Arizona. "Professor Distressed by Remarks on River," Letter to the Editor. *Sierra Vista Herald/Bisbee Daily Review,* 4 April 1999.

Melcher, Nick, Arizona District Chief, Water Resources Division, U.S. Geological Survey. Letter to Jim Rorabaugh, Arizona Ecological Services Field Office, U.S. Fish and Wildlife Service, *Re: Review of the Effects Analysis within the Draft Biological Opinion on the Huachuca Water Umbel of the San Pedro River Basin, Arizona.* 28 August 1998.

North, Oliver, Lt. Col. (Ret.), Honorary Chairman, Freedom Alliance. Petition to Protect U.S. Sovereignty to U.S. Secretary of State Madeline Albright, undated.

Rosenkrance, Lester. Letter to Rita Pearson, director, Arizona Dept. of Water Resources. 15 November 1993.

San Pedro Alliance. *Petition for a Rule to Designate the Upper San Pedro River Basin an Active Management Area under Title 45, Section 412 of the 1980 Groundwater Management Act.* Undated.

Silver, Robin, Conservation Chair, Southwest Center for Biological Diversity. Letter to Commander, U.S. Army Garrison, Ft. Huachuca, *Re: "The Draft Environmental*

Impact Statement (DEIS) Titled: Approval of Land Use and Real Estate Investment Strategies in Support of Real Property Master Planning, Fort Huachuca, Arizona" ["DEIS"] Is Biased and Fundamentally Flawed. Fort Huachuca Continues to Deny and Attempt to Cover-up Responsibility for Its Actions. 23 July 1998.

Silver, Robin, Conservation Chair, Southwest Center for Biological Diversity. Letter to Thomas G. Burbey, area manager, U.S. Department of the Interior, Bureau of Reclamation, Re: Draft Environmental Assessment for the City of Sierra Vista Water Reclamation Facility Effluent Recharge Project. 29 January 1999.

Silver, Robin, Conservation Chair, Southwest Center for Biological Diversity. Letter to Thomas G. Burbey, area manager, U.S. Department of Interior Bureau of Reclamation, Re: Failure to Include in the Proposed Sierra Vista Wastewater Treatment Plant Draft Environmental Assessment (DEA) an Evaluation of the City of Sierra Vista's Annexation Proceedings. The Annexation Proceedings Appear Related to the Predictable Failure of the Proposed Sierra Vista Wastewater Treatment Plant (WWTP) Recharge Basins and the City's Efforts to Provide for Future Compensatory Expansion. 12 February 1999.

Southwest Center for Biological Diversity. Notice of Intent to Sue. 30 June 1999.

Thomas, John, Major General, U.S. Army Commanding General. "Environmental Stewards," (Letter to the Editor). The Arizona Daily Star, 10 November 1999.

Upper San Pedro Partnership. San Pedro Conservation Plan: A Plan to Protect the People and Natural Resources of the Sierra Vista Sub-Watershed of the Upper San Pedro River (Draft). 7 September 1999.

Vandine, Donald. "Save the San Pedro," Letter to the Editor. The Arizona Daily Star, 29 June 1998.

Vandine, Donald. "Don't Blame Growth," Letter to the Editor. The Arizona Daily Star, 27 April 1999.

Vaughn, Carole, Mayor of Huachuca City. Letter to Robin Silver, conservation chair, Re: Notice of Intent to Sue Dated June 30, 1999. 20 August 1999.

Wallace, Greg, Chief Hydrologist, Arizona Department of Water Resources. Letter to Duane Turner, deputy commissioner, Tucson Division, Department of Real Estate, Re: The Cottonwoods of San Pedro—Lots 1 through 90. 1 February 1994.

Wilkinson, Todd. Letter to Harold Vangilder and to Readers, Re: Science inder Siege: The Politicians' War on Nature and Truth (Editorial Reviews) (visited 16 December 1999) <www.amazon.com/exec/obidos/tx/book-reviews/1555662110/102-3430079-8338419>

Chapter 5. Tampa Bay's Avarice: Cypress Groves, Wetlands, Springs, and Lakes in Florida

Books

Carroll, David M. Swampwalker's Journal: A Wetlands Year. New York: Houghton Mifflin Company, 2001.

Articles and Reports

Alley, William M. et al. *Sustainability of Ground-Water Resources*, U.S. Geological Survey Circular 1186, 1999.

Becker, Jo. "Pasco Pulled Two Ways on Desal." *St. Petersburg Times*, 29 July 1998.

Brainard, Jeffrey. "Two More Pasco Lakes May Be Refilled." *St. Petersburg Times*, 24 February 1997.

Brainard, Jeffrey. "Will Owner of Springs, Preserve Keep Getting Tax Break?" *St. Petersburg Times*, 22 May 1997.

Browning, Michael. "Whatever Happened to Florida's Water? From the Oasis to the Desert Beneath Our Feet, Unseen and Undefended, a Vast Sea Shrinks." *The Miami Herald*, 24 May 1998.

Browning, Michael. "A Desert Grows in Florida; Hidden Hamlet First to Feel Our Dry Future." *The Miami Herald*, 25 May 1998.

Browning, Michael. "Environmental Battles Swirl over Use of Peace River Flow." *The Miami Herald*, 26 May 1998.

Browning, Michael. "The Era of Cheap Water Ends As Supplies Dwindle and Populations Grow, Cities Look to the Sea." *The Miami Herald*, 27 May 1998.

Buettner, Michael. "Water Board Finds Itself in Middle of Firestorm." *Tampa Bay Business Journal*, 6 September 1996.

"Call Off the Lawyer Series" (Editorial). *St. Petersburg Times*, 14 December 1998.

"Clinton Inks Water Resource Bill to Replenish Florida Everglades." *The Arizona Daily Star*, 13 October 1996.

Davis, Cary. "Judge Hears Both Sides of Pasco Water Argument." *St. Petersburg Times*, 23 September 1999.

Davis, Cary. "Expert: Perrier Should Get Water Because It Sells." *St. Petersburg Times*, 25 September 1999.

Davis, Cary. "Judge Says No to More Water for Zephyrhills Bottler." *St. Petersburg Times*, 28 January 2000.

Dennis, Brady and Jean Heller. "Ranch May Pump More Water, if Replaced." *St. Petersburg Times*, 25 April 2001.

Devall, Cheryl. "Report on Competition for Water Supplies along Florida's Gulf Coast." National Public Radio, 25 November 1997.

DeWitt, Dan. "Water Pumping Possibilities Upset Officials." *St. Petersburg Times*, 6 June 2001.

Gotlieb, Andy. "Swiftmud: Perrier Too Thirsty." *The Tampa Tribune*, 26 January 1999.

Gotlieb, Andy. "Crystal Springs Owner Defends Pumping Request." *The Tampa Tribune*, 22 September 1999.

Gotlieb, Andy. "Crystal Springs Hearings End Sooner than Expected." *The Tampa Tribune*, 25 September 1999.

"Heavier Pumping of Crystal Springs" (Editorial). *The Tampa Tribune*, 9 August 1998.

Heller, Jean. "Rancher Floating a Water Solution." *St. Petersburg Times*, 13 April 1999.

Heller, Jean. "South Florida Still Soaked, Tampa Bay Needs Rain." *St. Petersburg Times*, 19 October 1999.

Heller, Jean. "Utility Official Warns of Area Water Shortage." *St. Petersburg Times*, 14 December 1999.

Hiaasen, Carl. "The Last Days of Florida Bay." *Sports Illustrated*, 18 September 1995.

Huettel, Steve. "Swiftmud's Lower Hillsborough River Plan Challenged on Two Fronts." *St. Petersburg Times*, 9 February 2000.

Jackson, Tom. "Water War Pushes Us to Boiling Point." *The Tampa Tribune*, 9 May 1999.

Jackson, Tom. "More Good Comes from Sipping Straw." *The Tampa Tribune*, 16 March 2000.

James, Ian. "Rainfall Nourishing Once-Dry Lake." *St. Petersburg Times*, 1 February 1998.

Jehl, Douglas. "Tampa Bay Looks to the Sea to Quench Its Thirst." *The New York Times*, 12 March 2000.

Leary, Alex. "Bottler Says It Would Not Harm Spring." *St. Petersburg Times*, 1 February 2001.

Leary, Alex. "A Rule on Springs Would Ban Bottlers." *St. Petersburg Times*, 11 June 2001.

Matthews, Frank E. and Gabriel E. Nieto. "Florida Water Policy: A Twenty-Five Year Mid-Course Correction." *Florida State University Law Review*, vol. 25, p. 365, 1998.

O'Brien, Kevin M. and Barbara Markham. "A Tale of Two Coasts: How Two States Link Water and Land Use Planning." *Natural Resources & Environment*, vol. 11, p. 3, 1996.

"Officials Give Go-Ahead to Build Huge Desalination Plant in Florida, Cost of Water Ranges from $1.71 to $2.08/1,000 Gallons." *U.S. Water News*, 1999.

Pedreira, David. "Wellfields Taking a Soaking: Pinellas Consumed Two-Thirds of the Water Pumped from Pasco." *St. Petersburg Times*, 1 September 1995.

Pedreira, David. "Replenishing Dream Lakes a Bittersweet Victory; Water from the Aquifer Has Been Siphoned to Refill Lakes Dry from Well Fields." *The Tampa Tribune*, 7 April 1996.

Pedreira, David. "Water Plan May Face Challenge." *St. Petersburg Times*, 2 December 1999.

"Pinellas' Costly Apology Series" (Editorial). *St. Petersburg Times*, 18 May 1999.

"Pinellas' Touting of Birding Event in Pasco Is Ironic." *St. Petersburg Times*, 8 April 1998.

"A Prudent Reply to Perrier Series" (Editorial). *St. Petersburg Times*, 27 February 2000.

"Questions Cloud Plan Series" (Editorial). *St. Petersburg Times*, 14 March 1999.

Rand, Honey. *In the Public Interest: A Story of Conflict, Communication, and Change in Tampa Bay's Water Wars*. Ph.D. dissertation, University of South Florida, December 2000.

Riddle, Amanda. "Everglades Drying as Florida Drought Holds." *Arizona Daily Star*, 18 March 2001.

"A Rudderless Water Board Series" (Editorial). *St. Petersburg Times*, 18 June 1999.

"Serving Perrier Series" (Editorial). *St. Petersburg Times*, 19 March 1998.

Southwest Florida Water Management District. "District Water Management Plan, Volume One." March 1995.

Southwest Florida Water Management District. "District Water Management Plan, Volume Two." March 1995.

Southwest Florida Water Management District. "Northern Tampa Bay Water Resources Assessment Project, Volume One: Surface-Water/Ground-Water Interrelationships." March 1996.

Southwest Florida Water Management District. "District Water Management Plan." July 2000.

Southwest Florida Water Management District State Regulation. "Notice of Change; Rule Title 40D-2.091: Water Use Permitting Basis of Review." 10 March 1996.

Squires, Chase. "Tampa Bay Water Admits Pumping Affected Well Field." *St. Petersburg Times*, 6 August 1999.

Squires, Chase. "Lawsuit over Well Field Moves Ahead." *St. Petersburg Times*, 24 November 1999.

"State Takes Dip in Source of Water at Zephyrhills." *Orlando Sentinel*, 25 September 1997.

"Stay Calm about Water Plan Series" (Editorial). *St. Petersburg Times*, 15 May 1999.

Tampa Bay Water and the Southwest Florida Water Management District. "Amended and Restated Interlocal Agreement Reorganizing the West Coast Regional Water Supply Authority." June 1998.

"Thirsty Floridans Sucking State Dry." *The Denver Post*, 5 September 1994.

Thompson, Bill. "Couple's Lawsuit Blames Wellfield for Damage." *The Tampa Tribune*, 26 June 1998.

Thorner, James. "Skeptics Spring Up on Water Proposal." *St. Petersburg Times*, 18 May 1999.

Thorner, James. "Agency Taking More Water, Activist Says." *St. Petersburg Times*, 5 October 1999.

Voyles, Karen. "Levy Residents Voice Concerns over Spring." *Gainesville Sun*, 3 January 2001.

"Water Resources Development Act of 1996." PL 104-303 (S 640), 12 October 1996.

Wing, John. "Water War Spills over to Marion." *The Tampa Tribune*, 31 January 2001.

Wing, John. "Rancher's Pumping Request Rejected." *The Tampa Tribune*, 8 February 2001.

Wing, John. "Water Deal Puts Larger Tap on Crystal Springs." *The Tampa Tribune*, 10 March 2002.

Letters, Memoranda, Miscellaneous

Benny Guy and Terry Sims v. Tampa Bay Water, A Regional Water Supply Authority (First Amended Complaint). 25 November 1998.

Florida Department of Environmental Protection. *In re: Petition of the West Coast Regional Water Supply Authority for Approval under Section 373.1962 of Its Amended and Restated Interlocal Agreement* (Final Order). 1998 WL 4602.01, 10 June 1988.

Florida Statutes, "Minimum Flows and Levels," ch 373.042, p. 1437, 1997.

Hatcher, Ruby. "Pasco Letters." Letter to the Editor, *The Tampa Tribune*, 1 September 1997.

Northern Tampa Bay New Water Supply and Ground Water Withdrawal Reduction Agreement. May 1998.

Wolfe, Terri. "About Our Water." Letter to the Editor, *The Tampa Tribune*, 30 September 1999.

Chapter 6. The Tourist's Mirage: San Antonio's River Walk, the Edwards Aquifer, and Endangered Species

Books

Brune, Gunnar. *Springs of Texas*, vol. 1. Fort Worth: Branch-Smith, Inc., 1981.

Fisher, Lewis. *Crown Jewel of Texas: The Story of San Antonio's River*. San Antonio: Maverick Publishing Company, 1997.

Articles and Reports

"Amarillo Man Wants to Offer Water Rights to South Texas." Associated Press Newswires, 24 January 2000.

"Aquifer Permits Given Boost." Associated Press Newswires, 20 January 2000.

"Aquifer Threatens Lawsuits for Water Abuse." Associated Press Newswires, 11 August 2000.

"Bid to Halt Ozarka Fails: Eustace-area Residents Plan to Appeal Ruling on Pumping." *The Dallas Morning News*, 5 December 1996.

Bohlen, Mary Painter. "Colorful Attractions and History Combine in San Antonio." *The State Journal-Register*, 14 March 1999.

Braley, Sarah. "Singing a Tejano Tune: The City Lures Groups with Its Latino Roots." *Reed Travel Group: Meetings and Conventions*, 1 May 1998.

Cagle, Molly and George Wilkinson. "The Legal Framework for Urban Growth and Water Supply in Texas: The San Antonio Example." 16th Annual American Bar Association Water Law Conference, 19 February 1998.

"Central Texas Residents Want to Reduce Aquifer Pumping Cutbacks." Associated Press Newswires, 3 March 2000.

Chapman, Art. "The Waterway to Wealth; Amarillo Businessman Sees Profit Potential in a Liquid, and It's Not Oil." *The Fort Worth Star-Telegram*, 20 June 2000.

Chunn, Sherri. "Cities Fight Dry Conditions, Warn of Decreased Supply." Associated Press Newswires, 13 January 2000.

City of San Antonio Planning Department. "The San Antonio River: A Brief Look at Its Colorful History" (visited 21 June 1999) <www.ci.sat.tx.us/pio/riverwalk.htm>.

"Court Orders Imposition Withdrawal Reduction Plan in Edwards Aquifer." *Water Intelligence Monthly*, September 1996.

Crouse, Jacque. "Judge Tells Barge Firm Suit Doesn't Hold Water." *San Antonio Express News*, 20 February 1998.

Earl, Richard and Robert Czerniak. "Sunbelt Water War: The El Paso–New Mexico Water Conflict." *The Social Science Journal*, 1 October 1996.

Easton, Pam. "Panhandle Ranchers Wary of Water Deal." *Austin American-Statesman*, 4 April 2000.

Easton, Pam. "Oilman Identifies Possible Routes in Selling Water Rights." *Austin American-Statesman*, 17 May 2000.

"Edwards Aquifer." *Western States Water*, 13 September 1996.

"Edwards Aquifer Authority Seeks Federal Funding for Land Fallowing Program." *Water Strategist*, October 1999.

"The Edwards Aquifer Is the Sole Supplier of Water for the City of San Antonio." *Talk of the Nation*, 4 December 1998.

Ellis, Gregory M., General Manager, Edwards Aquifer Authority. "Edwards Aquifer Authority Update." 18th Annual American Bar Association Water Law Conference, February 24–25, 2000.

"Endangered Species Keep Edwards Aquifer at Risk of Federal Intervention." *U.S. Water News*, November 1996.

Epstein, Kyra. "Edwards Aquifer Authority Paying Farmers Not to Irrigate Crops." *U.S. Water News*, April 2000.

Hancock, Lee. "Bottling Firm Blamed for Dried-up Well." *The Dallas Morning News*, 13 March 1996.

Haurwitz, Ralph K. M. "Drought or Drained? Family's Well Goes Dry After Ozarka Arrives; In Texas, Old Water Rule Says No One's to Blame." *Austin American-Statesman*, 18 January 1997.

Haurwitz, Ralph K. M. "Texas Justices to Explore Final Frontier of Water Law." *Austin American-Statesman*, 17 November 1998.

Haurwitz, Ralph K. M. "Underground Water Law Upheld/Texas Supreme Court Opens Door to Future 'Rule of Capture' Revisions." *Austin American-Statesman*, 7 May 1999.

Haurwitz, Ralph K. M. "State Agency Leaders Differ on LCRA Reservoir Proposal/Water Board Executive Calls Plan to Pipe Water to San Antonio 'Brilliant.'" *Austin American-Statesman*, 29 June 2000.

Haurwitz, Ralph K. M. "Water Supply Solution Is Approved with a Catch." *Austin-American Statesman*, 10 August 2000.

HDR Engineering, Inc. *Assessment of Groundwater Availability on CPS Property in Bastrop and Lee Counties, Texas*. Prepared for San Antonio Water System, July 1999.

HDR Engineering, Inc. *Preliminary Feasibility of Options to Deliver ALCOA/CPS Groundwater to Bexar County*. Prepared for San Antonio Water System, January 2000.

Jorden, Jay. "Ozarka Touts Test Results from Springs; Still, Lawmakers and Residents Are Not Convinced Northeast Texas Water Source Won't Be Harmed." *Austin American-Statesman*, 29 September 1995.

"Judge Bunton's Decision: The Order (2nd Take)." *San Antonio Express-News*, 26 August 1996.

Kaiser, Ronald A. and Laura M. Phillips. "Dividing the Waters: Water Marketing as a Conflict Resolution Strategy in the Edwards Aquifer Region." *Natural Resources Journal*, vol. 38, p. 411, 1998.

Karp, David. "When Perrier Came to Texas, the Water Left." *St. Petersburg Times*, 16 December 1997.

Kosub, Phil Steven. "Current Litigation Regarding Texas Groundwater." 17th Annual American Bar Association Water Law Conference: Evolving Federalism in Water Law and Policy, February 25–26, 1999.

Ledbetter, Kay. "Area Water Supply in Good Shape Thanks to Planning." *Amarillo Globe-News*, 25 July 2000.

Lofgren, Ruth. "Acceptable Water Plan the Goal." *San Antonio Express-News*, 20 September 1996.

McCorkle, Rob et al. "An Aquatic Phoenix Rises." *Texas Parks & Wildlife*, February 1998.

Mesa Water, Inc. Proposal to San Antonio Water System, Executive Summary, undated.

Needham, Jerry. "Some Central Texas Water Users Will Pay Higher Price." *San Antonio Express-News*, 30 April 1998.

Needham, Jerry. "San Antonio Water Plan Draws Criticism from Both Ends." *San Antonio Express-News*, 9 March 1999.

"Ozark's Plan for Pumping Water Has Residents Boiling." *San Antonio Express-News*, 11 November 1995.

Parks, Scott. "Water Investors Eye Liquid Assets; Demand Creates a Market for Aquifer Rights in Texas." *The Dallas Morning News*, 21 May 2000.

Pitts, John R. and Janet L. Hamilton. "Texas Water Law for the New Millennium." *Natural Resources & Environment*, vol. 14, p. 35, 1999.

Powell, Tracie. "A Long Walk for Water; Women March to San Antonio in Pipeline Protest." *Austin American-Statesman*, 20 May 2000.

Reagan, Brad. "Pickens Says Study Backs Water Pipe." *The Wall Street Journal*, 17 May 2000.

"Recycling Water on the River Walk." *Houston Chronicle*, 25 June 2000.

Richelieu, David Anthony. "River Tunnel Is Impressive; Its Future Inspiring." *San Antonio Express-News*, 26 October 1997.

"River Walk Keeps Flowing with Recycled Wastewater." Associated Press Newswires, 20 June 2000.

Rogers, Stephan. "Long-Awaited Water Payday Arrives for Bexar County Catfish Farmer; Case Sparks Unprecedented Changes in Texas Groundwater Law." *Western Water Law & Policy Reporter*, April 2001.

"San Antonio Faces Another Year of Water Restrictions." Associated Press Newswires, 11 June 1999.

"San Antonio Told Plans to Pipe in Water Expensive." *The Fort Worth Star-Telegram*, 8 July 2000.

San Antonio Water System. "City Council Approves Stage 2 Restrictions and Additional SAWS Drought Authority" (visited 31 July 2000) <www.saws.org/news/councilok.shtml>.

San Antonio Water System. "History of the San Antonio Water System" (visited 11 August 2000) <www.saw.org/yoursaws/history.shtml>.

"Saving Water by Sending It Away." *Austin American-Statesman*, 2 July 2000.

Shannon, Kelley. "Cities Likely to Spread Out, Not Sprout Up, with Growth." Associated Press Newswires, 6 November 1999.

Shay, Kevin. "A River Runs Through It, San Antonio Attraction Unrivaled." *The Dallas Morning News*, 22 March 1998.

"Sierra Club Sues to Limit Edwards Aquifer Water Use." *U.S. Water News*, September 1996.

Stanley, Dick. "Reservoirs Receding in Water Plans/Controversial Lakes Dropped." *Austin American-Statesman*, 6 April 2000.

"State Senate Passes Comprehensive Water Bill." *Water Intelligence Monthly*, April 1997.

"Texas: Court of Appeals Rejects Pecan Growers' Challenge to Edwards Aquifer Permitting Rules." *Western Water Law & Policy Reporter*, February 2000.

"Texas Judge Signs Final Order in Aquifer Pumping Lawsuit." *U.S. Water News*, February 1999.

"Texas Oil Men Busy Drilling for Water Rights." Associated Press Newswires, 20 January 2000.

Thorner, James. "Opponents of Perrier Turn Eyes to Texas," *St. Petersburg Times*, 24 November 1998.

Thorner, James. "Perrier's Texas Win Disappoints Local Activist." *St. Petersburg Times*, 13 May 1999.

"TX: GBRA, SAWS and SARA Sign Water Supply and Delivery Agreement." *Water Strategist*, June 2001.

"Ultrafiltration Plant Treats Surface Water in San Antonio." *Civil Engineering*, vol. 70, issue 2, 1 February 2000.

Vertuno, Jim. "Bush Declares 195 Texas Counties Disaster Areas Because of Drought." Associated Press Newswires, 28 July 2000.

Votteler, Todd H. "The Little Fish that Roared: The Endangered Species Act, State Groundwater Law, and Private Property Rights Collide over the Texas Edwards Aquifer." *Environmental Law*, vol. 28, p. 845, 1998.

Votteler, Todd H. "Guest Commentary: Guadalupe River Diversion Could Signal an End to Regional Water Conflict." *Water Strategist*, December 2001.

"Water Rationing to Start in San Antonio Area." *Houston Chronicle*, 2 May 2000.

"West Texas Oilman Identifies Possible Routes in Selling West Texas' Newest Commodity." Associated Press Newswires, 17 May 2000.

Wian, Casey. "Seeing Beneath the Surface to Find a Potential Fortune." CNNfn: *Moneyline News Hour*, 31 May 2000.

Wyatt, A. Wayne, Manager, High Plains Underground Water Conservation District No. 1. "Texas Supreme Court Rules on Edwards Aquifer Authority Case." *The Cross Section*, vol. 42, no. 8, August 1996.

Yardley, Jim. "For Texas Now, Water, Not Oil, Is Liquid Gold." *The New York Times*, 16 April 2001.

Letters, Memoranda, Miscellaneous

Friendswood Development Company v. Smith-Southwest Industries, Inc., 576 S.W.2d 21 (Tex. 1978).

Pecos County Water Control & Improvement District v. Williams, 271 S.W.2d 503 (Tex. Civ. App. 1954).

Phil Barshop v. Medina County Underground Water Conservation District, 925 S.W.2d 618 (Tex. 1996).

San Antonio Water System. "Securing Our Water Future Together: The ALCOA/CPS Water Resources Contracts." Undated.

Sierra Club v. Babbitt, 995 F.2d 571 (5th Cir. 1993).

Sierra Club v. City of San Antonio, et al., 112 F.3d 789 (5th Cir. 1997).

Sierra Club v. City of San Antonio, et al., 115 F.3d 311 (5th Cir. 1997).

Sierra Club v. Dan Glickman, 82 F.3d 106 (5th Cir. 1996).

Sierra Club v. Dan Glickman, 156 F.3d 606 (5th Cir. 1998).

Sipriano, Bart v. Great Spring Waters of America, Inc., 1 S.W. 3d 75 (Tex. 1999).

Thuss, Michael, President/CEO San Antonio Water System. Letter to Steve Stevens, Mesa Water, Inc., 22 June 2000.

Chapter 7. Suburban Development and Watershed Initiatives: Massachusetts' Ipswich River Basin

Books

Dow, George Francis. *The River Agawam: An Essex County Waterway*. Topsfield, Massachusetts, 1926.

Articles and Reports

Adams, Steve. "Water Limits Area's Growth; S. Shore Must Protect Supply." *The Patriot Ledger*, 2 October 1998.

Allen, Scott. "Already, N.E. Thirsty for Summer Showers." *The Boston Globe*, 23 June 1999.

Armstrong, David S. et al. U.S. Geological Survey. *Assessment of Habitat, Fish Communities, and Streamflow Requirements for Habitat Protection, Ipswich River, Massachusetts, 1998–99.* Water-Resources Investigations Report 01-4161. 2001.

Benson, Reed D. American Bar Association, Section of Environment, Energy, and Resources. "What Makes a Watershed Work? Ten Concerns about Watershed Processes." 19th Annual American Bar Association Water Law Conference, February 15–16, 2001.

Busse, Katherine M. Massachusetts Coastal Zone Management, Executive Office of Environmental Affairs. "Park River/Essex Bay Area of Critical Environmental Concern, Resource Inventory." Undated.

Clarke, Jack. "Act before the Ipswich River Disappears." *The Boston Globe*, 12 October 1997.

Cohen, Russell, Rivers Advocate, Riverways Program, Massachusetts Department of Fisheries, Wildlife and Environmental Law Enforcement. *Water Supply Development vs. River Protection: The Case for Water Conservation.* 29 January 1992.

Cole, Caroline Louise. "Low River Spurs Treatment Plant Call." *The Boston Globe*, 8 October 2000.

Cole, Caroline Louise. "4 River Towns Would Ally Under Plan." *The Boston Globe*, 14 January 2001.

Commonwealth of Massachusetts, Water Resources Commission. *Interbasin Transfer Act Performance Standards Guidance*. Undated.

Commonwealth of Massachusetts, Water Resources Commission. *Special Report of the Water Resources Commission Relative to Its Study of the Public Water Supply Resources of the Ipswich River*. 27 January 1965.

"Ebb & Flow: The State of the Ipswich River." *The Salem Evening News Online* (visited 20 June 2000) <www.salemnews.com/ipsriver/ipsriver.htm>.

Executive Office of Environmental Affairs. *Massachusetts Watershed Initiative*. 1999.

Franklin, James. "Taking Water Seriously." *Boston Sunday Globe*, 21 May 2000.

Guidelines for Interpreting the Interbasin Transfer Act's Criteria for Approval as Applied to: An Interbasin Transfer of Wastewater. 25 August 1987.

Higgins, Richard. "H$_2$O Aplenty, but . . . Sprawl, Overuse, Access of Concern." *Boston Sunday Globe*, 14 May 2000.

Hollmer, Mark. "Bostik: Finally Living in Harmony with the River." *The Salem Evening News Online* (visited 20 June 2000) <www.salemnews.com/ipsriver/ipbostic.htm>.

Hollmer, Mark. "A History: From Glaciers and Indians to Industry and Drought." *The Salem Evening News Online* (visited 20 June 2000) <www.salemnews.com/ipsriver/iphistor.htm>.

Hollmer, Mark. "Ipswich River Provides Fun and Respite from Busy World." *The Salem Evening News Online* (visited 20 June 2000) <www.salemnews.com/ipsriver/iprec.htm>.

Hollmer, Mark. "Leave Nothing but Footprints, Take Nothing but Water." *The Salem Evening News Online* (visited 20 June 2000) <www.salemnews.com/ipsriver/ipnature.htm>.

Howland, Dave. "Dry Weather, Water Users, Drinking Up Massachusetts Rivers." Associated Press Newswires, 30 June 1999.

"How to Help the River." *The Salem Evening News Online* (visited 20 June 2000) <www.salemnews.com/ipsriver/iprec.htm>.

The Interbasin Transfer Act. 313 CMR 4.00 et seq. (2000).

Ipswich River Watershed Association. *1997 Low Flow/No Flow Study*. 1998.

Ipswich River Watershed Association. *Macroinvertebrate Data Report for Fall 1997, Spring 1998, and Fall 1998 Samplings*. 1998.

Ipswich River Watershed Association. "Spring Floods." *River Currents*, April 2001.

Ipswich River Watershed Association. *The Voice of the River*. Undated.

Kirk, Bill. "Hamilton May Have Lost 1 Billion Gallons of Water in the '80s." *The Salem Evening News Online* (visited 20 June 2000) <www.salemnews.com/ipsriver/hamwoes.htm>.

Kirk, Bill. "Reasons and Methods of Water Conservation Vary from Town to Town and City to City." *The Salem Evening News Online* (visited 20 June 2000) <www.salemnews.com/ipsriver/townwoes.htm>.

Kirk, Bill. "Watershed Organizations Help Keep Rivers Clean." *The Salem Evening News Online* (visited 20 June 2000) <www.salemnews.com/ipsriver/porgs.htm>.

Kirk, Bill. "Water Shortage Hits Home Upstream." *The Salem Evening News Online* (visited 20 June 2000) <www.salemnews.com/ipsriver/ipbeliev.htm>.

Kirk, Bill. "Water Wars on the North Shore." *The Salem Evening News Online* (visited 20 June 2000) <www.salemnews.com/ipsriver/waterwar.htm>.

Kirk, Bill and Mark Hollmer. "Solutions Not Easy on the Ipswich River." *The Salem Evening News Online* (visited 20 June 2000) <www.salemnews.com/ipsriver/ipsolut.htm>.

Laidler, John. "Preserving Open Space Can Help the Cause." *The Boston Globe*, 7 May 2000.

Lawton, Millicent. "Tapped Out." *CommonWealth: Politics, Ideas, and Civic Life in Massachusetts*, Fall 2000.

Mackin, Kerry, Executive Director, Ipswich River Watershed Association and Lou Wagner, Water Resources Specialist, Massachusetts Audubon Society. *Ipswich River Basin Water Conservation Report Card Grading the Communities of the Ipswich River Basin on Water Conservation and Water Use Efficiency.* September 1999.

Massachusetts Audubon Society: North Shore Conservation Advocacy for the Massachusetts Bays Program and the Towns of Ipswich, Rowley, and Newbury. "Conserving the Plum Island Sound/River Ecosystems: A Research Report and Management Plan." May 1999.

Massachusetts Audubon Society. *Ipswich River Wildlife Sanctuary*, 2002 <www.massaudubon.org>.

Massachusetts Department of Housing and Community Development. "Community Profiles." <www.state.ma.us/dhcd/iprofile/>.

Massachusetts Executive Office of Environmental Affairs. *Ipswich River Watershed Brief.* Undated.

Massachusetts Geographic Information System and Executive Office of Environmental Affairs. "Massachusetts Watershed Initiative." 6 March 2000.

Massachusetts Watershed Initiative. *Ipswich River Watershed: FY 01 Annual Work Plan.* 2001.

McCabe, Coco. "Ipswich River Users Fail to Make Grade." *The Boston Globe*, 22 October 2000.

McLaughlin, Jeff. "Saving Our Water; Can We Keep Our Source Clean?" *The Boston Globe*, 7 May 2000.

"Mighty Ipswich Needs Our Protection" (Editorial). *The Salem Evening News Online* (visited 20 June 2000) <www.salemnews.com/ipsriver/sedi0821.htm>.

Smith, Mark P. "Watershed Teams Take Charge: Results from the Massachusetts Watershed Initiative," 19th Annual American Bar Association Water Law Conference, 15–16 February 2001.

U.S. Geological Survey. "U.S.G.S. Monitoring Activities on the Ipswich River" (visited 26 June 2000) <ma.water.usgs.gov/ipswich/>.

U.S. Geological Survey. "Ipswich River Drainage Basin—Surface Water" (visited 9 May 2001) <ma.water.usgs.gov/basins/ipswich>.

U.S. Geological Survey. *Effects of Water Withdrawals on Streamflow in the Ipswich River Basin, Massachusetts.* USGS Fact Sheet 00-160 (visited 17 January 2002) <pubs.water.usgs.gov/fs-160-00>.

Zarriello, Phillip J. and Kernell G. Ries III. U.S. Geological Survey. *A Precipitation-*

Runoff Model for Analysis of the Effects of Water Withdrawals on Streamflow, Ipswich River Basin, Massachusetts. Water-Resources Investigation Report 00-4029. 2000.

Zimmerman, Bob. "Old Problems Present New Opportunities." *Streamer*, vol. 29, no. 2, Spring 1998.

Chapter 8. A Game of Inches for Endangered Chinook Salmon: California's Cosumnes River, the Army Corps of Engineers, and Sacramento Sprawl

Books

Dietrich, William. *Northwest Passage, The Great Columbia River.* New York: Simon & Schuster, 1995.

Goodson, Gar. *Fishes of the Pacific Coast.* Stanford: Stanford University Press, 1988.

Groot, C. and L. Margolis. *Pacific Salmon Life Histories.* British Columbia: UBC Press, 1991.

Leopold, Luna and Thomas Maddock. *The Flood Control Controversy: Big Dams, Little Dams, and Land Management.* New York: Ronald Press Co., 1954.

Lichatowich, Jim. *Salmon Without Rivers, A History of the Pacific Salmon Crisis.* Washington, D.C.: Island Press, 1999.

Mount, Jeffrey. *California Rivers and Streams: The Conflict between Fluvial Process and Land Use.* Berkeley: University of California Press, 1995.

Reisner, Mark. *Cadillac Desert: The American West and Its Disappearing Water.* New York: Viking Press, 1986.

Safina, Carl. *Song for the Blue Ocean: Encounters along the World's Coasts and Beneath the Seas.* New York: Henry Holt & Company, Inc., 1997.

Articles and Reports

"As Levee Breaches." Associated Press Newswires, 9 November 2000.

Benston, Liz. "Mega-mall Planned in Elk Grove, California." *The Record*, 10 July 2001.

Bowman, Chris. "Risk Trickles Down to Cosumnes River." *The Sacramento Bee*, 31 July 2001.

Boyle, Robert. "Brother, Can You Spare a Dam?" *The Amicus Journal*, Fall 1998.

Boyle, Robert H. "A Hydro-History of the Bay-Delta." *The Amicus Journal*, Fall 1998.

Bureau of Land Management. "Cosumnes River Preserve" (visited 26 August 2001) <pub.4.ca.blm.gov>.

CALFED. "Bay-Delta Program Mission Statement" (visited 2 November 2001) <calfed.ca.gov>.

CALFED. "ERP Projects Tracking Table," 13 June 2001.

"California: After Five Years, Historic CALFED Framework Announced." *Western Water Law & Policy Reporter*, July 2000.

"California: State Water Resources Control Board Postpones Commencement of Phase 8 of the Bay-Delta Water Rights Hearings." *Western Water Law & Policy Reporter*, July 2000.

Chan, Gilbert. "Best Buy in Sacramento, California, Seeks Applicants." *The Sacramento Bee*, 14 July 2001.

"Cosumnes Questions: Would Pumping for Houses Dry Up River?" *The Sacramento Bee*, 2 August 2001.

"Cosumnes River Preserve" (visited 26 October 2001) <www.cosumnes.org>.

Cosumnes River Project. "Project Description" (visited 26 October 2001) <www.cosumnes.org>.

County of Sacramento Department of Environmental Review and Assessment. "Revised Recirculated Draft, Environmental Impact Report for the Sunrise Douglas Community Plan/Sun Ridge Specific Plan Project." 18 May 2001.

Crain, P. K. et al., Department of Wildlife, Fish, and Conservation Biology, University of California, Davis. "Fish Assemblages and Environmental Gradients in the Cosumnes River Basin." 1999–2000 Research Abstracts, CALFED Science Conference. October 2000.

Fleckenstein, Jan et al., Department of Land, Air and Water Resources—Hydrologic Sciences, University of California, Davis. "Options for Conjunctive Water Management to Restore Fall Flows in the Cosumnes River Basin, California." July 2000.

Fleckenstein, Jan et al., Department of Land, Air and Water Resources—Hydrologic Sciences, University of California, Davis. "Modeling Groundwater Surface Water Interactions to Restore Fall Flows in the Lower Cosumnes River Basin," 1999–2000 Research Abstracts, CALFED Science Conference. October 2000.

Florsheim, J. L. and J. F. Mount, Department of Geology and Center for Integrated Watershed Science and Management, University of California, Davis. "Restoration of Floodplain Geomorphology at Intentional Levee Breaches," 1999–2000 Research Abstracts, CALFED Science Conference. October 2000.

Florsheim, J. L. and J. F. Mount, Department of Geology and Center for Integrated Watershed Science and Management, University of California, Davis. "To Breach or Not to Breach: Levee Modifications to Support Floodplain Restoration," 1999–2000 Research Abstracts, CALFED Science Conference. October 2000.

Glennon, Robert Jerome and John E. Thorson. "Federal Environmental Restoration Initiatives: An Analysis of Agency Performance and the Capacity for Change." *Arizona Law Review*, vol. 42. p. 483, 2000.

Great Valley Center. "The State of the Great Central Valley of California, Assessing the Region via Indicators" (visited May 1999) <www.greatvalley.org>.

Green, Martha Hodgkins. "Cosumnes River, California." *The Nature Conservancy*, July/August 2001.

Kavvas, M. L. et al. Department of Civil and Environmental Engineering—Hydrologic Research Laboratory, University of California, Davis. "A Physically-Based Watershed Model for the Upper Cosumnes Basin, California," 1999–2000 Research Abstracts, CALFED Science Conference. October 2000.

Knudson, Tom. "Litigation Central: A Flood of Costly Lawsuits Raises Questions about Motive." *The Sacramento Bee*, 24 April 2001.

Knudson, Tom. "Seeds of Change: Solutions Sprouting from Grass-Roots Efforts." *The Sacramento Bee*, 26 April 2001.

Knudson, Tom and Nancy Vogel. "The Gathering Storm." *The Sacramento Bee*, 27 November 1997.

"Legacy of Protection: Cosumnes River Is on Key to Approving New Mall." *The Sacramento Bee*, 24 December 1999.

Levenworth, Stuart. "County Plans 22,000 Homes." *The Sacramento Bee*, 15 November 2001.

Morrisette, Peter M. "Conservation Easements and the Public Good: Preserving the Environment on Public Lands." *Natural Resources Journal*, vol. 41, p. 373, 2001.

Moyle, P. B. et al. Department of Wildlife, Fish, and Conservation Biology, University of California, Davis. "Importance of Cosumnes River Floodplain to Chinook Salmon and Sacramento Splittail," 1999–2000 Research Abstracts, CALFED Science Conference. October 2000.

Nature Conservancy, The. "Cosumnes/Mokelumne Corridor Floodplain Acquisitions, Management, and Restoration Planning" (Proposal to CALFED). 20 May 2000.

Philip Williams & Associates for The Nature Conservancy. "An Analysis of Opportunities for Restoring a Natural Flood Regime on the Cosumnes River Floodplain." San Francisco, California. 7 May 1997.

Sax, Joseph L. "Appropriations of Groundwater Classified as Subterranean Streams and the SWRCB's Implementation of Those Laws." Final Report to the California State Water Resources Control Board. 19 January 2002.

Steding, Anna. "Restoring Riparian Forests and Natural Flood Regimes: The Cosumnes River Preserve," in *Sustainable Use of Water: California Success Stories*. Hayward: Alonzo Printing Co., Inc., 1999.

Suzuki, E. et al., Department of Land, Air and Water Resources—Hydrologic Sciences, University of California, Davis. "Using Seepage Meters and Thermal Gradients to Quantify Groundwater Fluxes in the Lower Cosumnes River Basin," 1999–2000 Research Abstracts, CALFED Science Conference. October 2000.

Trochet, John. "Site Guide to the Cosumnes River Preserve" (visited 26 August 2001) <www.cosumnes.org>.

Trowbridge, W. B. et al., Department of Environmental Science and Policy and Center for Integrated Watershed Science and Management, University of California, Davis. "Restoration of Floodplain and Riparian Forests at Levee Breaches," 1999–2000 Research Abstracts, CALFED Science Conference. October 2000.

Umbach, Kenneth W. "A Statistical Tour of California's Great Central Valley," August 1997. Available at <www.library.ca.gov>.

U.S. Army Corps of Engineers. "Lower Cosumnes and Mokelumne Rivers, California Expedited Reconnaissance Study 905(b) Analysis." 3 February 1999.

U.S. Army Corps of Engineers. Draft: "Summary, Lower Cosumnes and Mokelume Rivers Feasibility Study." December 1999.

U.S. Fish and Wildlife Service. "Investigation of Groundwater Surface Water Interactions and their Role in Declining Fall River Flows in the Lower Cosumnes Basin." September 2001.

U.S. Geological Survey. "1999 California Hydrologic Data Report" (visited 8 November 2001) <ca.water.usgs.gov>.

Vellinga, Mary Lynne. "Elk Grove, California, Shopping Mall Project Sparks Suit." *The Sacramento Bee*, 31 July 2001.

Wicinas, David. "A Mellifluous Roar." *The Nature Conservancy*, September/October 1998.

Yoshiyama, Ronald et al. "Historical Abundance and Decline of Chinook Salmon in the Central Valley Region of California." *North American Journal of Fisheries Management*, vol. 18, pp. 487–521, 1998.

Yoshiyama, Ronald et al. "Chinook Salmon in the California Central Valley: An Assessment." *Fisheries*, vol. 25, no. 2, February 2000.

Letters, Memoranda, Miscellaneous

Mount, Jeffrey F. Letter to Mike Eaton. "Impact of Proposed Omo Ranch Resort Diversion on Middle Fork Flows." 2 March 2001.

Mount, Jeffrey F. Letter and Handouts re: "2001 State of the River Symposium: Hydrologic and Biologic Science in the Cosumnes and Mokelumne Watershed." University of California, Davis. 25 October 2001.

Mount, Jeffrey F. "Multidisciplinary Research in Support of Adaptive Floodplain Management and Restoration: The Cosumnes Research Group." Riparian Habitat and Floodplains Conference Proceedings. 2001.

Chapter 9. Wild Blueberries and Atlantic Salmon: Down East Maine

Books

Baum, Ed. *Maine Atlantic Salmon: A National Treasure*. Hermon: Atlantic Salmon Unlimited, 1997.

Safina, Carl. *Song for the Blue Ocean: Encounters along the World's Coasts and Beneath the Seas*. New York: Henry Holt and Company, Inc., 1997.

Taylor, Joseph III. *Making Salmon: An Environmental History of the Northwest Fisheries Crisis*. Seattle: University of Washington Press, 1999.

Articles and Reports

Allen, Scott. "Salmon Safeguard Called Overkill in Maine." *The Boston Globe*, 3 December 1999.

Allen, Scott. "Fish Fight." *The Boston Globe*, 27 December 1999.

"Allocation of Federal Salmon Funding Confounds Maine Officials." Associated Press Newswires, 2 August 2000.

Anderson, Ross. "Salmon Protection Relies on Old Tactics; Many Salmon Runs in the Pacific Northwest Have Been Listed under the Endangered Species Act for Years." *Portland Press Herald*, 14 November 1999.

"Atlantic Salmon Declared Endangered." *Trout*, Winter 2001.

Atlantic Salmon Federation. "Salmon Federation Says Endangered Species Listing an

Act of Last Resort" (visited 13 November 2000) <www.asf.ca/Communications/2000/nov00/listing.htm>.

Atlantic Salmon Federation and Trout Unlimited. "ASF and TU Sue to Protect United States' Last Wild Atlantic Salmon" (visited 12 August 1999) <www.asf.ca/Communications/Aug99/lawsuit.htm>.

Atlantic Salmon Unlimited. "Biology of Maine Atlantic Salmon" (visited 11 May 2001) <www.MaineAtlanticSalmon.com/biology.htm>.

Austin, Phyllis. "Cherryfield Foods Gets Water Permit, but Only for this Year." *Maine Times*, 23 July 1998.

Bell, David K. "Blueberry Irrigation Important State Issue." *Bangor Daily News*, 23 August 1999.

"Blueberries and Salmon." *Bangor Daily News*, February 15, 2000.

"Blueberry Growers Agree to Spending to Study River Water Level." Associated Press Newswires, 21 June 2000.

Bradbury, Dieter. "Devices Could Explain Why Salmon Are Dying, Finding the Cause of the High Death Rate May Then Help the State Better Preserve Them." *Portland Press Herald*, 10 May 1998.

Bradbury, Dieter. "Salmon Hearings Likely to be Stormy, Opponents to the Proposed Federal Listing Will Turn Out in Force." *Portland Press Herald*, 28 January 2000.

Bradbury, Dieter. "Fate of the Atlantic Salmon." *Portland Press Herald*, 30 January 2000.

Burke, Monte. "On the Brink." *Audubon*, November 2001.

Campbell, Richard H. "Atlantic Salmon Decision Dangerous." *Bangor Daily News*, 24 November 2000.

"Cherryfield Foods Receives Irrigation Permit." Associated Press Newswires, 22 May 2000.

Clancy, Mary Anne. "Salmon Group Seeks Dam Ban." *Bangor Daily News*, 24 February 1998.

Clancy, Mary Anne. "Salmon Win Fight Over Irrigation Water Use Strict on Down East Rivers." *Bangor Daily News*, 16 April 1999.

Clancy, Mary Anne. "Tribe, LURC Disagree on Water Pumps." *Bangor Daily News*, 30 June 1999.

Clancy, Mary Anne. "Blueberries, Salmon Vying for Scarce Water." *Bangor Daily News*, 10 July 1999.

Clancy, Mary Anne. "Dam Breach a New Spin on Down East Water Rift," *Bangor Daily News*, 6 August 1999.

Clancy, Mary Anne. "Feds Acting to Save Salmon, Authorities Move to Put Fish on List of Endangered Species, Proposal Raises Stakes for $60 Million Aquaculture." *Bangor Daily News*, 17 November 1999.

Clancy, Mary Anne. "Salmon Plan Science Argued, Snowe Seeks Independent Review." *Bangor Daily News*, 18 November 1999.

Clancy, Mary Anne. "LURC Vote Expected on Application to Dig Blueberry Land Irrigation Well, Staff Favors Cherryfield Foods' Proposal with Conditions." *Bangor Daily News*, 19 January 2000.

Clancy, Mary Anne. "Blueberry Grower Asks for Irrigation Permit." *Bangor Daily News*, 23 February 2000.

Clancy, Mary Anne. "Supporters, Critics Turn Out for Irrigation Hearing." *Bangor Daily News*, 24 March 2000.

Clancy, Mary Anne. "Official Predicts Salmon Solution, Opposing Groups Gather for Forum." *Bangor Daily News*, 27 March 2000.

Clancy, Mary Anne. "Regulators to Consider Blueberry Irrigation Request." *Bangor Daily News*, 15 May 2000.

Clancy, Mary Anne. "Cherryfield Irrigation Permit Strictest Yet." *Bangor Daily News*, 22 May 2000.

Clancy, Mary Anne. "Retiring Fish Expert to Continue Salmon Passion." *Bangor Daily News*, 1 June 2000.

Clancy, Mary Anne. "Reaction Mixed to EPA Rule, Recovery Proposal May Be Months Away." *Bangor Daily News*, 15 November 2000.

Clancy, Mary Anne. "Salmon Farm to Face Charges: Company Failed to Report Fish Virus." *Bangor Daily News*, 19 January 2002.

"Coalition Raises $600,000 to Attack Endangered Species Listing." Associated Press Newswires, 12 December 2000.

Cooke, Robert. "Battle on to Save Wild Atlantic Salmon from Extinction." *Chicago Tribune*, 6 May 2001.

Daley, Beth. "Maine Takes Its Turn in Salmon-Saving Dispute." *The Boston Globe*, 18 October 2000.

Daley, Beth. "Escaped Farm Salmon Raise Alarm in Maine." *The Boston Globe*, 23 February 2001.

Daley, Beth. "Virus Hits Salmon Industry in Maine." *The Chicago Tribune*, 7 September 2001.

Day, Clarence. "A History of the Blueberry Industry in Washington County." Prepared for Farm and Home Week Presentation, University of Maine, 1959.

"Firm Accused of Violating Reporting Rules." Associated Press Newswires, 19 January 2002.

FitzGerald, Des. "What We're Doing with Salmon." *The Providence Journal*, 22 November 2000.

Gaines, Charles L. III. "Swimming Upstream." *Audubon*, November 2001.

Handy, Matthew. "Trout in the Cold." *Trout*, Winter 2000.

Hennessey, Tom. "Chasing Bluefish and Pondering Blueberries, Salmon." *Bangor Daily News*, 7 August 1999.

King, Angus, Governor of Maine. "Restoration Not Regulation" (visited 2 December 1999) <janus.state.me.us/govoffice/salmon2_text.htm>.

King, Angus, Governor of Maine. "Statement of Gov. King on Salmon Decision" (visited 13 November 2000) <janus.state.me.us/govoffice/salmon2_text.htm>.

Land and Water Resource Council. "1998 Annual Progress Report" (visited 5 January 2000) <www.state.me.us/spo/salmon/annual.htm>.

Maine Atlantic Salmon Task Force. "Atlantic Salmon Conservation Plan for Seven Maine Rivers" (March 1997) <www.state.me.us/spo/salmon/a-plus.htm>.

Maine Council, Atlantic Salmon Federation. "100,000 Aquaculture Salmon Escape." *Casting*, Spring 2001.

Maine Council, Atlantic Salmon Federation. "Salmon Spawn in Restored Reach of Kennebec." *Casting*, Spring 2001.

Maine Department of Conservation: Natural Resources Information and Mapping Center. Aquifer Fact Sheet (visited 6 January 2000) <www.state.me.us/doc/nrimc/pubedinf/factsht/hydro/hydfact.htm>.

Maine Department of Conservation: Natural Resources Information and Mapping Center. Aquifer Mapping (visited 6 January 2000) <www.state.me.us/doc/nrimc/pubedinf/factsht/hydro/aquifmap.htm>.

Maine Department of Conservation: Natural Resources Information and Mapping Center. Bedrock Mapping Fact Sheet (visited 6 January 2000) <www.state.me.us/doc/nrimc/pubedinf/factsht/bedrock/bedfact.htm>.

Maine Department of Conservation: Natural Resources Information and Mapping Center. Generalized Bedrock Geologic Map of Maine (visited 6 January 2000) <www.state.me.us/doc/nrimc/pubedinf/factsht/bedrock/bedmap.gif>.

Maine Department of Conservation: Natural Resources Information and Mapping Center. Generalized Surficial Geologic Map of Maine (visited 6 January 2000) <www.state.me.us/doc/nrimc/pubedinf/factsht/surfical/surfmap.gif>.

Maine Department of Conservation: Natural Resources Information and Mapping Center. Glacial Geology Fact Sheet (visited 6 January 2000) <www.state.me.us.doc/nrimc/pubedinf/factsht/surfical/surffact.htm>.

"Maine Salmon Biologist Honored by TU and ASF." *Fly Rod & Reel*, January/February 2001.

Marvinney, Robert G. and Woodrow B. Thompson, Maine Department of Conservation: Natural Resources Information and Mapping Center. The Geology of Maine (visited January 6, 2000) <www.state.me.us/doc/nrimc/pubedinf/factsht/bedrock/megeol.htm>.

Moss, Ralph, Atlantic Salmon of Maine. *Federal Document Clearing House* (Congressional Testimony). 9 May 2001.

Moyer, Steve N., Vice President, Conservation Programs, Trout Unlimited. *Federal Document Clearing House* (Congressional Testimony). 9 May 2001.

Reisman, Jon. "Salmon Listing Bad News for Washington County." *Bangor Daily News*, 24 December 1999.

Richardson, John. "Salmon Farming Fights for Its Life: Slaughter Prompted by Virus Is Among Mounting Challenges." *Portland Press Herald*, 20 January 2002.

Salmon Letter, The, vol. 5, issue 4. December 2000.

"Salmon Restoration Funding Secured." Associated Press Newswires, 11 October 2000.

Scott, Matthew, Executive Secretary, Project Share. "Salmon Habitat and River Enhancement." Belgrade, Maine. 17 June 1999.

Sharp, David. "Salmon Farms Fear Higher Costs Because of Endangered Species Listing." Associated Press Newswires, 20 November 2000.

Sharp, David. "Salmon Destroyed to Stop Virus." Associated Press Newswires, 7 September 2001.

Snowe, Olympia. "Snowe Announces $5 Million in Salmon Funding." *Federal Documents Clearing House* (government press release), 12 July 2000.

Snowe, Olympia. "Snowe and Collins Announce $3.8 Million in Grants to Bolster Salmon Restoration throughout Maine." *Federal Document Clearing House* (government press release), 18 December 2000.

"State and Feds Should Now Work Together on Salmon Plan; The Federalism Fight Settled, the Focus Should Move to Recovery." *Portland Press Herald*, 15 November 2000.

"State Orders Slaughter of Cobscook Bay Salmon." Associated Press Newswires, 8 January 2002.

Taylor, Bill, Atlantic Salmon Federation. "Restoring Maine's Salmon" (visited 6 January 2000) <www.flyfishamerica.com/conservatio...icles/AtlanticSalmonFederation/99MAR.html>.

University of Maine Cooperative Extension. *Wild Blueberry Fact Sheet*, Fact Sheet No. 220 (Bulletin No. 2088). 1998.

"USDA Implements ISA Program." *Feedstuffs*, vol. 73, issue 54, 31 December 2001.

U.S. Fish and Wildlife Service. *Endangered and Threatened Species; Proposed Endangered Status for a Distinct Population Segment of Anadromous Atlantic Salmon* (Salmo salar) *in the Gulf of Maine*, Proposed Rules, 64 FR 62627. 17 November 1999.

U.S. Fish and Wildlife Service. "Biological Report on the Atlantic Salmon Report Shows Atlantic Salmon Stocks Need Additional Protection" (visited 30 December 1999) <news.fws.gov/salmon/asalmon.html>.

U.S. Fish and Wildlife Service and National Oceanic and Atmospheric Administration. *Endangered and Threatened Species; Final Endangered Status for a Distinct Population Segment of Anadromous Atlantic Salmon in the Gulf of Maine.* 17 November 2000.

Young, Susan. "Berry Grower Loses Water Request, LURC Tells Cherryfield Foods to Draw Less from Area Rivers, Ponds." *Bangor Daily News*, 21 May 1999.

Zakin, Susan. "Code Red." *Trout*, Spring 2000.

Letters, Memoranda, Miscellaneous

National Public Radio. "Profile: Gulf of Maine Atlantic Salmon to Be Declared an Endangered Species." *Morning Edition*, 14 November 2000.

National Public Radio. "Profile: Salmon Farming in Maine." *All Things Considered*, 8 January 2001.

State of Maine v. Bruce Babbitt et al. Complaint.

State of Maine Department of Conservation. *Permit Commission Decision in the Matter of Cherryfield Foods, Inc.* (Amendment F to Development Permit DP 3624). 16 July 1998.

State of Maine Department of Conservation. *Permit Commission Decision in the Matter of Cherryfield Foods, Inc.* (Approval in Part, Denial in Part of Amendment G to Development Permit DP 3624). 20 May 1999.

State of Maine Department of Conservation. *Development Permit Application DP 4513, Cherryfield Foods, Inc.* 11 January 2000.

State of Maine Department of Conservation. *Permit Commission Decision in the Matter of Cherryfield Foods, Inc.* 20 January 2000.

Chapter 10. Size Does Count, at Least for French Fries: Minnesota's Straight River

Books

Drache, Hiram M. *Creating Abundance: Visionary Entrepreneurs of Agriculture.* Danville, Illinois: Interstate Publishers, Inc., 2001.
Schlosser, Eric. *Fast Food Nation.* New York: Houghton, Miffllin Company, 2001.

Articles and Reports

Barboza, David. "Misery Is Abundant for Potato Farmers." *The New York Times*, 17 March 2001.
Gladwell, Malcolm. "Annals of Eating: The Trouble with Fries. Fast Food Is Killing Us: Can It Be Fixed?" *The New Yorker*, 5 March 2001.
National Agricultural Statistics Service, United States Department of Agriculture. "1997 Census of Agriculture AC97-SP-1 Farm and Ranch Irrigation Survey," vol. 3, Special Studies, Part 1. 1998.
Stark, J. R. et al. *Stream-Aquifer Interactions in the Straight River Area, Becker and Hubbard Counties, Minnesota,* Water-Resources Investigation Report 94-4009. Mounds View, Minnesota 1994.
U.S. Department of Agriculture. "Design and Operation of Farm Irrigation Systems," revised printing. St. Joseph: American Society of Agricultural Engineers, September 1983.
U.S. Geological Survey. "Water Fact Sheet: Effects of Ground-Water Withdrawals for Irrigation on the Quality of the Straight River, North-Central Minnesota." 1989.
U.S. Geological Survey. "Relation of Land Use to Nitrate in the Surficial Aquifer along the Straight River, North-Central Minnesota, 1992–93." March 1996.

Letters, Memoranda, Miscellaneous

Alberta Agriculture, Food and Rural Development. "The History of Potatoes" (last revised 2 May 1997) <www.agric.gov.ab.ca>.
"McDonald's USA French Fry Facts" (visited 18 September 2001) <www.mcdonalds.com>.

Chapter 11. The Black Mesa Coal Slurry Pipeline: The Hopi Reservation in Arizona

Books

Benedek, Emily. *The Wind Won't Know Me.* New York: Alfred A. Knopf, Inc., 1992.

Waters, Frank. *Book of the Hopi*. New York: Penguin Books, 1977.

Wilkinson, Charles. *Fire on the Plateau: Conflict and Endurance in the American Southwest*. Washington, D.C.: Island Press, 1999.

Articles and Reports

Beckman, David et al. "Drawdown, Groundwater Mining on Black Mesa." Natural Resources Defense Council, October 2000.

Black Mesa Trust. "Black Mesa Groundwater Preservation Plan, A Proposal by the Black Mesa Trust." Undated.

Black Mesa Trust. "Save Black Mesa Water." Undated.

"Coal Royalty Dispute Allowed to Proceed." *The Arizona Republic*, 20 March 2001.

Colarusso, Dan. "In an Energy Fog, Coal Starts to Shine." *New York Times*, 29 April 2001.

"Court Dismisses Navajo Claim." *Coal Outlook*, vol. 24, issue 7, 14 February 2000.

Cuza, Bobby. "California and the West, Navajo Faction Urges Edison to Shut Down Power Plant." *Los Angeles Times*, 21 April 2000.

Dougherty, John. "High and Dry." *New Times*, 24–30 April 1997.

Dougherty, John. "A People Betrayed." *New Times*, 1–7 May 1997.

Eskovitz, Joel. "Judge Allows Navajo Lawsuit to Continue." Associated Press Newswires, 19 March 2001.

Fischer, Howard. "U.S. May Owe Navajo Millions in Coal Funds." *Capitol Media Services/Arizona Daily Star*, 14 August 2001.

Foster Associates, Inc., Errol Montgomery & Associates, Ryley, Carlock & Applewite, and Woodward-Clyde Consultants. "Study of Alternatives to Transport Coal from the Black Mesa Mine to the Mohave Power Generating Station" (Phase II Draft Report for the U.S. Department of the Interior). 24 May 1993.

Geo Trans, Inc. "Hydrogeologic Studies Performed Related to the N Aquifer." Executive Summary. Undated.

Goodell, Jeff. "How Coal Got Its Glow Back—Blasts from the Past: Thanks to the Bush Administration, Big Coal Is Back. But Can It Be Taught to Behave?" *The New York Times Magazine*, 22 July 2001.

Industrial Environmental Research Laboratory, U.S. Environmental Protection Agency. "Environmental and Pollution Aspects of Coal Slurry Pipelines." March 1979.

Johnson, Angelee. "The Hopi and Their Legal Claim to Groundwater Reserved Rights." Student Report, The University of Arizona, James E. Rogers College of Law, January 2001.

"Judge Lets Navajo/Peabody Suit Proceed." *Coal Outlook*, vol. 26, issue 13, 26 March 2001.

Kammer, Jerry. "Tribes at Odds with Mine." *The Arizona Republic*, 25 October 2000.

Kao, David and Sandra Rusher, University of Kentucky Water Resources Research Institute. "Water Requirement for Coal Slurry Transportation," Research Report No. 146, U.S. Department of the Interior Agreement Number: 14-34-0001-2119 (FY 1982), P.L. 95-467. 1982.

Kim, Eun-Kyung. "Hopis, Navajos at Odds over Water Pipeline Plan." *The Phoenix Gazette*, 12 September 1994.

Leshy, John D. "The Babbitt Legacy at the Department of the Interior: A Preliminary View." *Environmental Law*, Northwestern School of Law of Lewis and Clark College, vol. 31, p. 199, 2 November 2001.

LeSure, Elizabeth. "American Indian Activists Protest Coal Mining in Arizona." Associated Press Newswires, 2 April 2001.

LeSure, Elizabeth. "Native Americans Protest, Say Mine Harms Tribal Land." *The Tucson Citizen*, 3 April 2001.

Masayesva, Vernon. "Guest Essay." *Colorado Plateau Advocate*, vol. 2, no. 5, Spring 1991.

"Mine Operator Says Pumping Not Harming Navajo Aquifer." Associated Press Newswires, 13 April 2001.

Natural Resources Defense Council. "Water Life: An Interview with Vernon Masayesva." 1998.

Natural Resources Defense Council. "Coal Company's Slurry Operation Depleting Sole Source of Drinking Water on Black Mesa Plateau." 24 October 2000.

Office of Technology Assessment, U.S. Congress. "A Technology Assessment of Coal Slurry Pipelines" (Summary). March 1978.

Office of Technology Assessment, U.S. Congress. "A Technology Assessment of Coal Slurry Pipelines" (Summary). September 1980.

Pay Dirt. "Peabody: The World's Best Coal Company" (January 2001) <www.voiceofmining.com>.

"Peabody Announces Name Change, New Web and E-Mail Addresses" (visited 20 April 2001) <www.PeabodyGroup.com>.

Peabody Group. "Annual Report" (Year ended 31 March 2000).

Peabody Group. "Peabody Group Files Registration Statement for Initial Public Offering of Common Stock" (visited 12 February 2001) <www.PeabodyGroup.com>.

Peabody Group. "Peabody Releases Latest Black Mesa Aquifer Study; Confirms Prior Studies Showing No Significant Harm" (visited 22 March 2001) <www.PeabodyGroup.com>.

Peabody Group. "Annual Report" (Year ended 31 March 2001).

Peabody Group. Company Profile (visited 30 April 2001) <www.PeabodyGroup.com>.

Peabody Group. Peabody's History (visited 30 April 2001) <www.PeabodyGroup.com>.

"Peabody Inches Along on Three Western Lawsuits." *Coal Outlook*, vol. 24; issue 27, 3 July 2000.

"Peabody, Navajo Nation Split Court Decision." *Mine Regulation Report*, vol. 12; issue 8, 17 April 2000.

Pollack, Stanley. "Little Colorado River Settlement." 9 February 2001.

Ramsey, Nikolai. "Beyond the Limits of the Land? Water and Politics of Growth in the Greater Grand Canyon." *Greater Grand Canyon*, undated.

Saquib, Muhammad et al., University of Kentucky Water Resources Research Institute. "Impact Assessment of Coal Slurry Pipelines on Water Resources Utilization and

Allocation," Research Report No. 153, U.S. Department of the Interior Agreement Number: G-844-06 (FY 1983), P.L. 95-467. 1984.

Torvik, Solveig. "Ruling Heaps Insult upon Injury to Tribes." *Seattle Post-Intelligencer*, 13 February 2000.

U.S. Geological Survey. *Results of Ground-Water, Surface-Water, and Water-Quality Monitoring, Black Mesa Area, Northeastern Arizona—1992–1993.* Water-Resources Investigations Report 95-4156, 1995.

U.S. Geological Survey. *Geochemical Analyses of Ground-Water Ages, Recharge Rates, and Hydraulic Conductivity of the N Aquifer, Black Mesa Area, Arizona.* Water-Resources Investigations Report 96-4190, 1997.

U.S. Geological Survey. *Monitoring the Effects of Ground-Water Withdrawals from the N Aquifer in the Black Mesa Area, Northeastern Arizona.* U.S.G.S. Fact Sheet 064-99, March 1999.

U.S. Geological Survey. *Ground-Water, Surface-Water, and Water-Chemistry Data, Black Mesa Area, Northeastern Arizona—1998.* Open-File Report 00-66, 2000.

Velush, Lukas. "Toxic Soup Threatens Water Supply of Hopis." *Arizona Daily Sun*, 20 June 1999.

Whiteley, Peter. "Paavahu and Paanaqawu: The Wellsprings of Life and the Slurry of Death." *Cultural Survival Quarterly*, Winter 1996.

Whiteley, Peter and Vernon Masayesva. "The Use and Abuse of Aquifers: Can the Hopi Indians Survive Multinational Mining?" in *Water, Culture, and Power: Local Struggles in a Global Context* (eds. John M. Donahue and Barbara Rose Johnston). Washington, D.C.: Island Press, 1998.

Wise, Katherine J. "A Matter of Trust: The Elimination of Federally Funded Legal Services on the Navajo Nation." *American Indian Law Review*, vol. 21, p. 157, 1997.

Yozwiak, Steve. "Activists Want to Shut Coal Mine on Reservation." *The Arizona Republic*, 22 August 1995.

Letters, Memoranda, Miscellaneous

Cohn, Cindy and Julie Berriault. "Risky Accommodation: Legal Analysis of the Accommodation Agreement between the U.S. Government, the Hopi Tribe and the Navajo Nation." Undated. The Hopi Tribe, official Web site (2001) <www.hopi.nsn. us>.

History of Hopi People (2001) <www.hopi.nsn.us/pages/history/history.htm>.

Hopi Climate and Geography (2001) <www.hopi.nsn.us/pages/statistics/geog.htm>.

Hopi Culture (2001) <www.hopi.nsn.us/pages/culture/hopi_1.htm>.

Hopi Demographic Summary (2001) <www.hopi.nsn.us/pages/statistics/demog.htm.

Hopi Farming (2001) <www.hopi.nsn.us/pages/culture/farming.htm>.

Hopi Villages on the Three Mesas (2001) <www.hopi.nsn.us/pages/villages/hopi_2. htm>.

Masayesva, Vernon, Hopi Tribe Chairman. Letter to Bruce Babbitt, Secretary of the Interior. 4 August 1993.

The Navajo Nation v. The United States, 46 Fed.Cl. 217 (Fed. C. 2000).

The Navajo Nation v. The United States, 263 F.3d 1325 (C.A. Fed 2001).

Oklahoma Statutes Annotated, 27 Okl. St. Ann §7.6 (2001).

Peabody Coal Company v. The Navajo Nation, 75 F.3d 457 (9th Cir. 1996).

Peabody Group. Peabody Energy Announces Improved Operating Results for the Quarter Ended June 30, 2001. 19 July 2001.

Peabody Group. Navajo Nation, Hopi Tribe and Energy Companies Join Efforts to Develop Water Resources, Tribal Economics, and Stable Energy Supplies. 15 August 2001.

Peabody Group. Validation Study Confirms No Material Harm to Navajo Aquifer from Mining Activities. 27 August 2001.

Sherman, Harris and David Neslin. Letter to Robert Armstrong, assistant secretary for land and mineral management, Department of the Interior, 9 May 1994.

U.S. Department of the Interior, Geological Survey. Memorandum from William M. Alley, chief, Office of Ground Water to the director, Office of Environmental Affairs, Department of the Interior, *Re: U.S. Geological Survey Evaluation of Various Studies and Hopi Tribe's Comments Regarding Impacts to the N-Aquifer from Withdrawal of Ground Water for Coal Slurry Transportation*. Reston, Virginia, 28 October 1999.

The Water Crisis at Hopi: Questions and Answers (2001) <www.hopi.nsn.us/Pages/Government/H3Water.htm>.

Chapter 12. Is Gold or Water More Precious?: Mining in Nevada

Books

Bernstein, Peter L. *The Power of Gold, The History of an Obsession*. New York: John Wiley & Sons, Inc., 2000.

Leshy, John D. *The Mining Law: A Study in Perpetual Motion*. Washington D.C.: Resources for the Future, 1987.

Watkins, T. H. *Gold and Silver in the West*. Palo Alto: America West Publishing Company, 1971.

Articles and Reports

Barrick Gold Corporation. *ABX 2001: Analysts' Briefing* (2001) <www.barrick.com>.

Bremner, Faith. "Abandoned Mines May Reduce Water Supplies." *Reno Gazette-Journal*, 20 October 1999.

"Canadian Gold Digger." *Maclean's*, 30 May 1994.

Carlton, Jim. "Gold Is Pitted against a Vital Resource." *Wall Street Journal*, 16 February 2000.

Chatterjee, Pratap. "Gold, Greed and Cyanide." *Dollars & Sense*, 1 January 1999.

Crompton, E. James. "Potential Hydrologic Effects of Mining in the Humboldt River Basin, Northern Nevada." U.S. Department of the Interior, U.S. Geological Survey, 1995.

Dobra, John L. *The U.S. Gold Industry 1998.* Nevada Bureau of Mines and Geology Special Publication 25, 1999.

Dreisner, Doug. "State and Federal Permits Required in Nevada before Mining or Milling Can Begin." Nevada Bureau of Mines and Geology, Special Publication L-6, December 1999.

Dreisner, Doug et al. *Major Mines of Nevada 1998: Mineral Industries in Nevada's Economy.* Nevada Bureau of Mines and Geology, Special Publication P-10, 1999.

Frans, Holly J. and Rebecca W. Watson. "Coalbed Natural Gas and Water Management: Water Appropriation, Water Quality and Water Conflicts." *Proceedings of the Rocky Mountain Mineral Law Institute,* vol. 47, p. 17-1, 2001.

Gerstenzang, James. "Mining Pact Reverses Historic Policies." *Los Angeles Times,* 18 November 1995.

"Hardball Politics and a 'Declaration of War.'" *Canada Stockwatch,* 4 May 1999.

Humboldt River Basin Hydrology. "A Proposed Program of Study to Evaluate the Regional Water Resources of the Humboldt River Basin, Nevada." U.S. Geological Survey (modified November 5, 1999) <nevada.usgs.gov/humb/proposal.htm>.

Kennedy/Jenks Consultants. *Evaluation of Water Resource Alternatives for the Humboldt River Basin.* April 2000.

Kenworthy, Tom. "Babbitt Rips Giveaway under 1872 Mining Act." *Chicago Sun-Times,* 17 May 1994.

McClure, Robert and Andrew Schneider. "The General Mining Act of 1872 Has Left a Legacy of Riches and Ruin." *Seattle Post-Intelligencer,* 11 June 2001.

McClure, Robert and Andrew Schneider. "More than a Century of Mining Has Left the West Deeply Scarred." *Seattle Post-Intelligencer,* 12 June 2001.

McClure, Robert and Andrew Schneider. "A Good Deal for Miners Often Isn't for Uncle Sam." *Seattle Post-Intelligencer,* 13 June 2001.

McClure, Robert et al. "Powerful Friends in Congress." *Seattle Post-Intelligencer,* 14 June 2001.

Mider, Zachary. "Kicking and Screaming in Nevada." *High Country News,* 31 July 2000.

"Mine Dewatering Threatens Northern Nevada." *Bristlecone,* Winter 2000.

"Mining Development May Damage Sacred Sites in the Rock Creek Area." *Newe News,* February 2000.

Mulligan, Belle. "Barrick Gold Corp—Barrick Second Quarter Results." *Canada Stockwatch,* 5 August 1999.

Myers, Tom. "Groundwater Management Implications of Open-Pit Mine Dewatering in Northern Nevada." *Conjunctive Use of Water Resources: Aquifer Storage and Recovery,* October 1997.

Myers, Tom. "Hydrogeology of the Humboldt River: Impacts of Open-Pit Mine Dewatering and Nevada Unified Watershed Assessment and Restoration Priorities." Nevada Division of Environmental Protection and USDA Natural Resources Conservation Service, 25 September 1998.

Myers, Tom. "Economic and Environmental Impacts of Mining in Eureka County." Center for Science in Public Participation, 13 June 2000.

Nailen, Richard L. "Using Big Submersibles to De-water the U.S.'s Largest Gold Mine." *The Nevada Mineral Industry.* 1998.

"Pit Lake Formation." Center for Science in Public Participation, April 1999.

Plume, Russell W. and David A. Ponce. *Hydrogeologic Framework and Ground-Water Levels, 1982 and 1996, Middle Humboldt River Basin, North-Central Nevada.* Water-Resources Investigations Report 98-4209, 1999.

Price, Jonathan G. et al. "Geology of Nevada," *Rocks and Minerals,* November 1999.

Ruling #5011 from Nevada State Engineer, re: Eureka County Protest. 5 April 2001.

Sewall, Christopher. *Digging Holes in the Spirit: Gold Mining and the Survival of the Western Shoshone Nation.* Western Shoshone Defense Project, June 1999.

Solnit, Rebecca. "The New Gold Rush." *Sierra,* July/August 2000.

Sonner, Scott. "Watertable Plummets in Nevada River Basin Drought: Decades of Irrigation and Pumping from Gold Mines Have Depleted Ground Water, Study Shows. Activists Fear Shortages." *Los Angeles Times,* 11 April 1999.

U.S. Department of the Interior, Bureau of Land Management, Elko District Office. *Betze Project, Environmental Impact Statement (Draft).* January 1991.

U.S. Department of the Interior, Bureau of Land Management, Elko District Office. *Betze Project, Environmental Impact Statement (Final).* June 1991.

U.S. Department of the Interior, Bureau of Land Management, Elko District Office. *Environmental Impact Statement, Newmont Gold Company's South Operations Area Project (Draft).* May 1993.

U.S. Department of the Interior, Bureau of Land Management, Elko District Office. *Environmental Impact Statement, Newmont Gold Company's South Operations Area Project (Final).* November 1993.

U.S. Department of the Interior, Bureau of Land Management, Elko Field Office, Elko, Nevada. *Cumulative Impact Analysis of Dewatering and Water Management Operations for the Betze Project, South Operations Area Project Amendment, and Leeville Project.* April 2000.

U.S. Department of the Interior, Bureau of Land Management, Elko Field Office, Elko, Nevada. *Draft Environmental Impact Statement Newmont Mining Corporation's South Operations Area Project Amendment.* September 2000.

U.S. Department of the Interior, Bureau of Land Management. Elko Field Office, Elko, Nevada. *Final Environmental Impact Statement Newmont Mining Corporation's South Operations Area Project Amendment.* April 2002.

U.S. Department of the Interior, Bureau of Land Management, Reno, Nevada. *Record of Decision, Newmont Gold Company's South Operations Area Project.* 18 November 1993.

U.S. Geological Survey. *Humboldt River Basin Hydrology, A Proposed Program of Study to Evaluate the Regional Water Resources of the Humboldt River Basin, Nevada* (last modified 5 November 1999) <nevada.usgs.gov>.

Vogel, Ed. "A Boom and Bust." *The Las Vegas Review-Journal,* 2 November 1997.

Watkins, T. H. "Hard Rock Legacy." *National Geographic,* March 2000.

Whaley, Sean. "State Gold Production Hits Record for 1998." *The Las Vegas Review-Journal*, 17 March 1999.

Van Der Werf, Martin. "Babbitt Blasts Mine Law 'Heist': Judge Forces $10 Billion Gold Giveaway." *The Arizona Republic*, 17 May 1994.

Williams, Ted. "Road to the Outhouse: Wise-use Zealots Bash Feds and Bull Trout in Nevada." *Fly Rod and Reel*, January/February 2001.

Letters, Memoranda, Miscellaneous

D'Esposito, Stephen, President, Mineral Policy Center. Testimony before the House Resources Subcommittee on Energy and Minerals. 23 February 1999.

Eureka County Protest, In the Office of the State Engineer of the State of Nevada, Ruling 5011. 5 April 2001.

Templeton, Billy R., Bureau of Land Management. Letter to Public, Reno, Nevada. 19 November 1993.

Chapter 13. All's Fair in Love and Water

Books

McKean, Lori, and Bill Whitbeck. *The Joy of Oysters*. Seattle: Speed Graphics, 2000.

Torak, Lynn et al. *Geohydrology and Evaluation of Stream-Aquifer Relations in the Apalachicola-Chattahoochee-Flint River Basin, Southeastern Alabama, Northwestern Florida, and Southwestern Georgia*. Washington, D.C.: The U.S. Government Printing Office, 1996.

Articles and Reports

"Apalachicola-Chattahoochee-Flint River Basin Compact PL 105-104 (HJRes91), *United States Public Laws*, 20 November 1997.

Apalachicola National Estuarine Research Reserve, Florida Department of Environmental Protection and The Sanctuaries and Reserves Division, Office of Ocean and Coastal Resource Management, National Oceanic and Atmospheric Administration. "Apalachicola National Estuarine Research Reserve: Management Plan 1993." 1993.

Beaverstock, Jeffrey Uhlman. "Learning to Get Along: Alabama, Georgia, Florida and the Chattahoochee River Compact." *Alabama Law Review*, vol. 49, p. 993, 1998.

Bragg, Rick. "An Oyster and a Way of Life, Both at Risk." *The New York Times*, 15 June 2002.

Couch, Carol A. et al. "Influences of Environmental Settings on Aquatic Ecosystems in the Apalachicola-Chattahoochee-Flint River Basin" <ga.water.usgs.gov>.

"Description of the ACF River Basin Study Area" <ga.water.usgs.gov>.

Dick, Jeff. "Drought Stricken Georgia Pays Farmers Not to Irrigate." *US Water News*, May 2001.

"Draft Environmental Impact Statement: Water Allocation for the Apalachicola-Chattahoochee-Flint (ACF) River Basin, Main Report." U.S. Army Corps of Engineers, September 1998.

Dumars, Charles T. "Interjurisdictional Compacts as Tools for Watershed Management." 19th Annual American Bar Association Water Law Conference, 15–16 February 2001.

"The Environment: Big Picture on Water. The State Needs a Water Policy with a Comprehensive, Statewide Focus Rather than a Collection of Misguided, Piecemeal Legislation." *The Atlanta Journal-Constitution*, 6 March 2001.

Erhardt, Carl. "The Battle over the 'Hooch': The Federal-Interstate Water Compact and the Resolution of Rights in the Chattahoochee River." *Stanford Environmental Law Journal*, vol. 11, p. 200, 1992.

Flint River Drought Protection Act. GA. ST. 12-5-54 Q et seq. (2000).

"Florida Wetland Resources." U.S. Geological Survey Water Supply Paper 2425. *National Water Summary*. Undated.

Fowler, Roy. "Florida's Stubborn: Keep Water Talks out of Court." *The Atlanta Journal-Constitution*, 28 December 2000.

"Georgia Floods and Droughts." U.S. Geological Survey Water Supply Paper 2375. *National Water Summary*, 1988–89.

"Georgia Ground-Water Quality." U.S. Geological Survey Water Supply Paper 2325. *National Water Summary*, 1986.

Georgia Irrigation Facts and Figures (2000) <nespal.cpes.peachnut.edu/agwateruse/facts/>.

"Georgia Stream Water Quality." U.S. Geological Survey Water Supply Paper 2400. *National Water Summary*, 1990–91.

Ghirardini, John. "States Near Water Accord Formula to Divide Three-River Basin." *The Atlanta Journal-Constitution*, 17 January 2002.

Hauserman, Julie. "Lawmakers See Effects of Dredging Apalachicola." *St. Petersburg Times*, 13 May 2001.

Hook, James E. "Sustainable Water Use and Management for the Southeast" (2000) <nespal.cpes.peachnut.edu>.

Horton, Tom. "Apalachicola, Making Choices in a Well-Watered World." *Nature Conservancy*, March/April 1999.

Jehl, Douglas. "Atlanta's Growing Thirst Creates Water War." *The New York Times*, 27 May 2002.

Kundell, James E. and Diana Tetens. "Whose Water Is It? Major Water Allocation Issues Facing Georgia." Carl Vinson Institute of Government, The University of Georgia, 1998.

Light, Helen M. et al. "Aquatic Habitats in Relation to River Flow in the Apalachicola River Floodplain, Florida." *United States Geological Survey Professional Paper* 159, 1998.

Livingston, Robert J. *Resource Atlas of the Apalachicola Estuary.* Florida Sea Grant College Program, 1983.

Livingston, Robert J. "Freshwater Input to a Gulf Estuary: Long-Term Control of Trophic Organization." *Ecological Applications*, vol. 7, no. 1, 1997.

Livingston, Robert J. "Trophic Response of Estuarine Fishes to Long-Term Changes of River Runoff." *Bulletin of Marine Science*, vol. 60, no. 3, 1997.

Livingston, Robert J. et al. "Recovery of Oyster Reefs (*Crassostrea virginica*) in a Gulf Estuary Following Disturbance by Two Hurricanes." *Bulletin of Marine Science*, vol. 7, no. 1, 1999.

Livingston, Robert J. et al. "Modelling Oyster Population Response to Variation in Freshwater Input." *Estuarine, Coastal and Shelf Science*, vol. 50, 2000.

Mackenzie, Clyde L., Jr. "History of Oystering in the United States and Canada, Featuring the Eight Greatest Oyster Estuaries." *Marine Fisheries Review*, vol. 58, no. 4, 1996.

Moore, C. Grady. "Water Wars: Interstate Water Allocation in the Southeast." *Natural Resources & Environment*, vol. 14, p. 5, 1999.

Mortazavi, Behzad et al. "Control of Phytoplankton Production and Biomass in a River-Dominated Estuary: Apalachicola Bay, Florida, USA." *Marine Ecology Progress Series*, vol. 198, 2000.

"Negotiators Reach Agreement in Water Dispute Between Georgia, Florida and Alabama." Associated Press Newswires, 15 January 2002.

Niu, X.-F. et al. "Time Series Models for Salinity and Other Environmental Factors in the Apalachicola Estuarine System." *Estuarine, Coastal and Shelf Science*, vol. 46, 1998.

"The Oystercatcher." The Apalachicola Estuarine Research Reserve, Winter 1998.

"Researchers Developing Smarter Irrigation System." *U.S. Water News*, August 2000.

Richter, Brian et al. "Ecologically Sustainable Water Management: Managing River Flows for Ecological Integrity." 28 August 2001.

Ritchie, Bruce. "River Provides Jobs, Recreation" and "River Houses Rare Breeds." *Tallahassee Democrat*, 4 November 2001.

Ritchie, Bruce. "Atlanta Needs Water to Grow On." *Tallahassee Democrat*, 5 November 2001.

Ritchie, Bruce. "Less Water Produces Less Power." *Tallahassee Democrat*, 6 November 2001.

Ritchie, Bruce. "Does Shipping Have a Future?" *Tallahassee Democrat*, 7 November 2001.

Ritchie, Bruce. "Researchers Study Farmers' Growing Water Needs." *Tallahassee Democrat*, 8 November 2001.

Ritchie, Bruce. "Lake's Low Level Has Residents Looking Downstream." *Tallahassee Democrat*, 9 November 2001.

Ritchie, Bruce. "River a Pearl for Oysters." *Tallahassee Democrat*, 10 November 2001.

Ritchie, Bruce. "States Weigh Conservation, Demands of Growth." *Tallahassee Democrat*, 11 November 2001.

Ritchie, Bruce. "Georgia, Florida Continue to Disagree over Water Use in Apalachicola River." *Tallahassee Democrat*, 14 November 2001.

Sachs, Jessica Snyder. "Problems and Promise in the Land of the 'Hooch.'" *National Wildlife Federation*, June/July 2001.

Seabrook, Charles. "River in Peril: Growth Poisons the Chattahoochee on Its Run to Atlanta, a Dirty, Dangerous Journey." *The Atlanta Journal-Constitution*, 23 November 1997.

Seabrook, Charles. "River in Peril: Solutions for the Chattahoochee Governments, Private Groups Step in to Save Watersheds." *The Atlanta Journal-Constitution*, 30 November 1997.

Seabrook, Charles. "River in Peril: Chattahoochee South of Atlanta, Fish Swim in a Toxic Soup." *The Atlanta Journal-Constitution*, 4 October 1998.

Seabrook, Charles. "Georgia to Pay Farmers Not to Irrigate." *The Atlanta Journal-Constitution*, 2 March 2001.

Seabrook, Charles. "EPD Chief Stays Ahead by Forging 'New Ways of Doing Things.'" *The Atlanta Journal-Constitution*, 7 March 2001.

Sharing the Water in Alabama, Florida, and Georgia, No. 3. U.S. Army Corps of Engineers, October 1998.

Sharing the Water in Alabama, Florida, and Georgia, No 4. U.S. Army Corps of Engineers, June 1999.

Torak, Lynn J. and Robin John McDowell. "Ground-Water Resources of the Lower Apalachicola-Chattahoochee-Flint River Basin in Parts of Alabama, Florida, and Georgia—Subarea 4 of the Apalachicola-Chattahoochee-Flint and Alabama-Coosa-Tallapoosa River Basins." U.S. Geological Survey, Open-File Report 95-321, 1996.

Water Laws for Georgia. Southwest Georgia Water Resources Taskforce (2000) <nespal.cpes.peachnet.edu>.

Water Resources Committee Newsletter, American Bar Association Section of Natural Resources, Energy, and the Environment, vol. 2, no. 2, December 1998.

Whitt, Richard and Julie B. Hairston. "Farmers Feel Sting of Water Payoffs." *The Atlanta Constitution*, 2 May 2001.

Wilbur, Dara H. "Associations between Freshwater Inflows and Oyster Productivity in Apalachicola Bay, Florida." *Estuarine, Coastal and Shelf Science*, vol. 35, 1992.

Wilbur, Dara H. "The Influence of Apalachicola River Flows on Blue Crab, *Callinectes spidus*, in North Florida." *Fishery Bulletin*, vol. 92, 1994.

Williams, James D. et al. "Unionid Mollusks of the Apalachicola Basin in Alabama, Florida and Georgia." *Bulletin 21*, 12 April 2000.

Chapter 14. The Future of Water: Tourism and Grand Canyon National Park

Articles and Reports

Ack, Bradley L. "Managing Growth at Grand Canyon—Canyon Forest Village." *Colorado Plateau Advocate*, Winter 2000.

"Babbitt Has a Serious Conflict of Interest in Land Ownership." *The Washington Times*, 3 April 2000.

"Canyon Forest Village." National Parks Conservation Association, Letters, Editorial Reply, 1 November 2000.

"Canyon Forest Village Compromise Hits Snag." Associated Press Newswires, 9 February 2000.

Canyon Forest Village Corporation. *Project Summary* and *Summary of Canyon Forest Village Project Water Resources Plan for Alternative H (Draft)*. 15 May 1998.

Carlton, Jim. "Arizona Coalition Sues to Block Swap of Land Between U.S., Hotel Developer." *The Wall Street Journal*, 12 January 2000.

Childs, Craig. "The Quest for Water: Natural Springs in the Grand Canyon Quench Hikers' Thirst for Adventure." *Arizona Highways*, April 2001.

"Court Rejects Most Arguments against Tusayan Development." Associated Press Newswires, 4 April 2001.

Elston, Catherine. "Alternative Water Plans Address Grand Canyon Needs." *Canyon Echoes*, vol. 1, undated.

Eskovitz, Joel. "Voters Say No to Development Outside Grand Canyon." Associated Press Newswires, 8 November 2000.

Graham, Judith. "Grand Canyon Facing Grand Problems with Overcrowding." *Chicago Tribune*, 16 April 2001.

"Grand Canyon-Area Development Issue Going before Voters." Associated Press Newswires, 5 May 2000.

Grand Canyon Trust. *Beyond the Boundaries: The Human and Natural Communities of the Greater Grand Canyon*, Flagstaff, Arizona. 1997.

Grand Canyon Trust. "7 Reasons to Support Alternative H." *Colorado Plateau Advocate*, July 1998.

Havasupai Tribal Council. *Comments of the Havasupai Tribe on Supplement to Draft Environmental Impact Statement for Tusayan Growth Coconino County, Arizona*. 9 October 1998.

Hyatt & Stubblefield, P.C. *Declaration of Covenants for Sustainable Water Use at Canyon Forest Village (Draft)*. 23 June 1999.

Ingley, Kathleen and Maureen West. "Critics Ask Who's Behind Canyon Plan." *The Arizona Republic*, 2 November 2000.

Janofsky, Michael. "Accord on Developing Land beside the Grand Canyon." *The New York Times*, 6 August 1999.

Kyl, Jon, U.S. Senator. "Problems in Grand Canyon Plan." *Arizona Daily Star*, 12 March 2001.

Laitos, Jan S. and Thomas A. Carr. "The Transformation on Public Lands." *Ecology Law Quarterly*, vol. 26, no. 2, p. 140, 1999.

Natural Resources Consulting Engineers, Inc. *Review and Analyses of Supplement to the Draft Environmental Impact Statement for Tusayan Growth Kaibab National Forest*. 6 October 1998.

"No Middle Ground in Debate over Development near Grand Canyon." Associated Press Newswires, 9 October 2000.

"Official Won't Participate in Rezoning Case." *The Las Vegas Review-Journal*, 21 January 2000.

Paige, Sean. "High Plains Gifter?" *The Washington Times*, 20 March 2000.

Rushlo, Michelle. "Development Set near Grand Canyon Riles Locals." *The San Diego Union-Tribune*, 30 April 2000.

Sander, Rhonda Bodfield. "Plans for Massive Canyon Village Win Endorsement of Zoning Board." *The Arizona Daily Star*, 19 November 1999.

Shaffer, Mark. "Canyon Developer Awaits Vote." *The Arizona Republic*, 12 February 2000.

Shaffer, Mark. "Grand Canyon Project Delayed, Touchy Proposal Returned for Further Review." *The Arizona Republic*, 17 February 2000.

Shaffer, Mark. "Village Foes Push Petition Drive." *The Arizona Republic*, 5 April 2000.

Shaffer, Mark. "Grand Canyon Plan Backers Outspend Critics in Ad Blitz." *The Arizona Republic*, 2 November 2000.

Shaffer, Mark. "Coconino County Rejects Village at Grand Canyon." *The Arizona Republic*, 9 November 2000.

Shaffer, Mark. "Cancel Swap near Canyon, U.S. Urged." *The Arizona Republic*, 19 December 2000.

Shaffer, Mark. "Canyon Village Plan Back to Forest Service." *The Arizona Republic*, 4 April 2001.

Shaffer, Mark. "Canyon Village Plan Remains on Track." *The Arizona Republic*, 5 April 2001.

"Sierra Club Sues to Stop Development Near Grand Canyon." *Associated Press Newswires*, 9 March 2000.

Sorvig, Kim. "Sustainability Disdained." *Landscape Architecture*, March 2001.

Storey, Lee A. and Adrian Hansen. "Canyon Forest Village—A Case Study." Arizona Water Law—8th Annual Conference. 2000.

"Supervisors May Vote on Canyon Forest Village in Mid-March." Associated Press Newswires, 1 March 2000.

"Supervisors OK Canyon Development; Referendum Planned." Associated Press Newswires, 16 March 2000.

Swan, William H. *Legal Feasibility of the Imported Water Supply Approach*. Included in Alternative H of the Tusayan Growth Supplemental EIS, 9 October 1998.

"$330M Project to Develop Grand Canyon Area Defeated." *The Tucson Citizen*, 10 November 2000.

"Tribes Support Canyon Plans." *The Denver Post*, 6 February 2000.

"Tusayan Land Owners Vow to Fight Canyon Forest Village." Associated Press Newswires, 14 March 2000.

U.S. Department of Agriculture, U.S. Forest Service, Southwestern Region. *Comments and Responses on the Supplement to the Draft Environmental Impact Statement for Tusayan Growth Kaibab National Forest*. May 1997.

U.S. Department of Agriculture, U.S. Forest Service, Southwestern Region. *Draft Environmental Impact Statement for Tusayan Growth Kaibab National Forest*. 20 June 1997.

U.S. Department of Agriculture, U.S. Forest Service, Southwestern Region. *Supplement to the Draft Environmental Impact Statement for Tusayan Growth Kaibab National Forest*. 17 July 1998.

U.S. Department of Agriculture, U.S. Forest Service, Southwestern Region. *Appendix of the Final Environmental Impact Statement for Tusayan Growth Kaibab National Forest*. July 1999.

U.S. Department of Agriculture, U.S. Forest Service, Southwestern Region. *Record of Decision, Final Environmental Impact Statement for Tusayan Growth Kaibab National Forest*. July 1999.

U.S. Department of Agriculture, U.S. Forest Service, Southwestern Region. *Executive*

Summary of the Final Environmental Impact Statement for Tusayan Growth Kaibab National Forest. 6 August 1999.

U.S. Department of Agriculture, U.S. Forest Service, Southwestern Region. *Final Environmental Impact Statement for Tusayan Growth Kaibab National Forest.* 6 August 1999.

Wilderness Society, The. "15 Most Endangered Wild Lands, 2000, Grand Canyon National Park, AZ" (visited on 30 May 2000) <www.wilderness.org/newsroom/15mostgrand_canyon.htm>.

Williams, Owen R. *Review and Analysis of Supplement to the Draft Environmental Impact Statement for Tusayan Growth,* Prepared for the Havasupai Tribe of the Havasupai Reservation, Supai, Arizona. 25 September 1998.

Letters, Memoranda, Miscellaneous

City of Williams, et al. v. Michael Dombeck, et al. 151 F.Supp.2d 9 (D.D.C. 2001).

Manajaka, Lincoln, Chairman, Havasupai Tribal Council. *Statement on the Supplemental DEIS for Tusayan Growth,* Supai, Arizona. September 1998.

The Sierra Club v. Michael Dombeck, 161 F.Supp.2d (D. Ariz. 2001).

Vick, Margaret J., Letter to Eleanor S. Towns, regional forester, Southwestern region, and Robert L. Arnberger, superintendent, Grand Canyon National Park. 10 June 1998.

Chapter 15: The Tragedy of Law and the Commons

Books

Anderson, Terry L. and Pamela Snyder. *Water Markets: Priming the Invisible Pump.* Washington, D.C.: Cato Institute, 1997.

Kinney, Clesson. *A Treatise on the Law of Irrigation,* Volumes I and II. Washington, D.C.: W. H. Lowdermilk & Co., 1894.

Mead, Elwood. *Irrigation Institutions: A Discussion of the Economic and Legal Questions Created by the Growth of Irrigated Agriculture in the West.* New York: The MacMillan Company, 1903.

Tarlock, A. Dan et al. *Water Resource Management: A Casebook in Law and Public Policy,* 4th ed. Westbury: The Foundation Press, Inc., 1993.

Articles and Reports

Colby, Bonnie G. "Markets as a Response to Water Scarcity: Policy Challenges and Economic Implications." *Advances in the Economics of Environmental Resources,* vol. 1, p. 211, 1996.

Colby, Bonnie G. et al. "Mitigating Environmental Externalities through Voluntary and Involuntary Water Reallocation: Nevada's Truckee-Carson River Basin." *Natural Resources Journal,* vol. 31, p. 757, 1991.

Congressional Research Service, The Library of Congress, *Farm Commodity Programs: A Short Primer*. CRS Report for Congress. 14 September 2001.

Couch, Dean A. "Supreme Court Decides Groundwater Case." *Water Law Newsletter*. Undated.

Davis, Peter. "Wells and Streams: Relationship at Law." *Missouri Law Review*, vol. 37, p. 189, 1972.

Glennon, Robert Jerome. "Because That's Where the Water Is: Retiring Current Water Uses to Achieve the Safe-Yield Objective of the Arizona Groundwater Management Act." *Arizona Law Review*, vol. 33, p. 88, 1991.

Goldberg, Carey. "Down East, the Lobster Hauls Are Up Big." *The New York Times*, 31 May 2001.

Land and Water Conservation Fund of 1965. 16 U.S.C. § 4601-4 to -11 (2000).

Olson, James M., representing Michigan Citizens for Water Conservation. Testimony before the Senate Committee on Natural Resources and Environmental Affairs. 26 November 2001.

Struhs, David B., Secretary, Florida Department of Environmental Protection. *Florida's Springs: Strategies for Protection and Restoration*, Florida Springs Task Force. November 2000.

Tierney, John. "A Tale of Two Fisheries." *The New York Times Magazine*, 27 August 2000.

"Washington: State Grapples with the Status of Small Wells as Exempt from Water Right Permit Requirements." *Western Water Law & Policy Reporter*, January 2002.

"Washington: Supreme Court Protects Stream Flows from Groundwater Withdrawals." *Western Water Law & Policy Reporter*, December 2000.

Letters, Memoranda, Miscellaneous

The Center for Biological Diversity et al. v. Joseph C. Smith in His Capacity as Director of the Arizona Department of Water Resources (Complaint) (2002).

Department of Ecology v. Campbell & Guinn, 146 Wash. 2d 1, 43 P.3d 4 (2002).

In re: Water Use Permit Applications. 9 P.3d 409 (Hawaii 2000).

Land and Water Conservation Fund, 16 U.S.C. § 460L-4 et seq. (2000).

Messer-Bowers Company, Inc., et al. v. State of Oklahoma ex rel. Oklahoma Water Resources Board and Kronseder Farms. 8 P.3d 877 (Okla. 2000).

Michigan Citizens for Water Conservation et al. v. Great Springs Waters of America, Inc., et al. No. 01-14563-CE (Second Amended Complaint) (25 January 2002).

Oregon Revised Statutes § 537.455.500 (1999).

Postema v. Pollution Control Hearings Board, 11 P.3d 726 (Wash. 2000).

Acknowledgments

Having written this book gives me the opportunity to thank friends, colleagues, and even perfect strangers who provided assistance. Their generosity, enthusiasm, and encouragement has been remarkable. I must begin with my good friend and sometimes coauthor, Thomas Maddock III, who is not only an extraordinarily gifted hydrologist but also a dedicated environmentalist. Tom believes that good science can and must inform public policy decisions. Through this entire project, he has generously and patiently helped me to improve my understanding of hydrology.

The University of Arizona James E. Rogers College of Law is an especially supportive environment. Jim Rogers' recent generosity opens new possibilities for collaborative, interdisciplinary work. My students and colleagues in the College of Law and elsewhere on campus, particularly in hydrology and economics, have nurtured this project by challenging me to think more clearly about its scope and consequences. In researching this book, I had the help of Peter Culp, College of Law class of 2001, who provided preliminary research on gold mining in Nevada and American consumers' fascination with bottled water. Rick Yarde, College of Law class of 2000, undertook initial research on Tampa Bay, the Black Mesa pipeline, and the Apalachicola-Chattahoochee-Flint Compact. I was fortunate to have the assistance of Peter Ghishan, College of Law class of 2002, in formatting and cite checking the Bibliography section. Mike Chiorazzi, director of the law library, has assembled a remarkable staff, especially Maureen Garmon, who graciously tracked down every request that I made for even the most obscure report. I enjoyed fantastic word processing services provided by Joni Coble, Kathy D'Assis, Carol Denis, Miriam Hochlaf, Norma Kelly, Davon May, Patricia Sesma, and Madeleine Sherman. I am especially

297

grateful to Sandy Davis, who labored long and hard on innumerable drafts and revisions.

I could not have written this book without enormous help from hundreds of people who granted me interviews, provided reports, studies, or photographs, suggested leads for further investigations, or bolstered my flagging energy with a comment such as: "It's a great topic. I'm so glad you're tackling it." For granting me interviews, I especially want to thank Brad Ack, Katherine Andrews, Dave Armstrong, Sydney Bacchus, Ed Baum, Dave Bell, Ted Beutel, Nancy Boatwright, Dick Bogart, Layne Bolen, Steve Born, Janette Brimmer, Dave Brooks, Susan Butler, Brad Caswell, Gilliam Clarke, Russ Cohen, Jock Conyngham, Tom De Paolo, Hiram Drache, Chuck DuMars, Mike Eaton, Lee Edmiston, Elwood Engle, Paul Firmani, Jay Fishman, Jan Fleckenstein, Graham Fogg, Kathy Fry, Bill Furbish, Grady Gammage, Jr., John Gardner, Vicki Gartland, Paul Hardy, Jim Hook, Terry Hudgins, John Hunt, Bill Kahrl, David Keeley, George Kraft, Jim Krohelski, Jim Kundell, Lealdon Langley, Andy Laurenzi, Diana Lefler, Steve Leitman, Duane LeVangie, Graham Lewis, Helen Light, Judith Light, Skip Livingston, Alan MacIntosh, Kerry Mackin, Tom Maddock, David Marlow, Bob Marvinney, Vernon Masayesva, Ruth Mathews, Ann Mesrobian, George Michaels, Woody Miley, Glenn Miller, Larry Monico, Anne Monnelly, Steve Monsees, Lynn Morgan, Jeff Mount, Peter Moyle, Tom Myers, Paul Nickerson, Al Niebur, Tom Nigus, Jim Olson, Fred Palmer, Kirk Patterson, Martin Pillsbury, Russ Plume, Stanley Pollock, Dale Pontius, Carolyn Raffensperger, Honey Rand, Todd Rasmussen, Jeff Reardon, Sid Reynolds, Brian Richter, Holly Richter, Stephan Rogers, Mary Jane Schmudlach, Matt Scott, Chris Sewell, Mark Smith, David Smolker, Jim Stark, Jon Steinhaus, John Stine, Lee Storey, Beth Sutton, Bill Swan, Ramona Swenson, Terry Swier, Fife Symington, Rich Tomczyk, Lynn Torak, Sarah Tufford, Lou Wagner, Tommy Ward, Jim Williams, John Williams, Terri Wolfe, Phil Zarriello, Jerry Ziewitz, and Bob Zimmerman.

Many people, too numerous to list, supplied information or suggested new avenues of inquiry. For special thanks, I would like to single out Emilie Cademartori, Roger Congdon, Raymond Dougan, Jim Hook, Daniele Lantagne, Bob MacNish, Linda Stitzer, Charlie Sugnet, Jeff Tannler, and Barbara Tellman.

I am extremely grateful to Mark Anderson, Brian Gray, Eric Handler, Kerry Mackin, Tom Myers, Suzanne Rabe, Sarah Van de Wetering, and Todd Votteler, who offered comments and suggestions on drafts of particular chapters, and to Kendra Gaines, Stephen Golden, and Martha Whitaker, who critiqued the entire manuscript. Martha also drew on her background in hydrology to help me with the glossary. A final reader, Ben Smith, was extraordinarily generous, drawing on experience as a copy editor. His remarkable sense of diction and syntax saved the manuscript from innumerable syntactical infelicities. He would have red-lined this last sentence had I shown it to him first.

I owe a special debt to the staffs of the United States Geological Survey (USGS) and The Nature Conservancy. The USGS, the arm of the federal government charged with conducting research on the nation's water resources, employs an incredible number of able and dedicated scientists who have produced absolutely first-rate studies of many watersheds throughout the country. As noted in the Bibliography section, I have drawn on this remarkable body of scholarship. Many of my illustrations and photographs originally appeared in USGS publications; for permission to reuse them I am extremely grateful. The real credit for the artwork goes to John Callahan, who tailored the originals to suit my purposes and created the maps for each story. The USGS recently changed its motto to "Science for a Changing World," a slogan that would have pleased its most famous director, John Wesley Powell. As for The Nature Conservancy, that organization deserves the nation's thanks for its sustained program of conservation. Since 1951, this privately funded, nonprofit organization has played a remarkable role in identifying sensitive lands and habitats that need protection and then figuring out some way to safeguard them. The Conservancy's strategy, which has emphasized the acquisition and management of key parcels of land, has resulted in protection of more than ten million acres in the United States and Canada. In my research, I received aid and suggestions from Conservancy employees too numerous to thank individually, but I want generally to acknowledge the Conservancy Freshwater Initiative Strategy Team, chaired by Brian Richter.

I received financial help from a number of sources along the way. I particularly want to acknowledge Deans Joel Seligman and Toni M. Massaro of the James E. Rogers College of Law at The University of Arizona for summer research grants that freed up my time to research and write. I benefited from the Ashby Lohse Fund at the college. I also received support from the Udall Center for Studies in Public Policy at The University of Arizona, thanks to the encouragement of its associate director, Bob Varady. Finally, I am a principal investigator on a project funded by the National

Science Foundation and the U.S. Environmental Protection Agency that allowed me to investigate the issues surrounding the San Pedro River.

Jolie Sibert and Joe Barbato introduced me to Deborah Grosvenor, who would become my agent. Deborah told me immediately that this book belonged at Island Press. Charles Wilkinson and Don Falk sang the praises of Island Press's Barbara Dean who, in turn, linked me up with my editor, Todd Baldwin. Todd's genuine interest in my project rekindled my enthusiasm at a most propitious time, and his aesthetic sensibility generated the title and helped me to reorient several chapters. From an author's perspective, Todd is a dream editor. He treated each of my obsessive concerns as though they were normal human worries. Others at Island Press were very helpful, especially Jonathan Cobb and Amelia Durand. The production process went smoothly, thanks to Cecilia González, Chace Caven, Brighid Willson, and Sherri Schultz. Joy Drohan did a splendid job as my copy editor.

Finally, my best friend, Karen Adam, who also happens to be my wife, has done more than anyone to help me finish this project. I dedicate this book to Karen.

Index

Island Press Board of Directors

Chair
HENRY REATH
President, Collectors Reprints, Inc.

Vice-Chair
VICTOR M. SHER
Miller Sher & Sawyer

Secretary
DANE A. NICHOLS
Chair, The Natural Step

Treasurer
DRUMMOND PIKE
President, The Tides Foundation

ROBERT E. BAENSCH
Director, Center for Publishing, New York University

MABEL H. CABOT
President, MHC & Associates

DAVID C. COLE
Owner, Sunnyside Farms

CATHERINE M. CONOVER

CAROLYN PEACHEY
Campbell, Peachey & Associates

WILL ROGERS
President, Trust for Public Land

CHARLES C. SAVITT
President, Center for Resource Economics/Island Press

SUSAN E. SECHLER
Senior Advisor on Biotechnology Policy, The Rockefeller Foundation

PETER R. STEIN
Managing Partner, The Lyme Timber Company

RICHARD TRUDELL
Executive Director, American Indian Resources Institute

DIANA WALL
Director and Professor, Natural Resource Ecology Laboratory, Colorado State University

WREN WIRTH
President, The Winslow Foundation

HAMILTON TOWNSHIP PUBLIC LIBRARY

3 1923 00427601 6

Free Public Library
Township of Hamilton
1 Municipal Drive
Hamilton, NJ 08619